JUSTICE INTERRUPTUS

JUSTICE INTERRUPTUS

Critical Reflections on the "Postsocialist" Condition

Nancy Fraser

Routledge

New York & London

Published in 1997 by

Routledge
29 West 35th Street
New York, NY 10001

Published in Great Britain by

Routledge
11 New Fetter Lane
London EC4P 4EE

Printed in the United States of America

The author gratefully ackowledges permission to reprint previously published material here. Chapter 1 originally appeared in *New Left Review*, July/August 1995, no. 212: 68–93. An earlier version of chapter 2 appeared as "After the Family Wage: Gender Equity and the Welfare State," in *Political Theory* 22, no. 4 (November 1994): 591–618, © Sage Publications, reprinted by permission. An earlier version of chapter 3 originally appeared in *Habermas and the Public Sphere*, ed. Craig Calhoun (Cambridge: MIT Press, 1991). An earlier version of chapter 4 appeared in *Critical Inquiry* 18 (spring 1992): 595–612, © University of Chicago Press, reprinted by permission. Chapter 5 originally appeared in *Signs* 19, no. 2 (winter 1994): 309–336. An earlier version of chapter 6 appeared as "The Uses and Abuses of French Discourse Theories for Feminist Politics," *boundary 2*, 17, no. 2 (summer 1990): 82–101. An earlier version of chapter 7 appeared as "Multiculturalism and Gender Equity: The U.S. 'Difference' Debates Revisited," *Constellations* 3, no. 1 (April 1996): 61–72. An earlier version of chapter 8 appeared as "Recognition or Redistribution? A Critical Reading of Iris Young's *Justice and the Politics of Difference*," *Journal of Political Philosophy* 3, no. 2 (June 1995): 166–180. An earlier version of chapter 9 appeared in *Praxis International* 11, no. 2 (July 1991): 166–177. An earlier version of chapter 10 appeared in *Social Text*, winter 1993, no. 37: 173–181.

Library of Congress Cataloging-in-Publication Data

Fraser, Nancy.
    Justice interruptus : critical reflections on the "postsocialist" condition / by Nancy Fraser.
      p. cm.
    Includes bibliographical references and index.
    ISBN 0-415-91794-8 (hb). — ISBN 0-415-91795-6 (pb)
    1. Justice. 2. Distributive justice. 3. Culture conflict.
I. Title.
JC578.F73   1996
320'.01'1—dc20   96-41608
                                    CIP

For Eli

Contents

Part III. Feminist Interventions

Acknowledgments

Research for material included in this book was supported by the American Council of Learned Societies; the Newberry Library; the National Endowment for the Humanities; the Center for Urban Affairs and Policy Research at Northwestern University; the Rockefeller Foundation Study and Conference Center, Bellagio, Italy; the *Institut für die Wissenschaften vom Menschen*, Vienna; the Humanities Research Institute, University of California, Irvine; and the Graduate Faculty of The New School for Social Research. I am grateful to the staff and administrators of all of these institutions, as well as to Cornelia Klinger, Wendy Brown, Judith Butler, and Judith Friedlander.

Many individuals read portions of this book in draft and/or discussed its ideas with me; I have acknowledged them in the notes to each chapter. But I owe thanks of a more overarching sort to Jane Mansbridge, Linda Nicholson, Judith Wittner, and Eli Zaretsky, who stimulated me and supported me more than they know. Thanks as well to Linda Gordon, who graciously allowed me to include our coauthored essay, "A Genealogy of 'Dependency'," and to Maureen MacGrogan, for editorial guidance and support.

Introduction

Justice Interruptus

Taken together, the essays collected here diagnose the "postsocialist" condition. I use this expression—with apologies to Jean-François Lyotard—to designate the general horizon within which political thought necessarily moves today.[1] I place the term "postsocialist" in quotation marks, however, to signal the effort to maintain a critical posture in relation to this horizon, despite being situated within it. I aim, in other words, not to reflect the "postsocialist" condition symptomatically, but rather to reflect on it critically.

What, then, is the "postsocialist" condition? Scarcely a definitive negative verdict on the relevance and viability of socialist ideals, it is, rather, a skeptical mood or structure of feeling that marks the post-1989 state of the Left. Fraught with a sense of "the morning after," this mood expresses authentic doubts bound to genuine opacities concerning the historical possibilities for progressive social change. Yet it is laced as well with ideological elements, which are difficult to disentangle and name. To begin to sort out the authentic from the ideological, I distinguish three constitutive features of the "postsocialist" condition.

The first is the absence of any credible progressive vision of an alternative to the present order. This, of course, is partly a matter of the increased delegitimation, in the wake of 1989, of socialism in the broad sense. What has collapsed, in other words, is not just a set of (erstwhile) actually existing institutional arrangements but belief in the principal ideal that inspired

1

struggles for social transformation for the last century and a half. The immediate consequence is what Jürgen Habermas has called "the exhaustion of
[leftwing] utopian energies."[2] The phrase is apt, I believe, despite the
impressive proliferation of differentiated progressive activisms currently in
evidence throughout the world. It signals that, for the present, at least, no
new comprehensive progressive vision of a just social order has emerged to
take socialism's place. Proposals to elevate "radical democracy" and "multiculturalism" to that status express the desire in some quarters for such a
vision. But they lack the power to convince, I contend, because they bracket
the question of political economy. The same holds for the still more anemic
notions of "political liberalism" and "communitarianism."

Of course, the current absence of utopian vision scarcely vindicates
Francis Fukuyama's shallow claim that 1989 represents "the end of history"[3]; there is no reason to believe it will last. But it does characterize our
situation. For the time being at least, progressive struggles are no longer
anchored in any credible vision of an alternative to the present order.
Political critique, accordingly, is under pressure to curtail its ambitions and
remain "oppositional." In a sense, then, we are flying blind.

The second constitutive feature of the "postsocialist" condition concerns
a shift in the grammar of political claims-making. Claims for the recognition
of group difference have become intensely salient in the recent period, at
times eclipsing claims for social equality. This phenomenon can be observed
at two levels. Empirically, of course, we have seen the rise of "identity politics," the decentering of class, and, until very recently, the corresponding
decline of social democracy.[4] More deeply, however, we are witnessing an
apparent shift in the political imaginary, especially in the terms in which justice is imagined. Many actors appear to be moving away from a socialist
political imaginary, in which the central problem of justice is redistribution,
to a "postsocialist" political imaginary, in which the central problem of justice is recognition. With this shift, the most salient social movements are no
longer economically defined "classes" who are struggling to defend their
"interests," end "exploitation," and win "redistribution." Instead, they are
culturally defined "groups" or "communities of value" who are struggling
to defend their "identities," end "cultural domination," and win "recognition." The result is a decoupling of cultural politics from social politics, and
the relative eclipse of the latter by the former.

Here, interlaced with historical developments, we encounter currents of
"postsocialist" ideology. Some celebrate the shift "from redistribution to
recognition" as if struggles for distributive justice were no longer relevant.
Others bemoan the decentering of class, which they equate with the decline

of egalitarian economic claims, as if struggles for racial and gender justice were "merely cultural" and not also addressed to distribution. Together, such responses construct what appears to be an either/or choice: class politics or identity politics? social politics or cultural politics? equality or difference? redistribution or recognition? The implication is that these are mutually exclusive alternatives, that we must choose between social equality and multiculturalism, that redistribution and recognition cannot be combined.

These, I maintain, are false antitheses, which I challenge throughout this book. They have structured an increasingly bitter split between "the social left" and "the cultural left" in the United States, a split that recently erupted in the *Social Text* hoax.[5] While one side insists in retrograde accents that "it's the economy, stupid," the other retorts in hypersophisticated tones that "it's the culture, stupid." Both thus evade what I take to be the crucial "postsocialist" tasks: first, interrogating the distinction between culture and economy; second, understanding how both work together to produce injustices; and third, figuring out how, as a prerequisite for remedying injustices, claims for recognition can be integrated with claims for redistribution in a comprehensive political project.

The context for these developments, and the third defining feature of the "postsocialist" condition, is a resurgent economic liberalism. As the center of political gravity seems to shift from redistribution to recognition, and egalitarian commitments appear to recede, a globalizing wall-to-wall capitalism is increasingly marketizing social relations, eroding social protections, and worsening the life-chances of billions. The United Nations reports in 1996 that inequality is rising sharply worldwide, as those who are positioned to prosper in the global information economy rapidly leave behind the many more who are not. In virtually every country in the world, the disparities mount—not only in income and wealth, but also in "capabilities" as measured by access to clean water and air; education, contraception, and health care; paid work and nutritious food; freedom from torture and rape.[6]

This, then, is the "postsocialist" condition: an absence of any credible overarching emancipatory project despite the proliferation of fronts of struggle; a general decoupling of the cultural politics of recognition from the social politics of redistribution; and a decentering of claims for equality in the face of aggressive marketization and sharply rising material inequality.

The "postsocialist" condition is also the horizon of contemporary political theorizing. Thus, it is crucial for theorists to ask: what constitutes a critical stance in this context? How can we distinguish those postures that critically interrogate the "postsocialist" condition from those that reflect it symptomatically?

It is a basic premise of the chapters that follow that all three constitutive features of the "postsocialist" condition need to be subject to critical scrutiny. This means, first, cultivating some skeptical distance from the fashionable "postsocialist" distrust of normative, programmatic, "totalizing" thinking. To eschew such thinking in the present context, whether in the name of "decon-struction," "postmodernism," or "piecemeal reformism," is symptomatically to express, rather than critically to interrogate, the current "exhaustion of [leftwing] utopian energies." It is to make a virtue out of what appears to be a necessity, instead of subjecting it to the pressure of critique.

Nor is it sufficient merely to speak abstractly of the need for "coalition," as is common today in U.S. multicultural circles. Such discussion is usually aimed at promoting additive combinations among already formed con-stituencies. Obscuring the social processes whereby constituencies are formed, it surrenders the possibility of an integrative prespective that seeks to grasp, and transform, the social whole. "Coalition politics" remains at the level of wishful thinking, moreover, in the absence of sustained, integrative, and holistic attempts to envision social arrangements that could transform the identities and harmonize the interests of diverse, currently fragmented constituencies.

In contrast to such approaches, a critical perspective must defend the possibility and desirability of comprehensive, integrative, normative, pro-grammatic thinking. It must diagnose the general "postsocialist" retreat from such thinking in recent political culture and lay the conceptual groundwork for redressing it. To be sure, we are not now in a position to envision a full-scale successor project to socialism. But we can try neverthe-less to conceive provisional alternatives to the present order that could supply a basis for a progressive politics.

A second imperative is to demystify "postsocialist" ideologies concerning the shift from redistribution to recognition. It should be axiomatic that no defensible successor project to socialism can simply jettison the commitment to social equality in favor of cultural difference. To assume otherwise is effectively to fall in line with the reigning neoliberal commonsense. This is not to say, however, that one should cling to socialist orthodoxy and eschew the politics of recognition altogether. On the contrary, critical theorists should rebut the claim that we must make an either/or choice between the politics of redistribution and the politics of recognition. We should aim instead to identify the emancipatory dimensions of both problematics and to integrate them into a single, comprehensive framework. The goal, in short, should be to create another "postsocialism," one that incorporates, rather than repudiates, the best of socialism.

It follows, too, that a critical approach must challenge one-sided, whole-sale dismissals of the politics of recognition. Such dismissals are often expressed today as rejections of "identity politics," a phrase that is subject to much abuse. It is paradigmatically associated with claims for national, regional, ethnic and religious recognition, some of which, to be sure, are genuinely pernicious. Yet in the United States today, the expression "identity politics" is increasingly used as a derogatory synonym for feminism, anti-racism, and anti-heterosexism. The implication is that the inherent thrust of such politics is a particularistic self-assertion that rejects the universalism of "common dreams"[7] and has nothing to do with justice. In fact, however, those movements arose in the first place precisely to protest the disguised particularisms—the masculinism, the white-Anglo ethnocentrism, the heterosexism—lurking behind what parades as universal. As such, they have everything to do with justice. These movements assume the guise of identity politics only under certain conditions, moreover, namely, when political currents that look to socioeconomic transformation as the remedy for gender, sexual, and racial-ethnic injustice are eclipsed by currents that look instead to the assertion and vindication of group identity.[8] Only in that case, as in the case of national and ethnic struggles, does a "postsocialist" stress on cultural difference displace the characteristic "socialist" stress on social equality.

Thus, a critical approach must reject facile dismissals that throw out the baby with the bath. Instead, it must develop a critical theory of recognition, distinguishing those claims for the recognition of difference that advance the cause of social equality from those that retard or undermine it.

This in turn requires challenging the current "postsocialist" decoupling of cultural politics from social politics, both practically and intellectually. In the U.S. academy today, cultural theorizing is largely dissociated from social theorizing, thus mirroring in intellectual life the practical decoupling of the politics of recognition from the politics of redistribution in social life. Within the discipline of political philosophy, for example, theorists of distributive justice tend simply to ignore identity politics, apparently assuming that it represents false consciousness. And theorists of recognition tend likewise to ignore distribution, as if the problematic of cultural difference had nothing to with that of social equality. Both parties, therefore, fail to interrogate the dissociation of political economy and culture that is a hallmark of the "postsocialist" condition.

A critical approach must be "bivalent," in contrast, integrating the social and the cultural, the economic and the discursive. This means exposing the limitations of fashionable neostructuralist models of discourse analysis that dissociate "the symbolic order" from the political economy. It requires culti-vating in their stead alternative models that connect the study of signification to institutions and social structures. Finally, it means connect-ing the theory of cultural justice with the theory of distributive justice.

The essays collected here attempt to develop such a critical approach. Their guiding assumption is that the cultural politics of recognition ought not simply to supplant the social politics of redistribution. Rather, the two need to be integrated with one another.

The chapters in Part One focus directly on the theory of justice. Chapter 1, "From Redistribution to Recognition?", argues that neither redistribu-tion alone nor recognition alone can suffice for remedying injustice in today's world. It proposes a critical theory of recognition that identifies, and supports, only those forms of identity politics that can be coherently com-bined with a politics of social equality. And it identifies the dilemmas that arise when we try to pursue both redistribution and recognition simultane-ously. Chapter 2, "After the Family Wage," examines such dilemmas with regard to gender and the welfare state. It exposes the limitations of two competing feminist visions of postindustrial gender justice, one aiming to make women "workers" like men, the other aiming to "make difference costless." And it sketches the outlines of a third approach that would inte-grate redistribution and recognition by deconstructing gender and changing men.

Part Two lays some groundwork for such an integration at the level of the theory of discourse. Surveying some of the main varieties of discourse analysis, I identify those approaches best suited to overcoming the current decoupling of the cultural from the social. Chapters 3 and 4 assess the potential of public-sphere theory to provide a hinge between the discursive and the institutional: "Rethinking the Public Sphere" identifies the insights and blindspots of Habermas's model and proposes a critical reconstruction; "Sex, Lies, and the Public Sphere" tests the revised model by analyzing the 1992 Clarence Thomas–Anita Hill confrontation as a struggle to define the line between the public and the private. Chapter 5, in contrast, seeks to remedy the social-structural deficits of Foucauldian genealogy by marrying it to Raymond Williams's cultural-materialism. Coauthored with Linda Gordon and titled "A Genealogy of 'Dependency'," this chapter situates the changing meanings of that "keyword" in relation to changing configurations of political economy so as to challenge current neoliberal ideology. Finally, chapter 6, "Structuralism or Pragmatics?", exposes the limitations of "Lacanianism," a neostructuralist model embraced by many feminists. Contending that "Lacanianism" reifies "the symbolic order" and dissociates it from political economy, this chapter defends the pragmatics tradition of discourse analysis as better able to connect the study of signification to the study of social inequality.

Part Three carries the project of integrating cultural politics and social politics into current debates in feminist theory. Chapter 7, "Multiculturalism, Antiessentialism, and Radical Democracy," charts the progressive uncoupling of redistribution and recognition in second-wave U.S. feminist theory, as the meaning of "difference" shifted from "gender difference" to "differences among women" and then again to "multiple intersecting differences." This trajectory brought major gains, to be sure, as gender ceased to be viewed in isolation from other axes of subordination; nevertheless, something important was lost: "differences" were assimilated to the model of cultural variations, thereby obscuring differentials rooted in political economy and truncating the scope of justice. Chapter 8, in contrast, examines a laudable effort to expand the scope of justice to encompass both culture and political economy. Titled "Culture, Political Economy, and Difference," it exposes some shortcomings of Iris Marion Young's approach, especially the latter's tendency to evade the hard political questions that arise when we try to pursue redistribution and recognition simultaneously. Chapter 9, "False Antitheses," seeks to integrate the discursive and the normative in the theory of subjectivity. Critiquing the unnecessarily polarized stances of Seyla Benhabib, on the one side, and Judith Butler, on the other, it analyzes what is involved in combining reconstruction and deconstruction, elements of Critical Theory and poststructuralism. Lastly, in chapter 10, "Beyond the Master/Subject Model," I examine Carole Pateman's effort to theorize the ways in which contractual relations modernize, rather than subvert, male dominance. Pateman underestimates, I argue, the degree to which gender inequality is today being transformed by a shift from dyadic relations of mastery and subjection to more impersonal structural mechanisms that are lived through more fluid cultural forms.

In every chapter my guiding aim is this: to *think through* the "postsocialist" condition in hopes of coming out on the other side. To be sure, we cannot now know precisely what lies on that other side. But we can nevertheless resist ideological pressures that would prematurely foreclose the possibilities. Above all, this means refusing the unacceptable either/or choices that "postsocialist" commonsense is currently constructing. The goal should be to open the way for another "postsocialism," one that incorporates what remains unsurpassable in the socialist project with what is compelling and defensible in the politics of recognition.

Notes

1. Jean-François Lyotard, *The Postmodern Condition: A Report on Knowledge,* trans. G. Bennington and B. Massumi (Minneapolis: University of Minnesota Press, 1984).

2. Jürgen Habermas, "The New Obscurity and the Exhaustion of Utopian Energies," in *Observations on the Spiritual Situation of the Age,* ed. Habermas, trans. Andrew Buchwalter (Cambridge: MIT Press, 1984).

3. Francis Fukuyama, *The End of History and the Last Man* (New York: Free Press, 1992).

4. As I write this in July 1996, social democracy appears to making a comeback in some countries: witness recent election results in Italy, Poland, and other former communist countries, as well as electoral polls in England.

5. In a special issue on the "Science Wars" (that is, recent debates over cultural studies scholarship about science), *Social Text* published an article by New York University physicist Alan Sokal. (Alan D. Sokal, "Transgressing the Boundaries: Toward a Transformative Hermeneutics of Quantam Gravity," *Social Text,* spring/summer 1996, no. 46–47: 217–252.) Sokal later claimed the article was a parody intended to expose the intellectual vacuity of cultural studies. (See Alan Sokal, "A Physicist Experiments with Cultural Studies," *Lingua Franca,* May/June 1996, pp. 62–64.) Aided in preparing his article by feminist scholars Ruth Rosen and Barbara Epstein, he cast himself as a defender of the "real left" (what I am calling the "social left") against the phony leftism of cultural studies (what I am calling "the cultural left"), which he took *Social Text* to epitomize. In my view, Sokal's hoax was most revealing for the reactions it generated. There was widespread gloating not only on the Right, as was to be expected, but also and more importantly within the social left. (Examples include Katha Pollitt, "Pomolotov Cocktail," *The Nation,* 10 June 1996, p. 9; and Tom Frank, "Textual Reckoning," *In These Times,* 27 May 1996, pp. 22–24.) In my view, the hoax cathected such intense feelings of resentful glee precisely because it crystallized a large, important fault line in the "postsocialist" condition. For a thoughtful analysis of the reaction, see Ellen Willis, "My Sokaled Life," *Village Voice,* 25 June 1996, pp. 22–23.

6. United Nations Development Program, *Human Development Report 1996* (Oxford: Oxford University Press, 1996). Highlights of the findings are reported by Barbara Crossette, "U.N. Survey Finds World Rich-Poor Gap Widening," *New York Times,* 15 July 1996, p. A4.

7. The reference is to Todd Gitlin, *The Twilight of Common Dreams: Why America is Wracked by Culture Wars* (New York: Metropolitan Books, 1995).

8. I mean here to contest the view that opposes "social politics," equated with the politics of class, to "identity politics," equated with the politics of feminism, anti-racism, and gay and lesbian liberation. This view treats identity-oriented currents within the latter movements as the whole story, rendering invisible alternative currents dedicated to righting gender-specific, race-specific, and sex-specific forms of economic injustice that traditional class movements ignored. In addition, it misses the ways in which even the identity-oriented currents are concerned with justice issues, albeit of a different sort. For a discussion of these issues, see chapter 1 of this volume, "From Redistribution to Recognition?"

PART I

REDISTRIBUTION AND RECOGNITION

1

From Redistribution to Recognition?

Dilemmas of Justice in a "Postsocialist" Age

The "struggle for recognition" is fast becoming the paradigmatic form of political conflict in the late twentieth century. Demands for "recognition of difference" fuel struggles of groups mobilized under the banners of nationality, ethnicity, "race," gender, and sexuality. In these "postsocialist" conflicts, group identity supplants class interest as the chief medium of political mobilization. Cultural domination supplants exploitation as the fundamental injustice. And cultural recognition displaces socioeconomic redistribution as the remedy for injustice and the goal of political struggle.[1]

This is not, of course, the whole story. Struggles for recognition occur in a world of exacerbated material inequality—in income and property ownership; in access to paid work, education, health care, and leisure time; but also, more starkly, in caloric intake and exposure to environmental toxicity, and hence in life expectancy and rates of morbidity and mortality. Material inequality is on the rise in most of the world's countries—in the United States and in China, in Sweden and in India, in Russia and in Brazil. It is also increasing global, most dramatically across the line that divides North from South.

How, then, should we view the eclipse of a socialist imaginary centered on terms such as "interest," "exploitation," and "redistribution"? And what should we make of the rise of a new political imaginary centered on notions of "identity," "difference," "cultural domination," and "recognition"? Does this shift represent a lapse into "false consciousness"? Or does it, rather, redress the culture-blindness of a materialist paradigm rightfully discredited by the collapse of Soviet communism?

Neither of those two stances is adequate, in my view. Both are too wholesale and unnuanced. Instead of simply endorsing or rejecting all of identity politics *simpliciter,* we should see ourselves as presented with a new intellectual and practical task: that of developing a *critical* theory of recognition, one that identifies and defends only those versions of the cultural politics of difference that can be coherently combined with the social politics of equality.

In formulating this project, I assume that justice today requires *both* redistribution *and* recognition. And I propose to examine the relation between them. In part, this means figuring out how to conceptualize cultural recognition and social equality in forms that support rather than undermine one another. (For there are many competing conceptions of both!) It also means theorizing the ways in which economic disadvantage and cultural disrespect are currently entwined with and support one another. Then, too, it requires clarifying the political dilemmas that arise when we try to combat both those injustices simultaneously.

My larger aim is to connect two political problematics that are currently dissociated from each other, for only by integrating recognition and redistribution can we arrive at a framework that is adequate to the demands of our age. That, however, is far too much to take on here. In what follows, I shall consider only one aspect of the problem: Under what circumstances can a politics of recognition help support a politics of redistribution? And when is it more likely to undermine it? Which of the many varieties of identity politics best synergize with struggles for social equality? And which tend to interfere with the latter?

In addressing these questions, I shall focus on axes of injustice that are simultaneously cultural and socioeconomic, paradigmatically gender and "race." (I shall not say much, in contrast, about ethnicity or nationality.)[2] And I must enter one crucial preliminary caveat: in proposing to assess recognition claims from the standpoint of social equality, I assume that varieties of recognition politics that fail to respect human rights are unacceptable, even if they promote social equality.[3]

Finally, a word about method. In what follows, I shall propose a set of analytical distinctions—for example, cultural injustices versus economic injustices, recognition versus redistribution. In the real world, of course, culture and political economy are always imbricated with each other, and virtually every struggle against injustice, when properly understood, implies demands for both redistribution and recognition. Nevertheless, for heuristic purposes, analytical distinctions are indispensable. Only by abstracting from the complexities of the real world can we devise a conceptual schema that can illuminate it. Thus, by distinguishing redistribution and recognition analytically, and by exposing their distinctive logics, I aim to clarify—and begin to resolve—some of the central political dilemmas of our age.

My discussion in this chapter proceeds in four parts. In the first section, I conceptualize redistribution and recognition as two analytically distinct paradigms of justice, and I formulate "the redistribution-recognition dilemma." In the second, I distinguish three ideal-typical modes of social collectivity in order to identify those vulnerable to the dilemma. In the third section, I distinguish between "affirmative" and "transformative" remedies for injustice, and I examine their respective logics of collectivity. I use these distinctions in the fourth section to propose a political strategy for integrating recognition claims with redistribution claims with a minimum of mutual interference.

The Redistribution-Recognition Dilemma

Let me begin by noting some complexities of contemporary "postsocialist" political life. With the decentering of class, diverse social movements are mobilized around crosscutting axes of difference. Contesting a range of injustices, their claims overlap and at times conflict. Demands for cultural change intermingle with demands for economic change, both within and among social movements. Increasingly, however, identity-based claims tend to predominate, as prospects for redistribution appear to recede. The result is a complex political field with little programmatic coherence.

To help clarify this situation and the political prospects it presents, I propose to distinguish two broadly conceived, analytically distinct understandings of injustice. The first is socioeconomic injustice, which is rooted in the political-economic structure of society. Examples include exploitation (having the fruits of one's labor appropriated for the benefit of others); economic marginalization (being confined to undesirable or poorly paid work or being denied access to income-generating labor altogether), and deprivation (being denied an adequate material standard of living).

Egalitarian theorists have long sought to conceptualize the nature of these socioeconomic injustices. Their accounts include Marx's theory of capitalist exploitation, John Rawls's account of justice as fairness in the choice of principles governing the distribution of "primary goods," Amartya Sen's view that justice requires ensuring that people have equal "capabilities to function," and Ronald Dworkin's view that it requires "equality of resources."[4]

For my purposes here, however, we need not commit ourselves to any one particular theoretical account. We need only subscribe to a rough and general understanding of socioeconomic injustice informed by a commitment to egalitarianism.

The second understanding of injustice is cultural or symbolic. Here injustice is rooted in social patterns of representation, interpretation, and communication. Examples include cultural domination (being subjected to patterns of interpretation and communication that are associated with another culture and are alien and/or hostile to one's own); nonrecognition (being rendered invisible by means of the authoritative representational, communicative, and interpretative practices of one's culture); and disrespect (being routinely maligned or disparaged in stereotypic public cultural representations and/or in everyday life interactions).

Some political theorists have recently sought to conceptualize the nature of these cultural or symbolic injustices. Charles Taylor, for example, has drawn on Hegelian notions to argue that

> nonrecognition or misrecognition . . . can be a form of oppression, imprisoning someone in a false, distorted, reduced mode of being. Beyond simple lack of respect, it can inflict a grievous wound, saddling people with crippling self-hatred. Due recognition is not just a courtesy but a vital human need.[5]

Likewise, Axel Honneth has argued that

> we owe our integrity . . . to the receipt of approval or recognition from other persons. [Negative concepts such as "insult" or "degradation"] are related to forms of disrespect, to the denial of recognition. [They] are used to characterize a form of behavior that does not represent an injustice solely because it constrains the subjects in their freedom for action or does them harm. Rather, such behavior is injurious because it impairs these persons in their positive understanding of self—an understanding acquired by intersubjective means.[6]

Similar conceptions inform the work of many other critical theorists, including Iris Marion Young and Patricia J. Williams, who do not use the term 'recognition.'[7] Once again, however, it is not necessary here to settle on a particular theoretical account. We need only subscribe to a general and rough understanding of cultural injustice, as distinct from socioeconomic injustice.

Despite the differences between them, both socioeconomic injustice and cultural injustice are pervasive in contemporary societies. Both are rooted in processes and practices that systematically disadvantage some groups of people vis-à-vis others. Both, consequently, should be remedied.

Of course, this distinction between economic injustice and cultural injustice is analytical. In practice, the two are intertwined. Even the most material economic institutions have a constitutive, irreducible cultural dimension; they are shot through with significations and norms. Conversely, even the most discursive cultural practices have a constitutive, irreducible political-economic dimension; they are underpinned by material supports. Thus, far from occupying two airtight separate spheres, economic injustice and cultural injustice are usually interimbricated so as to reinforce each other dialectically. Cultural norms that are unfairly biased against some are institutionalized in the state and the economy; meanwhile, economic disadvantage impedes equal participation in the making of culture, in public spheres and in everyday life. The result is often a vicious circle of cultural and economic subordination.[8]

Despite these mutual entwinements, I shall continue to distinguish economic injustice and cultural injustice analytically. And I shall also distinguish two correspondingly distinct kinds of remedy. The remedy for economic injustice is political-economic restructuring of some sort. This might involve redistributing income, reorganizing the division of labor, subjecting investment to democratic decision making, or transforming other basic economic structures. Although these various remedies differ importantly from one another, I shall henceforth refer to the whole group of them by the generic term "redistribution."[9] The remedy for cultural injustice, in contrast, is some sort of cultural or symbolic change. This could involve upwardly revaluing disrespected identities and the cultural products of maligned groups. It could also involve recognizing and positively valorizing cultural diversity. More radically still, it could involve the wholesale transformation of societal patterns of representation, interpretation, and communication in ways that would change *everybody's* sense of self.[10] Although these remedies differ importantly from one another, I shall henceforth refer to the whole group of them by the generic term "recognition."

Once again, this distinction between redistributive remedies and recognition remedies is analytical. Redistributive remedies generally presuppose an underlying conception of recognition. For example, some proponents of egalitarian socioeconomic redistribution ground their claims on the "equal moral worth of persons"; thus, they treat economic redistribution as an expression of recognition.[11] Conversely, recognition remedies sometimes presuppose an underlying conception of redistribution. For example, some proponents of multicultural recognition ground their claims on the impera-

tive of a just distribution of the "primary good" of an "intact cultural structure"; they therefore treat cultural recognition as a species of redistribution.[12]
Such conceptual entwinements notwithstanding, however, I shall leave to
one side questions such as, do redistribution and recognition constitute two
distinct, irreducible, *sui generis* concepts of justice, or alternatively, can
either one of them be reduced to the other?[13] Rather, I shall assume that
however we account for it metatheoretically, it will be useful to maintain a
working, first-order distinction between socioeconomic injustices and their
remedies, on the one hand, and cultural injustices and their remedies, on the
other.[14]

With these distinctions in place, I can now pose the following questions:
What is the relation between claims for recognition, aimed at remedying
cultural injustice, and claims for redistribution, aimed at redressing economic injustice? And what sorts of mutual interferences can arise when both
kinds of claims are made simultaneously?

There are good reasons to worry about such mutual interferences.
Recognition claims often take the form of calling attention to, if not performatively creating, the putative specificity of some group and then of
affirming its value. Thus, they tend to promote group differentiation.
Redistribution claims, in contrast, often call for abolishing economic
arrangements that underpin group specificity. (An example would be feminist demands to abolish the gender division of labor.) Thus, they tend to
promote group dedifferentiation. The upshot is that the politics of recognition and the politics of redistribution often appear to have mutually
contradictory aims. Whereas the first tends to promote group differentiation, the second tends to undermine it. Thus, the two kinds of claim stand
in tension with each other; they can interfere with, or even work against,
each other.

Here, then, is a difficult dilemma. I shall henceforth call it the redistribution-recognition dilemma. People who are subject to both cultural injustice
and economic injustice need both recognition and redistribution. They need
both to claim and to deny their specificity. How, if at all, is this possible?

Before taking up this question, let us consider precisely who faces the
recognition-redistribution dilemma.

Exploited Classes, Despised Sexualities, and Bivalent Collectivities

Imagine a conceptual spectrum of different kinds of social collectivities. At
one extreme are modes of collectivity that fit the redistribution model of jus-

tice. At the other extreme are modes of collectivity that fit the recognition model. In between are cases that prove difficult because they fit both models of justice simultaneously.

Consider, first, the redistribution end of the spectrum. At this end let us posit an ideal-typical mode of collectivity whose existence is rooted wholly in the political economy. It will be differentiated as a collectivity, in other words, by virtue of the economic structure, as opposed to the cultural order, of society. Thus, any structural injustices its members suffer will be traceable ultimately to the political economy. The root of the injustice, as well as its core, will be socioeconomic maldistribution, and any attendant cultural injustices will derive ultimately from that economic root. At bottom, there-fore, the remedy required to redress the injustice will be political-economic redistribution, as opposed to cultural recognition.

In the real world, to be sure, political economy and culture are mutually intertwined, as are injustices of distribution and recognition. Thus, we may question whether there exist any pure collectivities of this sort. For heuristic purposes, however, it is useful to examine their properties. To do so, let us consider a familiar example that can be interpreted as approximating the ideal type: the Marxian conception of the exploited class, understood in an orthodox way.[15] And let us bracket the question of whether this view of class fits the actual historical collectivities that have struggled for justice in the real world in the name of the working class.[16]

In the conception assumed here, class is a mode of social differentiation that is rooted in the political-economic structure of society. A class exists as a collectivity only by virtue of its position in that structure and of its relation to other classes. Thus, the Marxian working class is the body of persons in a capitalist society who must sell their labor power under arrangements that authorize the capitalist class to appropriate surplus productivity for its private benefit. The injustice of these arrangements, moreover, is quintessentially a matter of distribution. In the capitalist scheme of social reproduction, the proletariat receives an unjustly large share of the burdens and an unjustly small share of the rewards. To be sure, its members also suffer serious cultur-al injustices, the "hidden (and not so hidden) injuries of class." But far from being rooted directly in an autonomously unjust cultural structure, these derive from the political economy, as ideologies of class inferiority proliferate to justify exploitation.[17] The remedy for the injustice, consequently, is redis-tribution, not recognition. Overcoming class exploitation requires restructuring the political economy so as to alter the class distribution of social burdens and social benefits. In the Marxian conception, such restruc-turing takes the radical form of abolishing the class structure as such. The task of the proletariat, therefore, is not simply to cut itself a better deal but "to abolish itself as a class." The last thing it needs is recognition of its difference. On the contrary, the only way to remedy the injustice is to put the proletariat out of business as a group.

Now consider the other end of the conceptual spectrum. At this end we may posit an ideal-typical mode of collectivity that fits the recognition model of justice. A collectivity of this type is rooted wholly in culture, as opposed to in political economy. It is differentiated as a collectivity by virtue of the reigning social patterns of interpretation and evaluation, not by virtue of the division of labor. Thus, any structural injustices its members suffer will be traceable ultimately to the cultural-valuational structure. The root of the injustice, as well as its core, will be cultural misrecognition, while any attendant economic injustices will derive ultimately from that cultural root. At bottom, therefore, the remedy required to redress the injustice will be cultural recognition, as opposed to political-economic redistribution.

Once again, we may question whether there exist any pure collectivities of this sort, but it is useful to examine their properties for heuristic purposes. An example that can be interpreted as approximating the ideal type is the conception of a despised sexuality, understood in a specific way.[18] Let us consider this conception, while leaving aside the question of whether this view of sexuality fits the actual historical homosexual collectivities that are struggling for justice in the real world.

Sexuality in this conception is a mode of social differentiation whose roots do not lie in the political economy because homosexuals are distributed throughout the entire class structure of capitalist society, occupy no distinctive position in the division of labor, and do not constitute an exploited class. Rather, their mode of collectivity is that of a despised sexuality, rooted in the cultural-valuational structure of society. From this perspective, the injustice they suffer is quintessentially a matter of recognition. Gays and lesbians suffer from heterosexism: the authoritative construction of norms that privilege heterosexuality. Along with this goes homophobia: the cultural devaluation of homosexuality. Their sexuality thus disparaged, homosexuals are subject to shaming, harassment, discrimination, and violence, while being denied legal rights and equal protections—all fundamentally denials of recognition. To be sure, gays and lesbians also suffer serious economic injustices; they can be summarily dismissed from paid work and are denied family-based social-welfare benefits. But far from being rooted directly in the economic structure, these derive instead from an unjust cultural-valuational structure.[19] The remedy for the injustice, consequently, is recognition, not redistribution. Overcoming homophobia and heterosexism requires changing the cultural valuations (as well as their legal and practical expressions) that privilege heterosexuality, deny equal respect to gays and lesbians, and refuse to recognize homosexuality as a legitimate way of being sexual. It is to revalue a despised sexuality, to accord positive recognition to gay and lesbian sexual specificity.

Matters are thus fairly straightforward at the two extremes of our conceptual spectrum. When we deal with collectivities that approach the ideal type of the exploited working class, we face distributive injustices requiring redistributive remedies. When we deal with collectivities that approach the ideal type of the despised sexuality, in contrast, we face injustices of misrecognition requiring remedies of recognition. In the first case, the logic of the remedy is to put the group out of business as a group. In the second case, on the contrary, it is to valorize the group's "groupness" by recognizing its specificity.

Matters become murkier, however, once we move away from these extremes. When we consider collectivities located in the middle of the conceptual spectrum, we encounter hybrid modes that combine features of the exploited class with features of the despised sexuality. These collectivities are "bivalent." They are differentiated as collectivities by virtue of *both* the political-economic structure *and* the cultural-valuational structure of society. When oppressed or subordinated, therefore, they suffer injustices that are traceable to both political economy and culture simultaneously. Bivalent collectivities, in sum, may suffer both socioeconomic maldistribution and cultural misrecognition in forms where neither of these injustices is an indirect effect of the other, but where both are primary and co-original. In that case, neither redistributive remedies alone nor recognition remedies alone will suffice. Bivalent collectivities need both.

Both gender and "race" are paradigmatic bivalent collectivities. Although each has peculiarities not shared by the other, both encompass political-economic dimensions and cultural-valuational dimensions. Gender and "race," therefore, implicate both redistribution and recognition.

Gender, for example, has political-economic dimensions because it is a basic structuring principle of the political economy. On the one hand, gender structures the fundamental division between paid "productive" labor and unpaid "reproductive" and domestic labor, assigning women primary responsibility for the latter. On the other hand, gender also structures the division within paid labor between higher-paid, male-dominated, manufacturing and professional occupations and lower-paid, female-dominated "pink-collar" and domestic service occupations. The result is a political-economic structure that generates gender-specific modes of exploitation, marginalization, and deprivation. This structure constitutes gender as a political-economic differentiation endowed with certain classlike characteristics. When viewed under this aspect, gender injustice appears as a species of distributive injustice that cries out for redistributive redress. Much like class, gender justice requires transforming the political economy so as to eliminate its gender structuring. Eliminating gender-specific exploitation, marginalization, and deprivation requires abolishing the gender division of labor—both the gendered division between paid and unpaid labor and the gender division within paid labor. The logic of the remedy is akin to the logic with respect to class: it is to put gender out of business as such. If gender were nothing but a political-economic differentiation, in sum, justice would require its abolition.

That, however, is only half the story. In fact, gender is not only a political-economic differentiation but a cultural-valuational differentiation as well. As such, it also encompasses elements that are more like sexuality than class and that bring it squarely within the problematic of recognition. Certainly, a major feature of gender injustice is androcentrism: the authoritative construction of norms that privilege traits associated with masculinity. Along with this goes cultural sexism: the pervasive devaluation and disparagement of things coded as "feminine," paradigmatically—but not only—women.[20] This devaluation is expressed in a range of harms suffered by women, including sexual assault, sexual exploitation, and pervasive domestic violence; trivializing, objectifying, and demeaning stereotypical depictions in the media; harassment and disparagement in all spheres of everyday life; subjection to androcentric norms in relation to which women appear lesser or deviant and that work to disadvantage them, even in the absence of any intention to discriminate; attitudinal discrimination; exclusion or marginalization in public spheres and deliberative bodies; and denial of full legal rights and equal protections. These harms are injustices of recognition. They are relatively independent of political economy and are not merely "superstructural." Thus, they cannot be remedied by political-economic redistribution alone but require additional independent remedies of recognition. Overcoming androcentrism and sexism requires changing the cultural valuations (as well as their legal and practical expressions) that privilege masculinity and deny equal respect to women. It requires decentering androcentric norms and revaluing a despised gender. The logic of the remedy is akin to the logic with respect to sexuality: it is to accord positive recognition to a devalued group specificity.

Gender, in sum, is a bivalent mode of collectivity. It contains a political-economic face that brings it within the ambit of redistribution. Yet it also contains a cultural-valuational face that brings it simultaneously within the ambit of recognition. Of course, the two faces are not neatly separated from each other. Rather, they intertwine to reinforce each other dialectically because sexist and androcentric cultural norms are institutionalized in the state and the economy, and women's economic disadvantage restricts women's "voice," impeding equal participation in the making of culture, in public spheres and in everyday life. The result is a vicious circle of cultural and economic subordination. Redressing gender injustice, therefore, requires changing both political economy and culture.

But the bivalent character of gender is the source of a dilemma. Insofar as women suffer at least two analytically distinct kinds of injustice, they necessarily require at least two analytically distinct kinds of remedy: both redistribution and recognition. The two remedies pull in opposite directions, however, and are not easily pursued simultaneously. Whereas the logic of redistribution is to put gender out of business as such, the logic of recognition is to valorize gender specificity.[21] Here, then, is the feminist version of the redistribution-recognition dilemma: How can feminists fight simultaneously to abolish gender differentiation and to valorize gender specificity?

An analogous dilemma arises in the struggle against racism. "Race," like gender, is a bivalent mode of collectivity. On the one hand, it resembles class in being a structural principle of political economy. In this aspect, "race" structures the capitalist division of labor. It structures the division within paid work between low-paid, low-status, menial, dirty, and domestic occupations held disproportionately by people of color, and higher-paid, higher-status, white-collar, professional, technical, and managerial occupations held disproportionately by "whites."[22] Today's racial division of paid labor is part of the historic legacy of colonialism and slavery, which elaborated racial categorization to justify brutal new forms of appropriation and exploitation, effectively constituting "blacks" as a political-economic caste. Currently, moreover, "race" also structures access to official labor markets, constituting large segments of the population of color as a "superfluous," degraded subproletariat or underclass, unworthy even of exploitation and excluded from the productive system altogether. The result is a political-economic structure that generates "race"-specific modes of exploitation, marginalization, and deprivation. This structure constitutes "race" as a political-economic differentiation endowed with certain classlike characteristics. When viewed under this aspect, racial injustice appears as a species of distributive injustice that cries out for redistributive redress. Much like class, racial justice requires transforming the political economy so as to eliminate its racialization. Eliminating "race"-specific exploitation, marginalization, and deprivation requires abolishing the racial division of labor—both the racial division between exploitable and superfluous labor and the racial division within paid labor. The logic of the remedy is like the logic with respect to class: it is to put "race" out of business as such. If "race" were nothing but a political-economic differentiation, in sum, justice would require its abolition.

Yet "race," like gender, is not only political-economic. It also has cultural-valuational dimensions, which bring it into the universe of recognition. Thus, "race" too encompasses elements that are more like sexuality than class. A major aspect of racism is Eurocentrism: the authoritative construction of norms that privilege traits associated with "whiteness." Along with this goes cultural racism: the pervasive devaluation and disparagement[23] of things coded as "black," "brown," and "yellow," paradigmatically—but not only—people of color.[24] This depreciation is expressed in a range of harms suffered by people of color, including demeaning stereotypical depictions in the media as criminal, bestial, primitive, stupid, and so on; violence, harassment, and "dissing" in all spheres of everyday life; subjection to Eurocentric norms in relation to which people of color appear lesser or deviant and that work to disadvantage them, even in the absence of any intention to discriminate; attitudinal discrimination; exclusion from and/or marginalization in public spheres and deliberative bodies; and denial of full legal rights and equal protections. As in the case of gender, these harms are injustices of recognition. Thus, the logic of their remedy, too, is to accord positive recognition to devalued group specificity.

"Race," too, therefore, is a bivalent mode of collectivity with both a political-economic face and a cultural-valuational face. Its two faces intertwine to reinforce each other dialectically, moreover, because racist and Eurocentric cultural norms are institutionalized in the state and the economy, and the economic disadvantage suffered by people of color restricts their "voice." Redressing racial injustice, therefore, requires changing both political economy and culture. But as with gender, the bivalent character of "race" is the source of a dilemma. Insofar as people of color suffer at least two analytically distinct kinds of injustice, they necessarily require at least two analytically distinct kinds of remedy, redistribution and recognition, which are not easily pursued simultaneously. Whereas the logic of redistribution is to put "race" out of business as such, the logic of recognition is to valorize group specificity.[25] Here, then, is the antiracist version of the redistribution-recognition dilemma: How can antiracists fight simultaneously to abolish "race" and to valorize the cultural specificity of subordinated racialized groups?

Both gender and "race," in sum, are dilemmatic modes of collectivity. Unlike class, which occupies one end of the conceptual spectrum, and unlike sexuality, which occupies the other, gender and "race" are bivalent, implicated simultaneously in both the politics of redistribution and the politics of recognition. Both, consequently, face the redistribution-recognition dilemma. Feminists must pursue political-economic remedies that would undermine gender differentiation, while also pursuing cultural-valuational remedies that valorize the specificity of a despised collectivity. Antiracists, likewise, must pursue political-economic remedies that would undermine "racial" differentiation, while also pursuing cultural-valuational remedies that valorize the specificity of despised collectivities. How can they do both things at once?

Affirmation or Transformation?
Revisiting the Question of Remedy

So far I have posed the redistribution-recognition dilemma in a form that appears quite intractable. I have assumed that redistributive remedies for political-economic injustice always dedifferentiate social groups. Likewise, I have assumed that recognition remedies for cultural-valuational injustice always enhance social group differentiation. Given these assumptions, it is difficult to see how feminists and antiracists can pursue redistribution and recognition simultaneously.

Now, however, I want to complicate these assumptions. In this section, I shall examine alternative conceptions of redistribution, on the one hand, and alternative conceptions of recognition, on the other. My aim is to distinguish two broad approaches to remedying injustice that cut across the redistribution-recognition divide. I shall call them "affirmation" and "transformation" respectively. After sketching each of them generically, I shall show how each operates in regard to both redistribution and recognition. On this basis, finally, I shall reformulate the redistribution-recognition dilemma in a form that is more amenable to resolution.

Let me begin by briefly distinguishing affirmation and transformation. By affirmative remedies for injustice I mean remedies aimed at correcting inequitable outcomes of social arrangements without disturbing the underlying framework that generates them. By transformative remedies, in contrast, I mean remedies aimed at correcting inequitable outcomes precisely by restructuring the underlying generative framework. The crux of the contrast is end-state outcomes versus the processes that produce them. It is *not* gradual versus apocalyptic change.

This distinction can be applied, first of all, to remedies for cultural injustice. Affirmative remedies for such injustices are currently associated with what I shall call "mainstream multiculturalism."[26] This sort of multiculturalism proposes to redress disrespect by revaluing unjustly devalued group identities, while leaving intact both the contents of those identities and the group differentiations that underlie them. Transformative remedies, by contrast, are currently associated with deconstruction. They would redress disrespect by transforming the underlying cultural-valuational structure. By destabilizing existing group identities and differentiations, these remedies would not only raise the self-esteem of members of currently disrespected groups; they would change *everyone's* sense of self.

To illustrate the distinction, let us consider, once again, the case of the despised sexuality.[27] Affirmative remedies for homophobia and heterosexism are currently associated with gay-identity politics, which aims to revalue gay and lesbian identity.[28] Transformative remedies, in contrast, are associated with queer politics, which would deconstruct the homo-hetero dichotomy. Gay-identity politics treats homosexuality as a cultural positivity with its own substantive content, much like (the commonsense view of) an ethnicity.[29] This positivity is assumed to subsist in and of itself and to need only additional recognition. Queer politics, in contrast, treats homosexuality as the constructed and devalued correlate of heterosexuality; both are reifications of sexual ambiguity and are codefined only in virtue of each other.[30] The transformative aim is not to solidify a gay identity but to deconstruct the homo-hetero dichotomy so as to destabilize all fixed sexual identities. The point is not to dissolve all sexual difference in a single, universal human identity; it is, rather, to sustain a sexual field of multiple, debinarized, fluid, ever-shifting differences.

Both these approaches have considerable interest as remedies for misrecognition. But there is one crucial difference between them. Whereas gay-identity politics tends to enhance existing sexual group differentiation, queer politics tends to destabilize it—at least ostensibly and in the long run.[31] The point holds for recognition remedies more generally. Whereas affirmative recognition remedies tend to promote existing group differentiations, transformative recognition remedies tend, in the long run, to destabilize them so as to make room for future regroupments. I shall return to this point shortly.

Analogous distinctions hold for the remedies for economic injustice. Affirmative remedies for such injustices have been associated historically with the liberal welfare state.[32] They seek to redress end-state maldistribution, while leaving intact much of the underlying political-economic structure. Thus, they would increase the consumption share of economically disadvantaged groups, without otherwise restructuring the system of production. Transformative remedies, in contrast, have been historically associated with socialism. They would redress unjust distribution by transforming the underlying political-economic structure. By restructuring the relations of production, these remedies would not only alter the end-state distribution of consumption shares; they would also change the social division of labor and thus the conditions of existence for everyone.[33]

To illustrate the distinction, let us consider, once again, the case of the exploited class.[34] Affirmative redistributive remedies for class injustices typically include income transfers of two distinct kinds: social insurance programs share some of the costs of social reproduction for the stably employed, the so-called primary sectors of the working class; public assistance programs provide means-tested, "targeted" aid to the "reserve army" of the unemployed and underemployed. Far from abolishing class differentiation per se, these affirmative remedies support it and shape it. Their general effect is to shift attention from the class division between workers and capitalists to the division between employed and nonemployed fractions of the working class. Public assistance programs "target" the poor, not only for aid but for hostility. Such remedies, to be sure, provide needed material aid. But they also create strongly cathected, antagonistic group differentiations.

The logic here applies to affirmative redistribution in general. Although this approach aims to redress economic injustice, it leaves intact the deep structures that generate class disadvantage. Thus, it must make surface reallocations again and again. The result is to mark the most disadvantaged class as inherently deficient and insatiable, as always needing more and more. In time such a class can even come to appear privileged, the recipient of special treatment and undeserved largesse. Thus, an approach aimed at redressing injustices of distribution can end up creating injustices of recognition.

In a sense, this approach is self-contradictory. Affirmative redistribution generally presupposes a universalist conception of recognition, the equal moral worth of persons. Let us call this its "official recognition commitment." Yet the practice of affirmative redistribution, as iterated over time, tends to set in motion a second—stigmatizing—recognition dynamic, which contradicts its official commitment to universalism.[35] This second, stigmatizing, dynamic can be understood as the "practical recognition-effect" of affirmative redistribution.[36]

Now contrast this logic with transformative remedies for distributive injustices of class. Transformative remedies typically combine universalist

social-welfare programs, steeply progressive taxation, macroeconomic policies aimed at creating full employment, a large nonmarket public sector,
significant public and/or collective ownership, and democratic decision
making about basic socioeconomic priorities. They try to assure access to
employment for all, while also tending to delink basic consumption shares
from employment. Hence, their tendency is to undermine class differentiation. Transformative remedies reduce social inequality without, however,
creating stigmatized classes of vulnerable people perceived as beneficiaries
of special largesse.[37] They tend therefore to promote reciprocity and solidarity in the relations of recognition. Thus, an approach aimed at redressing
injustices of distribution can help redress (some) injustices of recognition
as well.[38]

This approach is self-consistent. Like affirmative redistribution, transformative redistribution generally presupposes a universalist conception of
recognition, the equal moral worth of persons. Unlike affirmative redistribution, however, its practice tends not to undermine this conception. Thus,
the two approaches generate different logics of group differentiation.
Whereas affirmative remedies can have the perverse effect of promoting class
differentiation, transformative remedies tend to blur it. In addition, the two
approaches generate different subliminal dynamics of recognition.
Affirmative redistribution can stigmatize the disadvantaged, adding the
insult of misrecognition to the injury of deprivation. Transformative redistribution, in contrast, can promote solidarity, helping to redress some forms of
misrecognition.

What, then, should we conclude from this discussion? In this section, we
have considered only the "pure" ideal-typical cases at the two extremes of
the conceptual spectrum. We have contrasted the divergent effects of affirmative and transformative remedies for the economically rooted distributive
injustices of class, on the one hand, and for the culturally rooted recognition
injustices of sexuality, on the other. We saw that affirmative remedies tend
generally to promote group differentiation, while transformative remedies
tend to destabilize or blur it. We also saw that affirmative redistribution
remedies can generate a backlash of misrecognition, while transformative
redistribution remedies can help redress some forms of misrecognition.

All this suggests a way of reformulating the redistribution-recognition
dilemma. We might ask: For groups who are subject to injustices of both
types, what combinations of remedies work best to minimize, if not altogether to eliminate, the mutual interferences that can arise when both
redistribution and recognition are pursued simultaneously?

Finessing the Dilemma: Revisiting Gender and "Race"

Imagine a four-celled matrix. The horizontal axis comprises the two general kinds of remedies we have just examined, namely, affirmation and transformation. The vertical axis comprises the two aspects of justice we have been considering, namely, redistribution and recognition. On this matrix we can locate the four political orientations just discussed. In the first cell, where redistribution and affirmation intersect, is the project of the liberal welfare state; centered on surface reallocations of distributive shares among existing groups, it tends to support group differentiation; it can also generate backlash misrecognition. In the second cell, where redistribution and transformation intersect, is the project of socialism; aimed at deep restructuring of the relations of production, it tends to blur group differentiation; it can also help redress some forms of misrecognition. In the third cell, where recognition and affirmation intersect, is the project of mainstream multiculturalism; focused on surface reallocations of respect among existing groups, it tends to support group differentiation. In the fourth cell, where recognition and transformation intersect, is the project of deconstruction; aimed at deep restructuring of the relations of recognition, it tends to destabilize group differentiations. (See Figure 1.1.)

Figure 1.1

	Affirmation	**Transformation**
Redistribution	*the liberal welfare state* surface reallocations of existing goods to existing groups; supports group differentiation; can generate misrecognition	*socialism* deep restructuring of relations of production; blurs group differentiation; can help remedy some forms of misrecognition
Recognition	*mainstream multiculturalism* surface reallocations of respect to existing identities of existing groups; supports group differentiations	*deconstruction* deep restructuring of relations of recognition; destabilizes group differentiation

This matrix casts mainstream multiculturalism as the cultural analogue of the liberal welfare state, while casting deconstruction as the cultural analogue of socialism. It thereby allows us to make some preliminary assessments of the mutual compatibility of various remedial strategies. We can gauge the extent to which pairs of remedies would work at cross-purposes with each other if they were pursued simultaneously. We can identify pairs that seem to land us squarely on the horns of the redistribution-recognition dilemma. We can also identify pairs that hold out the promise of enabling us to finesse it.

Prima facie at least, two pairs of remedies seem especially *un*promising. The affirmative redistribution politics of the liberal welfare state seems at odds with the transformative recognition politics of deconstruction; whereas the first tends to promote group differentiation, the second tends rather to destabilize it. Similarly, the transformative redistribution politics of socialism seems at odds with the affirmative recognition politics of mainstream multiculturalism; whereas the first tends to undermine group differentiation, the second tends rather to promote it.

Conversely, two pairs of remedies seem comparatively promising. The affirmative redistribution politics of the liberal welfare state seems compatible with the affirmative recognition politics of mainstream multiculturalism; both tend to promote group differentiation, although the former can generate backlash misrecognition. Similarly, the transformative redistribution politics of socialism seems compatible with the transformative recognition politics of deconstruction; both tend to undermine existing group differentiations.

To test these hypotheses, let us revisit gender and "race." Recall that these are bivalent differentiations, axes of both economic and cultural injustice. Thus, people subordinated by gender and/or "race" need both redistribution and recognition. They are the paradigmatic subjects of the redistribution-recognition dilemma. What happens in their cases, then, when various pairs of injustice remedies are pursued simultaneously? Are there pairs of remedies that permit feminists and antiracists to finesse, if not wholly to dispel, the redistribution-recognition dilemma?

Consider, first, the case of gender.[39] Recall that redressing gender injustice requires changing both political economy and culture, so as to undo the vicious circle of economic and cultural subordination. As we saw, the changes in question can take either of two forms, affirmation or transformation. Leaving aside the prima facie unpromising cases, let us consider, first, the prima facie promising case in which affirmative redistribution is combined with affirmative recognition.[40] As the name suggests, affirmative redistribution to redress gender injustice in the economy includes affirmative action, the effort to assure women their fair share of existing jobs and educational places, while leaving unchanged the nature and number of those jobs and places. Affirmative recognition to redress gender injustice in the culture includes cultural feminism, the effort to assure women respect by revaluing femininity, while leaving unchanged the binary gender code that gives the latter its sense. Thus, the scenario in question combines the socioeconomic politics of liberal feminism with the cultural politics of cultural feminism. Does this combination really finesse the redistribution-recognition dilemma?

Despite its initial appearance of promise, this scenario is problematic. Affirmative redistribution fails to engage the deep level at which the political economy is gendered. Aimed primarily at combating attitudinal discrimination, it does not attack the gendered division of paid and unpaid labor, nor the gendered division of masculine and feminine occupations within paid labor. Leaving intact the deep structures that generate gender disadvantage, it must make surface reallocations again and again. The result is not only to underline gender differentiation. It is also to mark women as deficient and insatiable, as always needing more and more. In time women can even come to appear privileged, recipients of special treatment and undeserved largesse. Thus, an approach aimed at redressing injustices of distribution can end up fueling backlash injustices of recognition.

This problem is exacerbated when we add the affirmative recognition strategy of cultural feminism. That approach insistently calls attention to, if it does not performatively create, women's putative cultural specificity or difference. In some contexts, such an approach can make progress toward decentering androcentric norms. In this context, however, it is more likely to have the effect of pouring oil onto the flames of resentment against affirmative action. Read through that lens, the cultural politics of affirming women's difference appears as an affront to the liberal welfare state's official commitment to the equal moral worth of persons.

The other route with a prima facie promise combines transformative redistribution with transformative recognition. Transformative redistribution to redress gender injustice in the economy consists in some form of socialist feminism or feminist social democracy. And transformative recognition to redress gender injustice in the culture consists in feminist deconstruction aimed at dismantling androcentrism by destabilizing gender dichotomies. Thus, the scenario in question combines the socioeconomic politics of socialist feminism with the cultural politics of deconstructive feminism. Does this combination really finesse the redistribution-recognition dilemma?

This scenario is far less problematic. The long-term goal of deconstructive feminism is a culture in which hierarchical gender dichotomies are replaced by networks of multiple intersecting differences that are demassified and shifting. This goal is consistent with transformative socialist-feminist redistribution. Deconstruction opposes the sort of sedimentation or congealing of gender difference that occurs in an unjustly gendered political economy. Its utopian image of a culture in which ever-new constructions of identity and difference are freely elaborated and then swiftly deconstructed is possible, after all, only on the basis of rough social equality.

As a transitional strategy, moreover, this combination avoids fanning the flames of resentment.[41] If it has a drawback, it is rather that both deconstructive-feminist cultural politics and socialist-feminist economic politics are far removed from the immediate interests and identities of most women, as these are currently culturally constructed.

Analogous results arise for "race," where the changes can again take either of two forms, affirmation or transformation.[42] Leaving aside once again the unpromising cases, let us consider the two prima facie promising scenarios. The first pairs affirmative redistribution with affirmative recognition. Affirmative redistribution to redress racial injustice in the economy includes affirmative action, the effort to assure people of color their fair share of existing jobs and educational places, while leaving unchanged the nature and number of those jobs and places. Affirmative recognition to redress racial injustice in the culture includes cultural nationalism, the effort to assure people of color respect by revaluing "blackness," while leaving unchanged the binary black-white code that gives the latter its sense. The scenario in question thus combines the socioeconomic politics of liberal antiracism with the cultural politics of black nationalism or black power. Does this combination really finesse the redistribution-recognition dilemma?

Such a scenario is again problematic. As in the case of gender, affirmative redistribution here fails to engage the deep level at which the political economy is racialized. It does not attack the racialized division of exploitable and surplus labor, nor the racialized division of menial and nonmenial occupations within paid labor. Leaving intact the deep structures that generate racial disadvantage, it must make surface reallocations again and again. The result is not only to underline racial differentiation; it is also to mark people of color as deficient and insatiable, as always needing more and more. Thus, they too can be cast as privileged recipients of special treatment. The problem is exacerbated when we add the affirmative recognition strategy of cultural nationalism. In some contexts, such an approach can make progress toward decentering Eurocentric norms, but in this context, the cultural politics of affirming black difference appears as an affront to the liberal welfare state. Fueling the resentment against affirmative action, it can elicit intense backlash misrecognition.

What, then, of the second prima facie promising case, which combines transformative redistribution with transformative recognition. Transformative redistribution to redress racial injustice in the economy consists of some form of antiracist democratic socialism or antiracist social democracy. And transformative recognition to redress racial injustice in the culture consists of antiracist deconstruction aimed at dismantling Eurocentrism by destabilizing racial dichotomies. Thus, the scenario in question combines the socioeconomic politics of socialist antiracism with the cultural politics of deconstructive antiracism.

This scenario, like its gender analogue, is far less problematic. The long-term goal of deconstructive antiracism is a culture in which hierarchical racial dichotomies are replaced by networks of multiple intersecting differences that are demassified and shifting. This goal, once again, is consistent with transformative socialist redistribution. Even as a transitional strategy, this combination, too, avoids fanning the flames of resentment.[43] Its principal drawback, again, is that both deconstructive-antiracist cultural politics and socialist-antiracist economic politics are far removed from the immediate interests and identities of most people of color, as these are currently culturally constructed.[44]

What, then, should we conclude from this discussion? For both gender and "race," the scenario that best finesses the redistribution-recognition dilemma is socialism in the economy plus deconstruction in the culture.[45] But for this scenario to be psychologically and politically feasible requires that all people be weaned from their attachment to current cultural constructions of their interests and identities.[46]

Conclusion

The redistribution-recognition dilemma is real. There is no neat theoretical move by which it can be wholly dissolved or resolved. The best we can do is to try to soften the dilemma by finding approaches that minimize conflicts between redistribution and recognition in cases where both must be pursued simultaneously.

I have argued here that socialist economics combined with deconstructive cultural politics works best to finesse the dilemma for the bivalent collectivities of gender and "race"—at least when they are considered separately. The next step would be to show that this combination also works for our larger sociocultural configuration. After all, gender and "race" are not neatly cordoned off from each other. Nor are they neatly cordoned off from sexuality and class. Rather, all these axes of injustice intersect one another in ways that affect everyone's interests and identities. No one is a member of only one such collectivity. And people who are subordinated along one axis of social division may well be dominant along another.[47]

The task, then, is to figure out how to finesse the redistribution-recognition dilemma when we situate the problem in this larger field of multiple, intersecting struggles against multiple, intersecting injustices. Although I cannot make the full argument here, I will venture three reasons for expecting that the combination of socialism and deconstruction will again prove superior to the other alternatives.

First, the arguments pursued here for gender and "race" hold for all bivalent collectivities. Thus, insofar as real-world collectivities mobilized under the banners of sexuality and class turn out to be more bivalent than the ideal-typical constructs posited above, they too should prefer socialism plus deconstruction. And that doubly transformative approach should become the orientation of choice for a broad range of disadvantaged groups.

Second, the redistribution-recognition dilemma does not arise only endogenously, as it were, within a single bivalent collectivity. It also arises exogenously, so to speak, across intersecting collectivities. Thus, anyone who is both gay and working-class will face a version of the dilemma, regardless of whether or not we interpret sexuality and class as bivalent. And anyone who is also female and black will encounter it in a multilayered and acute form. In general, then, as soon as we acknowledge that axes of injustice cut across one another, we must acknowledge crosscutting forms of the redistribution-recognition dilemma. And these forms are, if anything, even more resistant to resolution by combinations of affirmative remedies than the forms we considered above. For affirmative remedies work additively and are often at cross-purposes with one another. Thus, the intersection of class, "race," gender, and sexuality intensifies the need for transformative solutions, making the combination of socialism and deconstruction more attractive still.

Third, that combination best promotes coalition building. Coalition building is especially pressing today, given the multiplication of social antagonisms, the fissuring of social movements, and the growing appeal of the Right in the United States. In this context, the project of transforming the deep structures of both political economy and culture appears to be the one overarching programmatic orientation capable of doing justice to *all* current struggles against injustice. It alone does not assume a zero-sum game.

If that is right, then we can begin to see how badly off track is the current U.S. political scene. We are stuck in the vicious circles of mutually reinforcing cultural and economic subordination. Our best efforts to redress these injustices by means of the combination of the liberal welfare state plus mainstream multiculturalism are generating perverse effects. Only by looking to alternative conceptions of redistribution and recognition can we meet the requirements of justice for all.

Notes

1. Research for this chapter was supported by the Bohen Foundation, the Institut für die Wissenschaften vom Menschen in Vienna, the Humanities Research Institute at the University of California, Irvine, the Center for Urban Affairs and Policy Research at Northwestern University, and the Dean of the Graduate Faculty of the New School for Social Research. For helpful comments, I thank Robin Blackburn, Judith Butler, Angela Harris, Randall Kennedy, Ted Koditschek, Jane Mansbridge, Mika Manty, Linda Nicholson, Eli Zaretsky, and the members of the Feminism and the Discourses of Power work group at UCI Humanities Research Institute.

2. This omission notwithstanding, the framework elaborated below could prove fruitful for addressing struggles around ethnicity and nationality. It encourages us to pay attention in each case to the relative weight of claims for redistribution and claims for recognition, instead of assuming by default that groups mobilized along these lines are struggling only for recognition. Of course, insofar as such groups do not define themselves as sharing a situation of socioeconomic disadvantage and do not make redistributive claims, they can be understood as struggling primarily for recognition. National struggles are peculiar, however, in that the form of recognition they seek is political autonomy, whether in the form of a sovereign state of their own (e.g., the Palestinians) or in the form of more limited provincial sovereignty within a multinational state (e.g., the majority of Québècois). Struggles for ethnic recognition, in contrast, often seek rights of cultural expression within polyethnic nation-states. These distinctions are insightfully discussed in Will Kymlicka, "Three Forms of Group-Differentiated Citizenship in Canada," in *Democracy and Difference: Contesting the Boundaries of the Political,* ed. Seyla Benhabib (Princeton: Princeton University Press, 1996).

3. My principal concern in this essay is the relation between the recognition of cultural difference and social equality. I am not directly concerned, therefore, with the relation between recognition of cultural difference and liberalism. However, I assume that no identity politics is acceptable that fails to respect fundamental human rights of the sort usually championed by left-wing liberals.

4. Karl Marx, *Capital,* vol. 1; John Rawls, *A Theory of Justice* (Cambridge: Harvard University Press, 1971) and subsequent papers; Amartya Sen, *Commodities and Capabilities* (Amsterdam: North-Holland, 1985); and Ronald Dworkin, "What Is Equality? Part 2: Equality of Resources," *Philosophy and Public Affairs* 10, no. 4 (fall 1981): 283–345. Although I here classify all these writers as theorists of distributive economic justice, it is also true that most of them have some resources for dealing with issues of cultural justice as well. Rawls, for example, treats "the social bases of self-respect" as a primary good to be fairly distributed, and Sen treats a "sense of self" as relevant to the capability to function. (I am indebted to Mika Manty for this point.) Nevertheless, as Iris

Marion Young has suggested, the primary thrust of their thought leads in the direction of distributive economic justice. (See her *Justice and the Politics of Difference* [Princeton: Princeton University Press, 1990].)

5. Charles Taylor, *Multiculturalism and "The Politics of Recognition"* (Princeton: Princeton University Press, 1992), p. 25.

6. Axel Honneth, "Integrity and Disrespect: Principles of a Conception of Morality Based on the Theory of Recognition," *Political Theory* 20, no. 2 (May 1992): 188–89. It is no accident that both of the major contemporary theorists of recognition, Honneth and Taylor, are Hegelians.

7. See, for example, Patricia J. Williams, *The Alchemy of Race and Rights* (Cambridge: Harvard University Press, 1991) and Iris Marion Young, *Justice and the Politics of Difference* (Princeton: Princeton University Press, 1990).

8. The interimbrication of culture and political economy is a leitmotiv of all my work. I argued this point in several chapters of my *Unruly Practices: Power, Discourse and Gender in Contemporary Social Theory* (Minneapolis: University of Minnesota Press, 1989), including "What's Critical about Critical Theory? The Case of Habermas and Gender"; "Women, Welfare, and the Politics of Need Interpretation"; and "Struggle over Needs: Outline of a Socialist-Feminist Critical Theory of Late-Capitalist Political Culture." The point is central to many chapters of this volume as well, especially "Rethinking the Public Sphere: A Contribution to the Critique of Actually Existing Democracy" and "A Genealogy of 'Dependency': Tracing a Keyword of the U.S. Welfare State."

9. In fact, these remedies stand in some tension with one another, a problem I shall explore in a subsequent section of this chapter.

10. These various cultural remedies stand in some tension with one another. It is one thing to accord recognition to existing identities that are currently undervalued; it is another to transform symbolic structures and thereby alter people's identities. I shall explore the tensions among the various remedies in a subsequent section.

11. For a good example of this approach, see Ronald Dworkin, "Liberalism," in his *A Matter of Principle* (Cambridge: Harvard University Press, 1985), pp. 181–204.

12. For a good example of this approach, see Will Kymlicka, *Liberalism, Community and Culture* (Oxford: Oxford University Press, 1989). The case of Kymlicka suggests that the distinction between socioeconomic justice and cultural justice need not always map onto the distinction between distributive justice and relational or communicative justice.

13. Axel Honneth's *The Struggle for Recognition: The Moral Grammar of Social Conflicts,* trans. Joel Anderson (Cambridge: Polity Press, 1995) represents the most thorough and sophisticated attempt at such a reduction. He argues that recognition is the fundamental concept of justice and can encompass distribution. I argue against that view and for a "perspectival dualism" in my 1996 Tanner Lectures (unpublished typescript, forthcoming from the University of Utah Press).

14. Absent such a distinction, we foreclose the possibility of examining conflicts between them. We miss the chance to spot mutual interferences that could arise when redistribution claims and recognition claims are pursued simultaneously.

15. In what follows, I conceive class in a highly stylized, orthodox, and theoretical way in order to sharpen the contrast to the other ideal-typical kinds of collectivity discussed below. Of course, this is hardly the only interpretation of the Marxian conception of class. In other contexts and for other purposes, I myself would prefer a less economistic interpretation, one that gives more weight to the cultural, historical, and discursive dimensions of class emphasized by such writers as E. P. Thompson and Joan Wallach

Scott. See Thompson, *The Making of the English Working Class* (New York: Random House, 1963); and Scott, *Gender and the Politics of History* (New York: Columbia University Press, 1988).

16. It is doubtful that any collectivities mobilized in the real world today correspond to the notion of class presented below. Certainly, the history of social movements mobilized under the banner of class is more complex than this conception would suggest. Those movements have elaborated class not only as a structural category of political economy but also as a cultural-valuational category of identity—often in forms problematic for women and blacks. Thus, most varieties of socialism have asserted the dignity of labor and the worth of working people, mingling demands for redistribution with demands for recognition. Sometimes, moreover, having failed to abolish capitalism, class movements have adopted reformist strategies of seeking recognition of their "difference" within the system in order to augment their power and support demands for what I below call "affirmative redistribution." In general, then, historical class-based movements may be closer to what I below call "bivalent modes of collectivity" than to the interpretation of class sketched here.

17. This assumption does not require us to reject the view that distributive deficits are often (perhaps even always) accompanied by recognition deficits. But it does entail that the recognition deficits of class, in the sense elaborated here, derive from the political economy. Later, I shall consider other sorts of cases in which collectivities suffer from recognition deficits whose roots are not directly political-economic in this way.

18. In what follows, I conceive sexuality in a highly stylized theoretical way in order to sharpen the contrast to the other ideal-typical kinds of collectivity discussed here. I treat sexual differentiation as rooted wholly in the cultural structure, as opposed to in the political economy. Of course, this is not the only interpretation of sexuality. Judith Butler (personal communication) has suggested that one might hold that sexuality is inextricable from gender, which, as I argue below, is as much a matter of the division of labor as of the cultural-valuational structure. In that case, sexuality itself might be viewed as a "bivalent" collectivity, rooted simultaneously in culture and political economy. Then, the economic harms encountered by homosexuals might appear economically rooted rather than culturally rooted, as they are in the account I offer here. While this bivalent analysis is certainly possible, to my mind it has serious drawbacks. Yoking gender and sexuality together too tightly, it covers over the important distinction between a group that occupies a distinct position in the division of labor (and that owes its existence in large part to this fact), on the one hand, and one that occupies no such distinct position, on the other hand. I discuss this distinction below.

19. An example of an economic injustice rooted directly in the economic structure would be a division of labor that relegates homosexuals to a designated disadvantaged position and exploits them as homosexuals. To deny that this is the situation of homosexuals today is not to deny that they face economic injustices but to trace these to another root. In general, I assume that recognition deficits are often (perhaps even always) accompanied by distribution deficits. But I nevertheless hold that the distribution deficits of sexuality, in the sense elaborated here, derive ultimately from the cultural structure. Later, I shall consider other sorts of cases in which collectivities suffer from distribution deficits whose roots are not (only) directly cultural in this sense. I can perhaps further clarify the point by invoking Oliver Cromwell Cox's contrast between anti-Semitism and white supremacy. Cox suggested that for the anti-Semite, the very existence of the Jew is an abomination; hence, the aim is not to exploit the Jew but to eliminate him/her as such, whether by expulsion, forced conversion, or extermination. For the white supremacist, in contrast, the "Negro" is just fine—in his/her place: as an exploitable supply of cheap,

menial labor power. Here the preferred aim is exploitation, not elimination. (See Cox's unjustly neglected masterwork *Caste, Class, and Race* [New York: Monthly Review Press, 1970].) Contemporary homophobia appears in this respect to be more like anti-Semitism than white supremacy: it seeks to eliminate, not exploit, homosexuals. Thus, the economic disadvantages of homosexuality are derived effects of the more fundamental denial of cultural recognition. This makes it the mirror image of class, as just discussed, where the "hidden (and not so hidden) injuries" of misrecognition are derived effects of the more fundamental injustice of exploitation. White supremacy, in contrast, as I shall suggest shortly, is "bivalent," rooted simultaneously in political economy and culture, inflicting co-original and equally fundamental injustices of distribution and recognition. (On this last point, incidentally, I differ from Cox, who treats white supremacy as effectively reducible to class.)

20. Gender disparagement can take many forms, of course, including conservative stereotypes that appear to celebrate, rather than demean, "femininity."

21. This helps explain why the history of women's movements records a pattern of oscillation between integrationist equal-rights feminisms and "difference"-oriented "social" and "cultural" feminisms. It would be useful to specify the precise temporal logic that leads bivalent collectivities to shift their principal focus back and forth between redistribution and recognition. For a first attempt, see my "Multiculturalism, Antiessentialism, and Radical Democracy" in this volume.

22. In addition, "race" is implicitly implicated in the gender division between paid and unpaid labor. That division relies on a normative contrast between a domestic sphere and a sphere of paid work, associated with women and men respectively. Yet the division in the United States (and elsewhere) has always also been racialized in that domesticity has been implicitly a "white" prerogative. African Americans especially were never permitted the privilege of domesticity either as a (male) private "haven" or a (female) primary or exclusive focus on nurturing one's own kin. See Jacqueline Jones, *Labor of Love, Labor of Sorrow: Black Women, Work, and the Family from Slavery to the Present* (New York: Basic Books, 1985), and Evelyn Nakano Glenn, "From Servitude to Service Work: Historical Continuities in the Racial Division of Reproductive Labor." *Signs* 18, no. 1 (autumn 1992): 1–43.

23. In a previous draft of this paper I used the term 'denigration.' The ironic consequence was that I unintentionally perpetrated the exact sort of harm I aimed to criticize—in the very act of describing it. 'Denigration,' from the Latin *nigrare* (to blacken), figures disparagement as blackening, a racist valuation. I am grateful to the Saint Louis University student who called my attention to this point.

24. Racial disparagement can take many forms, of course, ranging from the stereotypical depiction of African Americans as intellectually inferior but musically and athletically gifted to the stereotypical depiction of Asian Americans as a "model minority."

25. This helps explain why the history of black liberation struggle in the United States records a pattern of oscillation between integration and separatism (or black nationalism). As with gender, it would be useful to specify the dynamics of these alternations.

26. Not all versions of multiculturalism fit the model I describe here. The latter is an ideal-typical reconstruction of what I take to be the majority understanding of multiculturalism. It is also mainstream in the sense of being the version that is usually debated in mainstream public spheres. Other versions are discussed in Linda Nicholson, "To Be or Not to Be: Charles Taylor on the Politics of Recognition," *Constellations* 3, no. 1 (1996): 1–16; and in Michael Warner et al., "Critical Multiculturalism," *Critical Inquiry* 18, no. 3 (spring 1992): 530–56.

27. Recall that sexuality is here assumed to be a mode of social differentiation rooted wholly in the cultural-valuational structure of society; thus, the issues here are unclouded by issues of political-economic structure, and the need is for recognition, not redistribution.

28. An alternative affirmative approach is gay-rights humanism, which would privatize existing sexualities. For reasons of space, I shall not discuss it here.

29. For a discussion of the tendency in gay-identity politics to cast sexuality tacitly in the mold of ethnicity, see Steven Epstein, "Gay Politics, Ethnic Identity: The Limits of Social Constructionism," *Socialist Review,* May–August 1987, no. 93/94: 9–54.

30. The technical term for this in Jacques Derrida's deconstructive philosophy is *supplement.*

31. Despite its professed long-term deconstructive goal, the practical effects of queer politics may be more ambiguous. Like gay-identity politics, it, too, seems likely to promote group solidarity in the here and now, even as it sets its sights on the promised land of deconstruction. Perhaps, then, we should distinguish what I below call its "official recognition commitment" of group dedifferentiation from its "practical recognition effect" of (transitional) group solidarity and even group solidification. The queer recognition strategy thus contains an internal tension: in order eventually to destabilize the homo-hetero dichotomy, it must first mobilize "queers." Whether this tension becomes fruitful or debilitating depends on factors too complex to discuss here. In either case, however, the queer recognition strategy remains distinct from that of gay-identity politics. Whereas the latter simply and straightforwardly underlines group differentiation, queer politics does so only indirectly, in the undertow of its principal dedifferentiating thrust. Accordingly, the two approaches construct qualitatively different kinds of groups. Whereas gay-identity politics mobilizes self-identified homosexuals qua homosexuals to vindicate a putatively determinate sexuality, queer politics mobilizes "queers" to demand liberation from determinate sexual identity. "Queers," of course, are not an identity group in the same sense as gays; perhaps they are better understood as an anti-identity group, one that can encompass the entire spectrum of sexual behaviors, from gay to straight to bi. (For a hilarious—and insightful—account of the difference, as well as for a sophisticated rendition of queer politics, see Lisa Duggan, "Queering the State," *Social Text,* summer 1994, no. 39: 1–14.) Complications aside, then, we can and should distinguish the (directly) differentiating effects of affirmative gay recognition from the (more) dedifferentiating (albeit complex) effects of transformative queer recognition.

32. By "liberal welfare state," I mean the sort of regime established in the United States in the aftermath of the New Deal. It has been usefully distinguished from the social-democratic welfare state and the conservative-corporatist welfare state by Gøsta Esping-Andersen in *The Three Worlds of Welfare Capitalism* (Princeton: Princeton University Press, 1990).

33. Today, of course, many specific features of socialism of the "really existing" variety appear problematic. Virtually no one continues to defend a pure "command" economy in which there is little place for markets. Nor is there agreement concerning the place and extent of public ownership in a democratic socialist society. For my purposes here, however, it is not necessary to assign a precise content to the socialist idea. It is sufficient, rather, to invoke the general conception of redressing distributive injustice by deep political-economic restructuring, as opposed to surface reallocations. In this light, incidentally, social democracy appears as a hybrid case that combines affirmative and transformative remedies; it can also be seen as a "middle position," which involves a moderate extent of economic restructuring, more than in the liberal welfare state but less than in socialism.

34. Recall that class, in the sense defined above, is a collectivity wholly rooted in the political-economic structure of society; the issues here are thus unclouded by issues of cultural-valuational structure, and the remedies required are those of redistribution, not recognition.

35. In some contexts, such as the United States today, the practical recognition-effect of affirmative redistribution can utterly swamp its official recognition commitment.

36. My terminology here is inspired by Pierre Bourdieu's distinction, in *Outline of a Theory of Practice* (Cambridge: Cambridge University Press, 1977), between "official kinship" and "practical kinship."

37. I have deliberately sketched a picture that is ambiguous between socialism and robust social democracy. The classic account of the latter remains T. H. Marshall's "Citizenship and Social Class," in *Class, Citizenship, and Social Development: Essays by T. H. Marshall*, ed. Seymour Martin Lipset (Chicago: University of Chicago Press, 1964). There, Marshall argues that a universalist social-democratic regime of "social citizenship" undermines class differentiation, even in the absence of full-scale socialism.

38. To be more precise: transformative redistribution can help redress those forms of misrecognition that derive from the political-economic structure. Redressing misrecognition rooted in the cultural structure, in contrast, requires additional independent recognition remedies.

39. Recall that gender, qua political-economic differentiation, structures the division of labor in ways that give rise to gender-specific forms of exploitation, marginalization, and deprivation. Recall, moreover, that qua cultural-valuational differentiation, gender also structures the relations of recognition in ways that give rise to androcentrism and cultural sexism. Recall, too, that for gender, as for all bivalent group differentiations, economic injustices and cultural injustices are not neatly separated from one another; rather, they intertwine to reinforce each other dialectically because sexist and androcentric cultural norms are institutionalized in the economy, while economic disadvantage impedes equal participation in the making of culture, both in everyday life and in public spheres.

40. With regard to the unpromising cases, let me simply stipulate that a cultural-feminist recognition politics aimed at revaluing femininity is hard to combine with a socialist-feminist redistributive politics aimed at degendering the political economy. The incompatibility is overt when we treat the recognition of "women's difference" as a long-term feminist goal. Of course, some feminists conceive the struggle for such recognition not as end in itself but as a stage in a process they envision as leading eventually to degenderization. Here, perhaps, there is no formal contradiction with socialism. At the same time, however, there remains a practical contradiction, or at least a practical difficulty: can a stress on women's difference in the here and now really end up dissolving gender difference in the by and by? The converse argument holds for the other unpromising case, the case of the liberal-feminist welfare state plus deconstructive-feminism. Affirmative action for women is usually seen as a transitional remedy aimed at achieving the long-term goal of "a sex-blind society." Here, again, there is perhaps no formal contradiction with deconstruction. But there remains nevertheless a practical contradiction, or at least a practical difficulty: can liberal-feminist affirmative action in the here and now really help lead us to deconstruction in the by and by?

41. Here I am assuming that the internal complexities of transformative recognition remedies, as discussed in note 31 above, do not generate perverse effects. If, however, the practical recognition effect of deconstructive-feminist cultural politics is strongly gender-differentiating, despite the latter's official recognition commitment to gender dedifferentiation, perverse effects could indeed arise. In that case, there could be interferences between socialist-feminist redistribution and deconstructive-feminist recognition. But these would probably be less debilitating than those associated with the other scenarios examined here.

42. The same can be said about "race" here as about gender in notes 39 and 40 above.

43. Once again, I am assuming that the internal complexities of transformative recognition remedies, as discussed in note 31 above, do not generate perverse effects. If, however, the practical recognition effect of deconstructive antiracist cultural politics is strongly color-differentiating, despite the latter's official recognition commitment to racial dedifferentiation, perverse effects could indeed arise. The result could be some mutual interferences between antiracist socialist redistribution and antiracist deconstructive recognition. But again, these would probably be less debilitating than those accompanying the other scenarios examined here.

44. Ted Koditschek (personal communication) has suggested to me that this scenario may have another serious drawback: "The deconstructive option may be less available to African Americans in the current situation. Where the structural exclusion of [many] black people from full economic citizenship pushes 'race' more and more into the forefront as a cultural category through which one is attacked, self-respecting people cannot help but aggressively affirm and embrace it as a source of pride." Koditschek goes on to suggest that Jews, in contrast, "have much more elbow room for negotiating a healthier balance between ethnic affirmation, self-criticism, and cosmopolitan universalism—not because we are better deconstructionists (or more inherently disposed toward socialism) but because we have more space to make these moves."

45. Whether this conclusion holds as well for nationality and ethnicity remains a question. Certainly bivalent collectivities of indigenous peoples do not seek to put themselves out of business as groups.

46. This has always been the problem with socialism. Although cognitively compelling, it is experientially remote. The addition of deconstruction seems to exacerbate the problem. It could turn out to be too negative and reactive, i.e., too *deconstructive,* to inspire struggles on behalf of subordinated collectivities attached to their existing identities.

47. Much recent work has been devoted to the "intersection" of the various axes of subordination that I have treated separately in this essay for heuristic purposes. A lot of this work concerns the dimension of recognition; it aims to demonstrate that various collective identifications and identity categories have been mutually co-constituted or co-constructed. Scott, for example, has argued (in *Gender and the Politics of History*) that French working-class identities have been discursively constructed through gender-coded symbolization; and David R. Roediger has argued (in *The Wages of Whiteness: Race and the Making of the American Working Class* [London: Verso, 1991]) that U.S. working-class identities have been racially coded. Meanwhile, many feminists of color have argued both that gender identities have been racially coded and that racialized identities have been gender coded. In chapter 5 of this volume, "A Genealogy of 'Dependency'," Linda Gordon and I argue that gender, "race," and class ideologies have intersected to construct current U.S. understandings of "welfare dependency" and "the underclass."

2

After the Family Wage

A Postindustrial Thought Experiment

The current crisis of the welfare state has many roots—global economic trends, massive movements of refugees and immigrants, popular hostility to taxes, the weakening of trade unions and labor parties, the rise of national and "racial"-ethnic antagonisms, the decline of solidaristic ideologies, and the collapse of state socialism. One absolutely crucial factor, however, is the crumbling of the old gender order. Existing welfare states are premised on assumptions about gender that are increasingly out of phase with many people's lives and self-understandings. They therefore do not provide adequate social protections, especially for women and children.[1]

The gender order that is now disappearing descends from the industrial era of capitalism and reflects the social world of its origin. It was centered on the ideal of *the family wage*. In this world people were supposed to be organized into heterosexual, male-headed nuclear families, which lived principally from the man's labor-market earnings. The male head of the household would be paid a family wage, sufficient to support children and a full-time wife-and-mother, who performed domestic labor without pay. Of course, countless lives never fit this pattern. Still, it provided the normative picture of a proper family.

The family-wage ideal was inscribed in the structure of most industrial-era welfare states.[2] That structure had three tiers, with social-insurance programs occupying the first rank. Designed to protect people from the vagaries of the labor market (and to protect the economy from shortages of

41

demand), these programs replaced the breadwinner's wage in case of sickness, disability, unemployment, or old age. Many countries also featured a second tier of programs, providing direct support for full-time female homemaking and mothering. A third tier served the "residuum." Largely a holdover from traditional poor relief, public assistance programs provided paltry, stigmatized, means-tested aid to needy people who had no claim to honorable support because they did not fit the family-wage scenario.[3]

Today, however, the family-wage assumption is no longer tenable—either empirically or normatively. We are currently experiencing the death throes of the old, industrial gender order with the transition to a new, *postindustrial* phase of capitalism. The crisis of the welfare state is bound up with these epochal changes. It is rooted in part in the collapse of the world of the family wage, and of its central assumptions about labor markets and families.

In the labor markets of postindustrial capitalism, few jobs pay wages sufficient to support a family single-handedly; many, in fact, are temporary or part-time and do not carry standard benefits.[4] Women's employment is increasingly common, moreover—although far less well paid than men's.[5] Postindustrial families, meanwhile, are less conventional and more diverse.[6] Heterosexuals are marrying less and later, and divorcing more and sooner. And gays and lesbians are pioneering new kinds of domestic arrangements.[7] Gender norms and family forms are highly contested, finally. Thanks in part to the feminist and gay-and-lesbian liberation movements, many people no longer prefer the male breadwinner/female homemaker model. One result of these trends is a steep increase in solo-mother families: growing numbers of women, both divorced and never married, are struggling to support themselves and their families without access to a male breadwinner's wage. Their families have high rates of poverty.

In short, a new world of economic production and social reproduction is emerging—a world of less stable employment and more diverse families. Though no one can be certain about its ultimate shape, this much seems clear: the emerging world, no less than the world of the family wage, will require a welfare state that effectively insures people against uncertainties. It is clear, too, that the old forms of welfare state, built on assumptions of male-headed families and relatively stable jobs, are no longer suited to providing this protection. We need something new, a postindustrial welfare state suited to radically new conditions of employment and reproduction.

What, then, should a postindustrial welfare state look like? Conservatives have lately had a lot to say about "restructuring the welfare state," but their vision is counterhistorical and contradictory; they seek to reinstate the male breadwinner/female homemaker family for the middle class, while demanding that poor single mothers "work." Neoliberal policies have recently been instituted in the United States but they, too, are inadequate in the current context. Punitive, androcentric, and obsessed with employment despite the absence of good jobs, they are unable to provide security in a postindustrial world.[8] Both these approaches ignore one crucial thing: a postindustrial welfare state, like its industrial predecessor, must support a gender order. But the only kind of gender order that can be acceptable today is one premised on *gender equity.*

Feminists, therefore, are in a good position to generate an emancipatory vision for the coming period. They, more than anyone, appreciate the importance of gender relations to the current crisis of the industrial welfare state and the centrality of gender equity to any satisfactory resolution. Feminists also appreciate the importance of carework for human well-being and the effects of its social organization on women's standing. They are attuned, finally, to potential conflicts of interest within families and to the inadequacy of androcentric definitions of work.

To date, however, feminists have tended to shy away from systematic reconstructive thinking about the welfare state. Nor have we yet developed a satisfactory account of gender equity that can inform an emancipatory vision. We need now to undertake such thinking. We should ask: What new, postindustrial gender order should replace the family wage? And what sort of welfare state can best support such a new gender order? What account of gender equity best captures our highest aspirations? And what vision of social welfare comes closest to embodying it?

Two different sorts of answers are currently conceivable, I think, both of which qualify as feminist. The first I call the Universal Breadwinner model. It is the vision implicit in the current political practice of most U.S. feminists and liberals. It aims to foster gender equity by promoting women's employment; the centerpiece of this model is state provision of employment-enabling services such as day care. The second possible answer I call the Caregiver Parity model. It is the vision implicit in the current political practice of most Western European feminists and social democrats. It aims to promote gender equity chiefly by supporting informal carework; the centerpiece of this model is state provision of caregiver allowances.

Which of these two approaches should command our loyalties in the coming period? Which expresses the most attractive vision of a postindustrial gender order? Which best embodies the ideal of gender equity?

In this chapter, I outline a framework for thinking systematically about these questions. I analyze highly idealized versions of Universal Breadwinner and Caregiver Parity in the manner of a thought experiment. I postulate, contrary to fact, a world in which both these models are feasible in that their economic and political preconditions are in place. Assuming very favorable conditions, then, I assess the respective strengths and weaknesses of each.

The result is not a standard policy analysis, however, for neither Universal Breadwinner nor Caregiver Parity will in fact be realized in the near future; and my discussion is not directed primarily at policy-making elites. My intent, rather, is theoretical and political in a broader sense. I aim, first, to clarify some dilemmas surrounding "equality" and "difference" by reconsidering what is meant by gender equity. In so doing, I also aim to spur increased reflection on feminist strategies and goals by spelling out some assumptions that are implicit in current practice and subjecting them to critical scrutiny.

My discussion proceeds in four parts. In the first section, I propose an analysis of gender equity that generates a set of evaluative standards. Then, in the second and third sections, I apply those standards to Universal Breadwinner and Caregiver Parity, respectively. I conclude, in the fourth section, that neither of those approaches, even in an idealized form, can deliver full gender equity. To have a shot at *that,* I contend, we must develop a new vision of a postindustrial welfare state that effectively dismantles the gender division of labor.

Gender Equity: A Complex Conception

To evaluate alternative visions of a postindustrial welfare state, we need some normative criteria. Gender equity, I have said, is one indispensable standard. But of what precisely does it consist?

Feminists have so far associated gender equity with either equality or difference, where "equality" means treating women exactly like men, and where "difference" means treating women differently insofar as they differ from men. Theorists have debated the relative merits of these two approaches as if they represented two antithetical poles of an absolute dichotomy. These arguments have generally ended in stalemate. Proponents of "difference" have successfully shown that equality strategies typically presuppose "the male as norm," thereby disadvantaging women and imposing a distorted standard on everyone. Egalitarians have argued just as cogently, however, that difference approaches typically rely on essentialist notions of femininity, thereby reinforcing existing stereotypes and confining women within existing gender divisions.[9] Neither equality nor difference, then, is a workable conception of gender equity.

Feminists have responded to this stalemate in several ways. Some have tried to resolve the dilemma by reconceiving one or another of its horns;

they have reinterpreted difference or equality in what they consider a more defensible form. Others have concluded "a plague on both your houses" and sought some third, wholly other, normative principle. Still others have tried to embrace the dilemma as an enabling paradox, a resource to be treasured, not an impasse to be gotten round. Many feminists, finally, have retreated altogether from normative theorizing—into cultural positivism, piecemeal reformism, or postmodern antinomianism.

None of these responses is satisfactory. Normative theorizing remains an indispensable intellectual enterprise for feminism, indeed for all emancipatory social movements. We need a vision or picture of where we are trying to go, and a set of standards for evaluating various proposals as to how we might get there. The equality/difference theoretical impasse is real, moreover; it cannot be simply sidestepped or embraced. Nor is there any "wholly other" third term that can magically catapult us beyond it. What, then, should feminist theorists do?

I propose we reconceptualize gender equity as a complex, not a simple, idea. This means breaking with the assumption that gender equity can be identified with any single value or norm, whether it be equality, difference, or something else. Instead, we should treat it as a complex notion comprising a plurality of distinct normative principles. The plurality will include some notions associated with the equality side of the debate, as well as some associated with the difference side. It will also encompass still other normative ideas that neither side has accorded due weight. Wherever they come from, however, the important point is this: each of several distinct norms must be respected simultaneously in order that gender equity be achieved. Failure to satisfy any one of them means failure to realize the full meaning of gender equity.

In what follows, I assume that gender equity is complex in this way. And I propose an account of it that is designed for the specific purpose of evaluating alternative pictures of a postindustrial welfare state. For issues other than welfare, a somewhat different package of norms might be called for. Nevertheless, I believe that the general idea of treating gender equity as a complex conception is widely applicable. The analysis here may serve as a paradigm case demonstrating the usefulness of this approach.

For this particular thought experiment, in any case, I unpack the idea of gender equity as a compound of seven distinct normative principles. Let me enumerate them one by one.

1. The Antipoverty Principle. The first and most obvious objective of social-welfare provision is to prevent poverty. Preventing poverty is crucial to achieving gender equity now, after the family wage, given the high rates of poverty in solo-mother families and the vastly increased likelihood that U.S. women and children will live in such families.[10] If it accomplishes nothing else, a welfare state should at least relieve suffering by meeting otherwise unmet basic needs. Arrangements, such as those in the United States, that leave women, children, and men in poverty, are unacceptable according to this criterion. Any postindustrial welfare state that prevented such poverty would constitute a major advance. So far, however, this does not say enough. The antipoverty principle might be satisfied in a variety of different ways, not all of which are acceptable. Some ways, such as the provision of targeted, isolating, and stigmatized poor relief for solo-mother families, fail to respect several of the following normative principles, which are also essential to gender equity in social welfare.

2. The Antiexploitation Principle. Antipoverty measures are important not only in themselves but also as a means to another basic objective: preventing exploitation of vulnerable people.[11] This principle, too, is central to achieving gender equity after the family wage. Needy women with no other way to feed themselves and their children, for example, are liable to exploitation—by abusive husbands, by sweatshop foremen, and by pimps. In guaranteeing relief of poverty, then, welfare provision should also aim to mitigate exploitable dependency.[12] The availability of an alternative source of income enhances the bargaining position of subordinates in unequal relationships. The nonemployed wife who knows she can support herself and her children outside her marriage has more leverage within it; her "voice" is enhanced as her possibilities of "exit" increase.[13] The same holds for the low-paid nursing-home attendant in relation to her boss.[14] For welfare measures to have this effect, however, support must be provided as a matter of right. When receipt of aid is highly stigmatized or discretionary, the antiexploitation principle is not satisfied.[15] At best the claimant would trade exploitable dependence on a husband or a boss for exploitable dependence on a caseworker's whim.[16] The goal should be to prevent at least three kinds of exploitable dependencies: exploitable dependence on an individual family member, such as a husband or an adult child; exploitable dependence on employers and supervisors; and exploitable dependence on the personal whims of state officials. Rather than shuttle people back and forth among these exploitable dependencies, an adequate approach must prevent all three simultaneously.[17] This principle rules out arrangements that channel a homemaker's benefits through her husband. It is likewise incompatible with arrangements that provide essential goods, such as health insurance, only in forms linked conditionally to scarce employment. Any postindustrial welfare state that satisfied the antiexploitation principle would represent a major improvement over current U.S. arrangements. But even it might not be satisfactory. Some ways of satisfying this principle would fail to respect several of the following normative principles, which are also essential to gender equity in social welfare.

A postindustrial welfare state could prevent women's poverty and exploitation and yet still tolerate severe gender inequality. Such a welfare state is not satisfactory. A further dimension of gender equity in social provision is redistribution, reducing inequality between women and men. Equality, as we saw, has been criticized by some feminists. They have argued that it entails treating women exactly like men according to male-defined standards, and that this necessarily disadvantages women. That argument expresses a legitimate worry, which I shall address under another rubric below, but it does not undermine the ideal of equality per se. The worry pertains only to certain inadequate ways of conceiving equality, which I do not presuppose here. At least three distinct conceptions of equality escape the objection. These are essential to gender equity in social welfare.

3. The Income-Equality Principle. One form of equality that is crucial to gender equity concerns the distribution of real per capita income. This sort of equality is highly pressing now, after the family wage, when U.S. women's earnings are approximately 70 percent of men's, when much of women's labor is not compensated at all, and when many women suffer from "hidden poverty" due to unequal distribution within families.[18] As I interpret it, the principle of income equality does not require absolute leveling, but it does rule out arrangements that reduce women's incomes after divorce by nearly half, while men's incomes nearly double.[19] It likewise rules out unequal pay for equal work and the wholesale undervaluation of women's labor and skills. The income-equality principle requires a substantial reduction in the vast discrepancy between men's and women's incomes. In so doing, it tends, as well, to help equalize the life-chances of children in that a majority of U.S. children are currently likely to live at some point in solo-mother families.[20]

4. The Leisure-Time-Equality Principle. Another kind of equality that is crucial to gender equity concerns the distribution of leisure time. This sort of equality is highly pressing now, after the family wage, when many women, but only a few men, do both paid work and unpaid primary carework and when women suffer disproportionately from "time poverty."[21] One recent British study found that 52 percent of women surveyed, compared to 21 percent of men, said they "felt tired most of the time."[22] The leisure-time-equality principle rules out welfare arrangements that would equalize incomes while requiring a double shift of work from women but only a single shift from men. It likewise rules out arrangements that would require women, but not men, to do either the "work of claiming" or the time-consuming "patchwork" of piecing together income from several sources and of coordinating services from different agencies and associations.[23]

5. *The Equality-of-Respect Principle.* Equality of respect is also crucial to gender equity. This kind of equality is especially pressing now, after the family wage, when postindustrial culture routinely represents women as sexual objects for the pleasure of male subjects. The principle of equal respect rules out social arrangements that objectify and deprecate women—even if those arrangements prevent poverty and exploitation, and even if in addition they equalize income and leisure time. It is incompatible with welfare programs that trivialize women's activities and ignore women's contributions—hence with "welfare reforms" in the United States that assume AFDC claimants do not "work." Equality of respect requires recognition of women's personhood and recognition of women's work.

A postindustrial welfare state should promote equality in all three of these dimensions. Such a state would constitute an enormous advance over present arrangements, but even it might not go far enough. Some ways of satisfying the equality principles would fail to respect the following principle, which is also essential to gender equity in social welfare.

6. *The Antimarginalization Principle.* A welfare state could satisfy all the preceding principles and still function to marginalize women. By limiting support to generous mothers' pensions, for example, it could render women independent, well provided for, well rested, and respected but enclaved in a separate domestic sphere, removed from the life of the larger society. Such a welfare state would be unacceptable. Social policy should promote women's full participation on a par with men in all areas of social life—in employment, in politics, in the associational life of civil society. The antimarginalization principle requires provision of the necessary conditions for women's participation, including day care, elder care, and provision for breast-feeding in public. It also requires the dismantling of masculinist work cultures and woman-hostile political environments. Any postindustrial welfare state that provided these things would represent a great improvement over current arrangements. Yet even it might leave something to be desired. Some ways of satisfying the antimarginalization principle would fail to respect the last principle, which is also essential to gender equity in social welfare.

7. *The Antiandrocentrism Principle.* A welfare state that satisfied many of the foregoing principles could still entrench some obnoxious gender norms. It could assume the androcentric view that men's current life patterns represent the human norm and that women ought to assimilate to

them. (This is the real issue behind the previously noted worry about equality.) Such a welfare state is unacceptable. Social policy should not require women to become like men nor to fit into institutions designed for men, in order to enjoy comparable levels of well-being. Policy should aim instead to restructure androcentric institutions so as to welcome human beings who can give birth and who often care for relatives and friends, treating them not as exceptions but as ideal-typical participants. The antiandrocentrism principle requires decentering masculinist norms—in part by revaluing practices and traits that are currently undervalued because they are associated with women. It entails changing men as well as changing women.

Here, then, is an account of gender equity in social welfare. On this account, gender equity is a complex idea comprising seven distinct normative principles, each of which is necessary and essential. No postindustrial welfare state can realize gender equity unless it satisfies them all.

How, then, do the principles interrelate? Here everything depends on context. Some institutional arrangements permit simultaneous satisfaction of several principles with a minimum of mutual interference; other arrangements, in contrast, set up zero-sum situations, in which attempts to satisfy one principle interfere with attempts to satisfy another. Promoting gender equity after the family wage, therefore, means attending to multiple aims that are potentially in conflict. The goal should be to find approaches that avoid trade-offs and maximize prospects for satisfying all—or at least most—of the seven principles.

In the next sections, I use this approach to assess two alternative models of a postindustrial welfare state. First, however, I want to flag four sets of relevant issues. One concerns the social organization of carework. Precisely how this work is organized is crucial to human well-being in general and to the social standing of women in particular. In the era of the family wage, carework was treated as the private responsibility of individual women. Today, however, it can no longer be treated in that way. Some other way of organizing it is required, but a number of different scenarios are conceivable. In evaluating postindustrial welfare state models, then, we must ask: How is responsibility for carework allocated between such institutions as the family, the market, civil society, and the state? And how is responsibility for this work assigned within such institutions: by gender? by class? by "race"-ethnicity? by age?

A second set of issues concerns the bases of entitlement to provision. Every welfare state assigns its benefits according to a specific mix of distributive principles, which defines its basic moral quality. That mix, in each case, needs to be scrutinized. Usually, it contains varying proportions of three basic principles of entitlement: need, desert, and citizenship. Need-based provision is the most redistributive, but it risks isolating and stigmatizing the needy; it has been the basis of traditional poor relief and of modern public assistance, the least honorable forms of provision. The most honorable, in contrast, is entitlement based on desert, but it tends to be antiegalitarian and exclusionary. Here one receives benefits according to one's "contributions," usually tax payments, work, and service—where "tax payments" means wage deductions paid into a special fund, "work" means primary labor-force employment, and "service" means the military, all interpretations of those terms that disadvantage women. Desert has usually been seen as the primary basis of earnings-linked social insurance in the industrial welfare state.[24] The third principle, citizenship, allocates provision on the basis of membership in society. It is honorable, egalitarian, and universalist, but also expensive, hence hard to sustain at high levels of quality and generosity; some theorists worry, too, that it encourages free-riding, which they define, however, androcentrically.[25] Citizenship-based entitlements are most often found in social-democratic countries, where they may include single-payer universal health insurance systems and universal family or child allowances; they are virtually unknown in the United States—except for public education. In examining models of postindustrial welfare states, then, one must look closely at the construction of entitlement. It makes considerable difference to women's and children's well-being, for example, whether day-care places are distributed as citizenship entitlements or as desert-based entitlements, that is, whether or not they are conditional on prior employment. It likewise matters, to take another example, whether carework is supported on the basis of need, in the form of a means-tested benefit for the poor, or whether it is supported on the basis of desert, as return for "work" or "service," now interpreted nonandrocentrically, or whether, finally, it is supported on the basis of citizenship under a universal Basic Income scheme.

A third set of issues concerns differences among women. Gender is the principal focus of this chapter, to be sure, but it cannot be treated en bloc. The lives of women and men are crosscut by several other salient social divisions, including class, "race"-ethnicity, sexuality, and age. Models of postindustrial welfare states, then, will not affect all women—nor all men—in the same way; they will generate different outcomes for differently situated people. For example, some policies will affect women who have children differently from those who do not; some, likewise, will affect women who have access to a second income differently from those who do not; and some, finally, will affect women employed full-time differently from those employed part-time, and differently yet again from those who are not employed. For each model, then, we must ask: Which groups of women would be advantaged and which groups disadvantaged?

A fourth set of issues concerns desiderata for postindustrial welfare states other than gender equity. Gender equity, after all, is not the only goal of social welfare. Also important are nonequity goals, such as efficiency, community, and individual liberty. In addition there remain other equity goals, such as "racial"-ethnic equity, generational equity, class equity, and equity among nations. All of these issues are necessarily backgrounded here. Some of them, however, such as "racial"-ethnic equity, could be handled by means of parallel thought experiments: one might define "racial"-ethnic equity as a complex idea, analogous to the way gender equity is treated here, and then use it, too, to assess competing visions of a postindustrial welfare state.

With these considerations in mind, let us now examine two strikingly different feminist visions of a postindustrial welfare state. And let us ask: Which comes closer to achieving gender equity in the sense I have elaborated here?

The Universal-Breadwinner Model

In one vision of postindustrial society, the age of the family wage would give way to the age of the Universal Breadwinner. This is the vision implicit in the current political practice of most U.S. feminists and liberals. (It was also assumed in the former communist countries!) It aims to achieve gender equity principally by promoting women's employment. The point is to enable women to support themselves and their families through their own wage-earning. The breadwinner role is to be universalized, in sum, so that women, too, can be citizen-workers.

Universal Breadwinner is a very ambitious postindustrial scenario, requiring major new programs and policies. One crucial element is a set of employment-enabling services, such as day care and elder care, aimed at freeing women from unpaid responsibilities so they could take full-time employment on terms comparable to men.[26] Another essential element is a set of workplace reforms aimed at removing equal-opportunity obstacles, such as sex discrimination and sexual harassment. Reforming the workplace requires reforming the culture, however—eliminating sexist stereotypes and breaking the cultural association of breadwinning with masculinity. Also required are policies to help change socialization, so as, first, to reorient women's aspirations toward employment and away from domesticity, and second, to reorient men's expectations toward acceptance of women's new role. None of this would work, however, without one additional ingredient: macroeconomic policies to create full-time, high-paying, permanent jobs for women.[27] These would have to be true breadwinner jobs in the primary labor force, carrying full, first-class social-insurance entitlements. Social insurance, finally, is central to Universal Breadwinner. The aim here is to bring women up to parity with men in an institution that has traditionally disadvantaged them.

How would this model organize carework? The bulk of such work would be shifted from the family to the market and the state, where it would be performed by employees for pay.[28] Who, then, are these employees likely to be? In many countries today, including the United States, paid institutional carework is poorly remunerated, feminized, and largely racialized and/or performed by immigrants.[29] But such arrangements are precluded in this model. If the model is to succeed in enabling *all* women to be breadwinners, it must upgrade the status and pay attached to carework employment, making it, too, into primary-labor-force work. Universal Breadwinner, then, is necessarily committed to a policy of "comparable worth"; it must redress the widespread undervaluation of skills and jobs currently coded as feminine and/or "nonwhite," and it must remunerate such jobs with breadwinner-level pay.

Universal Breadwinner would link many benefits to employment and distribute them through social insurance, with levels varying according to earnings. In this respect, the model resembles the industrial-era welfare state.[30] The difference is that many more women would be covered on the basis of their own employment records. And many more women's employment records would look considerably more like men's.

Not all adults can be employed, however. Some will be unable to work for medical reasons, including some adults not previously employed. Others will be unable to get jobs. Some, finally, will have carework responsibilities that they are unable or unwilling to shift elsewhere. Most of these last will be women. To provide for these people, Universal Breadwinner must include a residual tier of social welfare that provides need-based, means-tested wage replacements.[31]

Universal Breadwinner is far removed from present realities. It requires massive creation of primary-labor-force jobs—jobs sufficient to support a family single-handedly. That, of course, is wildly askew of current postindustrial trends, which generate jobs not for breadwinners but for "disposable workers."[32] Let us assume for the sake of the thought experiment, however, that its conditions of possibility could be met. And let us consider whether the resulting postindustrial welfare state could claim title to gender equity.

1. Antipoverty. We can acknowledge straight off that Universal Breadwinner would do a good job of preventing poverty. A policy that created secure breadwinner-quality jobs for all employable women and men—while providing the services that would enable women to take such jobs—would keep most families out of poverty. And generous levels of residual support would keep the rest out of poverty through transfers.[33]

2. Antiexploitation. The model should also succeed in preventing exploitable dependency for most women. Women with secure breadwinner jobs are able to exit unsatisfactory relations with men. And those who do not have such jobs but know they can get them will also be less vulnerable to exploitation. Failing that, the residual system of income support provides backup protection against exploitable dependency—assuming that it is generous, nondiscretionary, and honorable.[34]

3. Income equality. Universal Breadwinner is only fair, however, at achieving income equality. Granted, secure breadwinner jobs for women—plus the services that would enable women to take them—would narrow the gender wage gap.[35] Reduced inequality in earnings, moreover, translates into reduced inequality in social-insurance benefits. And the availability of exit options from marriage should encourage a more equitable distribution of resources within it. But the model is not otherwise egalitarian. It contains a basic social fault line dividing breadwinners from others, to the considerable disadvantage of the others—most of whom would be women. Apart from comparable worth, moreover, it does not reduce pay inequality among breadwinner jobs. To be sure, the model reduces the weight of gender in assigning individuals to unequally compensated breadwinner jobs, but it thereby increases the weight of other variables, presumably class, education, "race"-ethnicity, and age. Women—and men—who are disadvantaged in relation to those axes of social differentiation will earn less than those who are not.

4. Leisure-time equality. The model is quite poor, moreover, with respect to equality of leisure time, as we know from the communist experience. It assumes that all of women's current domestic and carework responsibilities can be shifted to the market and/or the state. But that assumption is patently unrealistic. Some things, such as childbearing, attending to family emergencies, and much parenting work, cannot be shifted—short of universal surrogacy and other presumably undesirable arrangements. Other things, such as cooking and (some) housekeeping, could—provided we were prepared to accept collective living arrangements or high levels of commodification. Even those tasks that are shifted, finally, do not disappear without a trace but give rise to burdensome new tasks of coordination. Women's chances for equal leisure, then, depend on whether men can be induced to do their fair share of this work. On this, the model does not inspire confidence. Not only does it offer no disincentives to free-riding, but in valorizing paid work, it implicitly devalues unpaid work, thereby fueling the motivation to shirk.[36] Women without partners would in any case be on their own. And those in lower-income households would be less able to purchase replacement services. Employed women would have a second shift on this model, then, albeit a less burdensome one than some have now; and there would be many more women employed full-time. Universal Breadwinner, in sum, is not likely to deliver equal leisure. Anyone who does not free-ride in this possible postindustrial world is likely to be harried and tired.

5. Equality of respect. The model is only fair, moreover, at delivering equality of respect. Because it holds men and women to the single standard of the citizen-worker, its only chance of eliminating the gender respect gap is to admit women to that status on the same terms as men. This, however, is unlikely to occur. A more likely outcome is that women would retain more connection to reproduction and domesticity than men, thus appearing as breadwinners manqué. In addition, the model is likely to generate another kind of respect gap. By putting a high premium on breadwinner status, it invites disrespect for others. Participants in the means-tested residual system will be liable to stigmatization, and most of these will be women. Any employment-centered model, even a feminist one, has a hard time constructing an honorable status for those it defines as "nonworkers."

6. Antimarginalization. This model is also only fair at combating women's marginalization. Granted, it promotes women's participation in employment, but its definition of participation is narrow. Expecting full-time employment of all who are able, the model may actually impede participation in politics and civil society. Certainly, it does nothing to promote women's participation in those arenas. It fights women's marginalization, then, in a one-sided, "workerist" way.

7. Antiandrocentrism. Last, the model performs poorly in overcoming androcentrism. It valorizes men's traditional sphere—employment—and simply tries to help women fit in. Traditionally female carework, in contrast, is treated instrumentally; it is what must be sloughed off in order to become a breadwinner. It is not itself accorded social value. The ideal-typical citizen here is the breadwinner, now nominally gender-neutral. But the content of the status is implicitly masculine; it is the male half of the old breadwinner/homemaker couple, now universalized and required of everyone. The female half of the couple has simply disappeared. None of her distinctive virtues and capacities has been preserved for women, let alone universalized to men. The model is androcentric.

We can summarize the merits of Universal Breadwinner in Figure 2.1. Not surprisingly, Universal Breadwinner delivers the best outcomes to women whose lives most closely resemble the male half of the old family-wage ideal couple. It is especially good to childless women and to women without other major domestic responsibilities that cannot easily be shifted to social services. But for those women, as well as for others, it falls short of full gender equity.

Figure 2.1

Principle	Universal Breadwinner
Antipoverty	good
Antiexploitation	good
Income equality	fair
Leisure-time equality	poor
Equality of respect	fair
Antimarginalization	fair
Antiandrocentrism	poor

The Caregiver-Parity Model

In a second vision of postindustrial society, the era of the family wage would give way to the era of Caregiver Parity. This is the picture implicit in the political practice of most Western European feminists and social democrats. It aims to promote gender equity principally by supporting informal carework. The point is to enable women with significant domestic responsibilities to support themselves and their families either through carework alone or through carework plus part-time employment. (Women without significant domestic responsibilities would presumably support themselves through employment.) The aim is not to make women's lives the same as men's but, rather, to "make difference costless."[37] Thus, childbearing, child rearing, and informal domestic labor are to be elevated to parity with formal paid labor. The caregiver role is to be put on a par with the breadwinner role—so that women and men can enjoy equivalent levels of dignity and well-being.

Caregiver Parity is also extremely ambitious. On this model, many (though not all) women will follow the current U.S. female practice of alternating spells of full-time employment, spells of full-time carework, and spells that combine part-time carework with part-time employment. The aim is to make such a life-pattern costless. To this end, several major new programs are necessary. One is a program of caregiver allowances to compensate childbearing, child rearing, housework, and other forms of socially necessary domestic labor; the allowances must be sufficiently generous at the full-time rate to support a family—hence equivalent to a breadwinner wage.[38] Also required is a program of workplace reforms. These must facilitate the possibility of combining supported carework with part-time employment and of making transitions between different life-states. The key here is flexibility. One obvious necessity is a generous program of mandated pregnancy and family leaves so that caregivers can exit and enter employment without losing security or seniority. Another is a program of retraining and job search for those not returning to old jobs. Also essential is mandated flextime so that caregivers can shift their hours to accommodate their carework responsibilities, including shifts between full- and part-time employment. Finally, in the wake of all this flexibility, there must be programs to ensure continuity of all the basic social-welfare benefits, including health, unemployment, disability, and retirement insurance.

This model organizes carework very differently from Universal Breadwinner. Whereas that approach shifted carework to the market and the state, this one keeps the bulk of such work in the household and supports it with public funds. Caregiver Parity's social-insurance system also differs sharply. To assure continuous coverage for people alternating between carework and employment, benefits attached to both must be integrated in a single system. In this system, part-time jobs and supported carework must be covered on the same basis as full-time jobs. Thus, a woman finishing a spell of supported carework would be eligible for unemployment insurance benefits on the same basis as a recently laid off employee in the event she could not find a suitable job. And a supported careworker who became disabled would receive disability payments on the same basis as a disabled employee. Years of supported carework would count on a par with years of employment toward eligibility for retirement pensions. Benefit levels would be fixed in ways that treat carework and employment equivalently.[39]

Caregiver Parity also requires another, residual tier of social welfare. Some adults will be unable to do either carework or waged work, including some adults without prior work records of either type. Most of these people will probably be men. To provide for them, the model must offer means-tested wage-and-allowance replacements.[40] Caregiver Parity's residual tier should be smaller than Universal Breadwinner's, however; nearly all adults should be covered in the integrated breadwinner-caregiver system of social insurance.

Caregiver Parity, too, is far removed from current U.S. arrangements. It requires large outlays of public funds to pay caregiver allowances, hence major structural tax reform and a sea change in political culture. Let us assume for the sake of the thought experiment, however, that its conditions of possibility could be met. And let us consider whether the resulting postindustrial welfare state could claim title to gender equity.

1. Antipoverty. Caregiver Parity would do a good job of preventing poverty—including for those women and children who are currently most vulnerable. Sufficiently generous allowances would keep solo-mother families out of poverty during spells of full-time carework. And a combination of allowances and wages would do the same during spells of part-time supported carework and part-time employment.[41] Since each of these options would carry the basic social-insurance package, moreover, women with "feminine" work patterns would have considerable security.[42]

2. Antiexploitation. Caregiver Parity should also succeed in preventing exploitation for most women, including for those who are most vulnerable today. By providing income directly to nonemployed wives, it reduces their economic dependence on husbands. It also provides economic security to single women with children, reducing their liability to exploitation by employers. Insofar as caregiver allowances are honorable and nondiscretionary, finally, recipients are not subject to caseworkers' whims.[43]

3. Income equality. Caregiver Parity performs quite poorly, however, with respect to income equality, as we know from the Nordic experience. Although the system of allowances-plus-wages provides the equivalent of a basic minimum breadwinner wage, it also institutes a "mommy track" in employment—a market in flexible, noncontinuous full- and/or part-time jobs. Most of these jobs will pay considerably less even at the full-time rate than comparable breadwinner-track jobs. Two-partner families will have an economic incentive to keep one partner on the breadwinner track rather than to share spells of carework between them, and given current labor markets, making the breadwinner the man will be most advantageous for heterosexual couples. Given current culture and socialization, moreover, men are generally unlikely to choose the mommy track in the same proportions as women. So the two employment tracks will carry traditional gender associations. Those associations are likely in turn to produce discrimination against women in the breadwinner track. Caregiver Parity may make difference cost less, then, but it will not make difference costless.

   4. *Leisure-time equality.* Caregiver Parity does somewhat better, however, with respect to equality of leisure time. It makes it possible for all women to avoid the double shift, if they choose, by opting for full- or part-time supported carework at various stages in their lives. (Currently, this choice is available only to a small percentage of privileged U.S. women.) We just saw, however, that this choice is not truly costless. Some women with families will not want to forego the benefits of breadwinner-track employment and will try to combine it with carework. Those not partnered with someone on the caregiver track will be significantly disadvantaged with respect to leisure time, and probably in their employment as well. Men, in contrast, will largely be insulated from this dilemma. On leisure time, then, the model is only fair.

   5. *Equality of respect.* Caregiver Parity is also only fair at promoting equality of respect. Unlike Universal Breadwinner, it offers two different routes to that end. Theoretically, citizen-workers and citizen-caregivers are statuses of equivalent dignity. But are they really on a par with each other? Caregiving is certainly treated more respectfully in this model than in current U.S. society, but it remains associated with femininity. Breadwinning likewise remains associated with masculinity. Given those traditional gender associations, plus the economic differential between the two lifestyles, caregiving is unlikely to attain true parity with breadwinning. In general, it is hard to imagine how "separate but equal" gender roles could provide genuine equality of respect today.

   6. *Antimarginalization.* Caregiver Parity performs poorly, moreover, in preventing women's marginalization. By supporting women's informal carework, it reinforces the view of such work as women's work and consolidates the gender division of domestic labor. By consolidating dual labor markets for breadwinners and caregivers, moreover, the model marginalizes women within the employment sector. By reinforcing the association of caregiving with femininity, finally, it may also impede women's participation in other spheres of life, such as politics and civil society.

   7. *Antiandrocentrism.* Yet Caregiver Parity is better than Universal Breadwinner at combating androcentrism. It treats caregiving as intrinsically valuable, not as a mere obstacle to employment, thus challenging the view that only men's traditional activities are fully human. It also accommodates "feminine" life-patterns, thereby rejecting the demand that women assimilate to "masculine" patterns. But the model still leaves something to be desired. Caregiver Parity stops short of affirming the universal value of activities and life-patterns associated with women. It does not value caregiving enough to demand that men do it, too; it does not ask men to change. Thus, Caregiver Parity represents only one-half of a full-scale challenge to androcentrism. Here, too, its performance is only fair.

Caregiver Parity's strengths and weaknesses are summarized in Figure 2.2. In general, Caregiver Parity improves the lot of women with significant care-work responsibilities, but for those women, as well as for others, it fails to deliver full gender equity.

Figure 2.2

Principle	Caregiver Parity
Antipoverty	good
Antiexploitation	good
Income equality	poor
Leisure-time equality	fair
Equality of respect	fair
Antimarginalization	poor
Antiandrocentrism	fair

Toward a Universal Caregiver Model

Both Universal Breadwinner and Caregiver Parity are highly utopian visions of a postindustrial welfare state. Either would represent a major improvement over current U.S. arrangements, yet neither is likely to be realized soon. Both models assume background preconditions that are strikingly absent today. Both presuppose major political-economic restructuring, including significant public control over corporations, the capacity to direct investment to create high-quality permanent jobs, and the ability to tax profits *and wealth* at rates sufficient to fund expanded high-quality social programs. Both models also assume broad popular support for a postindustrial welfare state that is committed to gender equity.

If both models are utopian in this sense, neither is utopian enough. Neither Universal Breadwinner nor Caregiver Parity can actually make good on its promise of gender equity—even under very favorable conditions. Although both are good at preventing women's poverty and exploitation, both are only fair at redressing inequality of respect: Universal Breadwinner holds women to the same standard as men, while constructing arrangements that prevent them from meeting it fully; Caregiver Parity, in contrast, sets up a double standard to accommodate gender difference, while institutionalizing policies that fail to assure equivalent respect for "feminine" activities and life-patterns. When we turn to the remaining principles, moreover, the two models' strengths and weaknesses diverge. Universal Breadwinner fails especially to promote equality of leisure time and to combat androcentrism, while Caregiver Parity fails especially to promote income equality and to prevent women's marginalization. Neither model, in addition, promotes women's full participation on a par with men in politics and civil society. And neither values female-associated practices enough to ask men to do them too; neither asks men to change. (The relative merits of Universal Breadwinner and Caregiver Parity are summarized in Figure 2.3.) Neither model, in sum, provides everything feminists want. Even in a highly idealized form neither delivers full gender equity.

Figure 2.3

Principle	Universal Breadwinner	Caregiver Parity
Antipoverty	good	good
Antiexploitation	good	good
Income equality	fair	poor
Leisure-time equality	poor	fair
Equality of respect	fair	fair
Antimarginalization	fair	poor
Antiandrocentrism	poor	fair

If these were the only possibilities, we would face a very difficult set of trade-offs. Suppose, however, we reject this Hobson's choice and try to develop a third alternative. The trick is to envision a postindustrial welfare state that combines the best of Universal Breadwinner with the best of Caregiver Parity, while jettisoning the worst features of each. What third alternative is possible?

So far we have examined—and found wanting—two initially plausible approaches: one aiming to make women more like men are now; the other leaving men and women pretty much unchanged, while aiming to make women's difference costless. A third possibility is to *induce men to become more like most women are now,* namely, people who do primary carework.

Consider the effects of this one change on the models we have just examined. If men were to do their fair share of carework, Universal Breadwinner would come much closer to equalizing leisure time and eliminating androcentrism, and Caregiver Parity would do a much better job of equalizing income and reducing women's marginalization. Both models, in addition, would tend to promote equality of respect. If men were to become more like women are now, in sum, both models would begin to approach gender equity.

The key to achieving gender equity in a postindustrial welfare state, then, is to make women's current life-patterns the norm for everyone. Women today often combine breadwinning and caregiving, albeit with great difficulty and strain. A postindustrial welfare state must ensure that men do the same, while redesigning institutions so as to eliminate the difficulty and strain. We might call this vision *Universal Caregiver*.

What, then, might such a welfare state look like? Unlike Caregiver Parity, its employment sector would not be divided into two different tracks; all jobs would be designed for workers who are caregivers, too; all would have a shorter workweek than full-time jobs have now; and all would have the support of employment-enabling services. Unlike Universal Breadwinner, however, employees would not be assumed to shift all carework to social services. Some informal carework would be publicly supported and integrated on a par with paid work in a single social-insurance system. Some would be performed in households by relatives and friends, but such households would not necessarily be heterosexual nuclear families. Other supported carework would be located outside households altogether—in civil society. In state-funded but locally organized institutions, childless adults, older people, and others without kin-based responsibilities would join parents and others in democratic, self-managed carework activities.

A Universal Caregiver welfare state would promote gender equity by effectively dismantling the gendered opposition between breadwinning and caregiving. It would integrate activities that are currently separated from one another, eliminate their gender-coding, and encourage men to perform them too. This, however, is tantamount to a wholesale restructuring of the institution of gender. The construction of breadwinning and caregiving as separate roles, coded masculine and feminine respectively, is a principal undergirding of the current gender order. To dismantle those roles and their cultural coding is in effect to overturn that order. It means subverting the existing gender division of labor and reducing the salience of gender as a structural principle of social organization.[44] At the limit, it suggests deconstructing gender.[45] By deconstructing the opposition between breadwinning and caregiving, moreover, Universal Caregiver would simultaneously deconstruct the associated opposition between bureaucratized public institutional settings and intimate private domestic settings. Treating civil society as an additional site for carework, it would overcome both the "workerism" of Universal Breadwinner and the domestic privatism of Caregiver Parity. Thus, Universal Caregiver promises expansive new possibilities for enriching the substance of social life and for promoting equal participation.

Only by embracing the Universal Caregiver vision, moreover, can we mitigate potential conflicts among our seven component principles of gender equity and minimize the need for trade-offs. Rejecting this approach, in contrast, makes such conflicts, and hence trade-offs, more likely. *Achieving gender equity in a postindustrial welfare state, then, requires deconstructing gender.*

Much more work needs to be done to develop this third—Universal Caregiver—vision of a postindustrial welfare state. A key is to develop policies that discourage free-riding. *Contra* conservatives, the real free-riders in the current system are not poor solo mothers who shirk employment. Instead, they are men of all classes who shirk carework and domestic labor, as well as corporations who free-ride on the labor of working people, both underpaid and unpaid.

A good statement of the Universal Caregiver vision comes from the Swedish Ministry of Labor: "To make it possible for both men and women to combine parenthood and gainful employment, a new view of the male role and a radical change in the organization of working life are required."[46] The trick is to imagine a social world in which citizens' lives integrate wage earning, caregiving, community activism, political participation, and involvement in the associational life of civil society—while also leaving time for some fun. This world is not likely to come into being in the immediate future, but it is the only imaginable postindustrial world that promises true gender equity. And unless we are guided by this vision now, we will never get any closer to achieving it.

Notes

1. Research for this chapter was supported by the Center for Urban Affairs and Policy Research, Northwestern University. For helpful comments, I am indebted to Rebecca Blank, Joshua Cohen, Fay Cook, Barbara Hobson, Axel Honneth, Jenny Mansbridge, Linda Nicholson, Ann Shola Orloff, John Roemer, Ian Schapiro, Tracy Strong, Peter Taylor-Gooby, Judy Wittner, Eli Zaretsky, and the members of the Feminist Public Policy Work Group of the Center for Urban Affairs and Policy Research, Northwestern University.

2. Mimi Abramowitz, *Regulating the Lives of Women: Social Welfare Policy from Colonial Times to the Present* (Boston: South End Press, 1988); Nancy Fraser, "Women, Welfare, and the Politics of Need Interpretation," in Fraser, *Unruly Practices: Power, Discourse,*

and Gender in Contemporary Social Theory (Minneapolis: University of Minnesota Press, 1989); Linda Gordon, "What Does Welfare Regulate?" *Social Research* 55, no. 4 (winter 1988): 609–30; Hilary Land, "Who Cares for the Family?" *Journal of Social Policy* 7, no. 3 (July 1978): 257–84. An exception to the built-in family-wage assumption is France, which from early on accepted high levels of female waged work. See Jane Jenson, "Representations of Gender: Policies to 'Protect' Women Workers and Infants in France and the United States before 1914," in *Women, the State, and Welfare,* ed. Linda Gordon (Madison: University of Wisconsin Press, 1990).

3. This account of the tripartite structure of the welfare state represents a modification of the account I proposed in "Women, Welfare, and the Politics of Need Interpretation." There I followed Barbara Nelson in positing a two-tier structure of ideal-typically "masculine" social insurance programs and ideal-typically "feminine" family support programs. (See her "Women's Poverty and Women's Citizenship: Some Political Consequences of Economic Marginality," *Signs* 10, no. 2 [winter 1984]: 209–31, and "The Origins of the Two-Channel Welfare State: Workmen's Compensation and Mothers' Aid," in *Women, the State, and Welfare,* ed. Linda Gordon, [Madison: University of Wisconsin Press, 1990].) Although that view was a relatively accurate picture of the U.S. social-welfare system, I now consider it analytically misleading. The United States is unusual in that the second and third tiers are conflated. The main program of means-tested poor relief—Aid to Families with Dependent Children (AFDC)—is also the main program that supports women's child rearing. Analytically, these are best understood as two distinct tiers of social welfare. When social insurance is added, we get a three-tier welfare state.

4. David Harvey, *The Condition of Postmodernity: An Inquiry into the Origins of Cultural Change* (Oxford: Blackwell, 1989); Scott Lash and John Urry, *The End of Organized Capitalism* (Cambridge: Polity Press, 1987); Robert Reich, *The Work of Nations: Preparing Ourselves for 21st Century Capitalism* (New York: Knopf, 1991).

5. Joan Smith, "The Paradox of Women's Poverty: Wage-earning Women and Economic Transformation," *Signs* 9, no. 2 (winter 1984): 291–310.

6. Judith Stacey, "Sexism by a Subtler Name? Postindustrial Conditions and Postfeminist Consciousness in the Silicon Valley," *Socialist Review,* 1987, no. 96: 7–28.

7. Kath Weston, *Families We Choose: Lesbians, Gays, Kinship* (New York: Columbia University Press, 1991).

8. Nancy Fraser, "Clintonism, Welfare, and the Antisocial Wage: The Emergence of a Neoliberal Political Imaginary," *Rethinking Marxism* 6, no. 1 (spring 1993): 9–23.

9. Some of the most sophisticated discussions are found in *Feminist Legal Theory: Readings in Law and Gender,* ed. Katharine T. Bartlett and Rosanne Kennedy (Boulder: Westview Press, 1991).

10. David T. Ellwood, *Poor Support: Poverty in the American Family* (New York: Basic Books, 1988).

11. Robert Goodin, *Reasons for Welfare: The Political Theory of the Welfare State* (Princeton: Princeton University Press, 1988).

12. Not all dependencies are exploitable. Goodin, in *Reasons for Welfare* (pp. 175–76), specifies the following four conditions that must be met if a dependency is to be exploitable: (1) the relationship must be asymmetrical; (2) the subordinate party must need the resource that the superordinate supplies; (3) the subordinate must depend on some particular superordinate for the supply of needed resources; (4) the superordinate must enjoy discretionary control over the resources that the subordinate needs from him/her.

13. Albert O. Hirschman, *Exit, Voice, and Loyalty: Responses to Decline in Firms, Organizations, and States* (Cambridge: Harvard University Press, 1970); Susan Moller

Okin, *Justice, Gender, and the Family* (New York: Basic Books, 1989); Barbara Hobson, "No Exit, No Voice: Women's Economic Dependency and the Welfare State," *Acta Sociologica* 33, no. 3 (fall 1990): 235–50.

14. Frances Fox Piven and Richard A. Cloward, *Regulating the Poor* (New York: Random House, 1971); Gøsta Esping-Andersen, *The Three Worlds of Welfare Capitalism* (Princeton: Princeton University Press, 1990).

15. Goodin, *Reasons for Welfare*.

16. Edward V. Sparer, "The Right to Welfare," in *The Rights of Americans: What They Are—What They Should Be*, ed. Norman Dorsen (New York: Pantheon, 1970).

17. Ann Shola Orloff, "Gender and the Social Rights of Citizenship: The Comparative Analysis of Gender Relations and Welfare States," *American Sociological Review* 58, no. 3 (June 1993): 303–28. The antiexploitation objective should not be confused with current U.S. attacks on "welfare dependency," which are highly ideological. These attacks define "dependency" exclusively as receipt of public assistance. They ignore the ways in which such receipt can promote claimants' independence by preventing exploitable dependence on husbands and employers. For a critique of such views, see Nancy Fraser and Linda Gordon, "A Genealogy of 'Dependency': Tracing a Keyword of the U.S. Welfare State," in this volume.

18. Ruth Lister, "Women, Economic Dependency, and Citizenship," *Journal of Social Policy* 19, no. 4 (1990): 445–67; Amartya Sen, "More Than 100 Million Women Are Missing," *New York Review of Books* 37, no. 20 (20 December 1990): 61–66.

19. Lenore Weitzman, *The Divorce Revolution: The Unexpected Social Consequences for Women and Children in America* (New York: Free Press, 1985).

20. Ellwood, *Poor Support*, p. 45.

21. Lois Bryson, "Citizenship, Caring and Commodification" (paper presented at "Crossing Borders: International Dialogues on Gender, Social Politics and Citizenship," conference, Stockholm, 27–29 May, 1994); Arlie Hochschild, *The Second Shift: Working Parents and the Revolution at Home* (New York: Viking Press, 1989); Juliet Schor, *The Overworked American: The Unexpected Decline of Leisure* (New York: Basic Books, 1991).

22. Lister, "Women, Economic Dependency, and Citizenship."

23. Laura Balbo, "Crazy Quilts," in *Women and the State*, ed. Ann Showstack Sassoon (London: Hutchinson, 1987).

24. Actually, there is a heavy ideological component in the usual view that public assistance is need-based, while social insurance is desert-based. Benefit levels in social insurance do not strictly reflect "contributions." Moreover, all government programs are financed by "contributions" in the form of taxation. Public assistance programs are financed from general revenues, both federal and state. Welfare recipients, like others, "contribute" to these funds, for example, through payment of sales taxes. See Nancy Fraser and Linda Gordon, "Contract versus Charity: Why Is There No Social Citizenship in the United States?" *Socialist Review* 22, no. 3 (July–September 1992): 45–68.

25. The free-rider worry is usually posed androcentrically as a worry about shirking paid employment. Little attention is paid, in contrast, to a far more widespread problem, namely, men's free-riding on women's unpaid domestic labor. A welcome exception is Peter Taylor-Gooby, "Scrounging, Moral Hazard, and Unwaged Work: Citizenship and Human Need," Darwin College, University of Kent, 1993, typescript.

26. Employment-enabling services could be distributed according to need, desert, or citizenship, but citizenship accords best with the spirit of the model. Means-tested day care targeted for the poor cannot help but signify a failure to achieve genuine breadwinner sta-

tus; and desert-based day care sets up a catch-22: one must already be employed in order to get what is needed for employment. Citizenship-based entitlement is best, then, but it must make services available to all. This rules out Swedish-type arrangements, which fail to guarantee sufficient day-care places and are plagued by long queues. For the Swedish problem, see Barbara Hobson, "Welfare Policy Regimes, Solo Mothers, and the Logics of Gender," in *Gendering Welfare States,* ed. Diane Sainsbury (London: Sage, 1994).

27. That incidentally would be to break decisively with U.S. policy, which has assumed since the New Deal that job creation is principally for men. Clinton's 1992 campaign proposals for "industrial" and "infrastructural investment" policies were no exception in this regard. See Fraser, "Clintonism, Welfare, and the Antisocial Wage."

28. Government could itself provide carework services in the form of public goods or it could fund marketized provision through a system of vouchers. Alternatively, employers could be mandated to provide employment-enabling services for their employees, either through vouchers or in-house arrangements. The state option means higher taxes, of course, but it may be preferable nevertheless. Mandating employer responsibility creates a disincentive to hire workers with dependents, to the likely disadvantage of women.

29. Evelyn Nakano Glenn, "From Servitude to Service Work: Historical Continuities in the Racial Division of Paid Reproductive Labor," *Signs* 18, no. 1 (autumn 1992): 1–43.

30. It, too, conditions entitlement on desert and defines "contribution" in traditional androcentric terms as employment and wage deductions.

31. Exactly what else must be provided inside the residual system will depend on the balance of entitlements outside it. If health insurance is provided universally as a citizen benefit, for example, then there need be no means-tested health system for the nonemployed. If, however, mainstream health insurance is linked to employment, then a residual health care system will be necessary. The same holds for unemployment, retirement, and disability insurance. In general, the more that is provided on the basis of citizenship, instead of on the basis of desert, the less has to be provided on the basis of need. One could even say that desert-based entitlements create the necessity of need-based provision; thus, employment-linked social insurance creates the need for means-tested public assistance.

32. Peter Kilborn, "New Jobs Lack the Old Security in Time of 'Disposable Workers,'" *New York Times,* March 15, 1993, pp. A1, A6.

33. Failing that, however, several groups are especially vulnerable to poverty in this model: those who cannot work, those who cannot get secure, permanent, full-time, good-paying jobs (disproportionately women and/or people of color); and those with heavy, hard-to-shift, unpaid carework responsibilities (disproportionately women).

34. Failing that, however, the groups mentioned in the previous note remain especially vulnerable to exploitation—by abusive men, by unfair or predatory employers, by capricious state officials.

35. Exactly how much remains depends on the government's success in eliminating discrimination and in implementing comparable worth.

36. Universal Breadwinner presumably relies on persuasion to induce men to do their fair share of unpaid work. The chances of that working would be improved if the model succeeded in promoting cultural change and in enhancing women's voice within marriage. But it is doubtful that this alone would suffice, as the communist experience suggests.

37. Christine A. Littleton, "Reconstructing Sexual Equality," in *Feminist Legal Theory,* ed. Katharine T. Bartlett and Rosanne Kennedy (Boulder: Westview Press, 1991).

38. Caregiver allowances could be distributed on the basis of need, as a means-tested benefit for the poor—as they have always been in the United States. But that would contravene

the spirit of Caregiver Parity. One cannot consistently claim that the caregiver life is equivalent in dignity to the breadwinner life, while supporting it only as a last-resort stop-gap against poverty. (This contradiction has always bedeviled mothers' pensions—and later Aid to Dependent Children—in the United States. Although these programs were intended by some advocates to exalt motherhood, they sent a contradictory message by virtue of being means-tested and morals-tested.) Means-tested allowances, moreover, would impede easy transitions between employment and carework. Since the aim is to make caregiving as deserving as breadwinning, caregiver allowances must be based on desert. Treated as compensation for socially necessary "service" or "work," they alter the standard androcentric meanings of those terms.

39. In *Justice, Gender, and the Family,* Okin has proposed an alternative way to fund care-work. In her scheme the funds would come from what are now considered to be the earnings of the caregiver's partner. A man with a nonemployed wife, for example, would receive a paycheck for one-half of "his" salary; his employer would cut a second check in the same amount payable directly to the wife. Intriguing as this idea is, one may wonder whether it is really the best way to promote a wife's independence from her husband, for it ties her income so directly to his. In addition, Okin's proposal does not provide any carework support for women without employed partners. Caregiver Parity, in contrast, provides public support for all who perform informal carework. Who, then, are its benefi-ciaries likely to be? With the exception of pregnancy leave, all the model's benefits are open to everyone; so men as well as women can opt for a "feminine" life. Women, how-ever, are considerably more likely to do so. Although the model aims to make such a life costless, it includes no positive incentives for men to change. Some men, of course, may simply prefer such a life and will choose it when offered the chance; most will not, howev-er, given current socialization and culture. We shall see, moreover, that Caregiver Parity contains some hidden disincentives to male caregiving.

40. In this respect, it resembles the Universal Breadwinner model: whatever additional essen-tial goods are normally offered on the basis of desert must be offered here too on the basis of need.

41. Wages from full-time employment must also be sufficient to support a family with dig-nity.

42. Adults with neither carework nor employment records would be most vulnerable to poverty in this model; most of these would be men. Children, in contrast, would be well protected.

43. Once again, it is adults with neither carework nor employment records who are most vul-nerable to exploitation in this model; the majority of them would be men.

44. Okin, *Justice, Gender, and the Family.*

45. Joan Williams, "Deconstructing Gender," in *Feminist Legal Theory,* ed. Katharine T. Bartlett and Rosanne Kennedy (Boulder: Westview Press, 1991).

46. Quoted in Lister, "Women, Economic Dependency, and Citizenship," p. 463.

PART II

PUBLIC SPHERES,
GENEALOGIES,
AND SYMBOLIC ORDERS

3

Rethinking the Public Sphere

A Contribution to the Critique of
Actually Existing Democracy

I n the wake of 1989 we have heard a great deal of ballyhoo about "the triumph of liberal democracy" and even "the end of history." Yet there is still quite a lot to object to in our own "actually existing democracy," and the project of a critical theory of the limits of democracy in late-capitalist societies remains as relevant as ever. In fact, this project seems to me to have acquired a new urgency at a time when "liberal democracy" is being touted as the *ne plus ultra* of social systems for countries that are emerging from Soviet-style state socialism, Latin American military dictatorships, and southern African regimes of racial domination.[1]

Those of us who remain committed to theorizing the limits of democracy in late-capitalist societies will find in the work of Jürgen Habermas an indispensable resource. I mean the concept of "the public sphere," originally elaborated in his 1962 book, *The Structural Transformation of the Public Sphere,* and subsequently resituated but never abandoned in his later work.[2]

The political and theoretical importance of this idea is easy to explain. Habermas's concept of the public sphere provides a way of circumventing some confusions that have plagued progressive social movements and the political theories associated with them. Take, for example, the long-standing failure in the dominant wing of the socialist and Marxist tradition to appreciate the full force of the distinction between the apparatuses of the state, on the one hand, and public arenas of citizen discourse and association, on the other. All too often it was assumed in this tradition that to subject the economy to the control of the socialist state was to subject it to the control of the socialist citizenry. Of course that was not so. But the conflation of the state apparatus with the public sphere of discourse and association provided ballast to processes whereby the socialist vision became institutionalized in an authoritarian statist form instead of in a participatory democratic form. The result has been to jeopardize the very idea of socialist democracy.

A second problem, albeit one that has so far been much less historically momentous and certainly less tragic, is a confusion one encounters at times in contemporary feminisms. I mean a confusion that involves the use of the very same expression "the public sphere," but in a sense that is less precise and less useful than Habermas's. This expression has been used by many feminists to refer to everything that is outside the domestic or familial sphere. "The public sphere" in this usage conflates at least three analytically distinct things: the state, the official-economy of paid employment, and arenas of public discourse.[3] It should not be thought that the conflation of these three things is a merely theoretical issue. On the contrary, it has practical political consequences, for example, when agitational campaigns against misogynist cultural representations are confounded with programs for state censorship, or when struggles to deprivatize housework and child care are equated with their commodification. In both these cases, the result is to occlude the question whether to subject gender issues to the logic of the market or the administrative state is to promote the liberation of women.

The idea of "the public sphere" in Habermas's sense is a conceptual resource that can help overcome such problems. It designates a theater in modern societies in which political participation is enacted through the medium of talk. It is the space in which citizens deliberate about their common affairs, hence, an institutionalized arena of discursive interaction. This arena is conceptually distinct from the state; it a site for the production and circulation of discourses that can in principle be critical of the state. The public sphere in Habermas's sense is also conceptually distinct from the official-economy; it is not an arena of market relations but rather one of discursive relations, a theater for debating and deliberating rather than for buying and selling. Thus, this concept of the public sphere permits us to keep in view the distinctions between state apparatuses, economic markets, and democratic associations, distinctions that are essential to democratic theory.

For these reasons, I am going to take as a basic premise for this chapter that something like Habermas's idea of the public sphere is indispensable to critical social theory and to democratic political practice. I assume that no attempt to understand the limits of actually existing late-capitalist democracy can succeed without in some way or another making use of it. I assume that the same goes for urgently needed constructive efforts to develop alternative models of democracy.

If you will grant me that the general idea of the public sphere is indispensable to critical theory, then I shall go on to argue that the specific form in which Habermas has elaborated this idea is not wholly satisfactory. On the contrary, I contend that his analysis of the public sphere needs to undergo some critical interrogation and reconstruction if it is to yield a category capable of theorizing the limits of actually existing democracy.

Recall that the subtitle of *Structural Transformation* is *An Inquiry into a Category of Bourgeois Society*. The object of the inquiry is twofold. On the one hand, Habermas charts the rise and decline of a historically specific and limited form of the public sphere, which he calls the "bourgeois public sphere." On the other hand, he interrogates the status of the idealized normative model associated with that institution, which he calls "the liberal model of the bourgeois public sphere." His aim, once again, is twofold: first, to identify the conditions that made possible the bourgeois public sphere and to chart their devolution; and second, to assess the consequences for the continuing normative viability of the liberal model. The upshot is an argument that, under altered conditions of late-twentieth-century "welfare state mass democracy," neither the bourgeois public sphere nor its liberal model is still feasible. Some new form of public sphere is required to salvage that arena's critical function and to institutionalize democracy.

Oddly, Habermas stops short of developing a new, postbourgeois model of the public sphere. Moreover, he never explicitly problematizes some dubious assumptions that underlie the liberal model. As a result, we are left at the end of *Structural Transformation* without a conception that is sufficiently distinct from the liberal model of the bourgeois public sphere to serve the needs of critical theory today.

That, at any rate, is the thesis I intend to argue. To make my case, I shall proceed as follows: I shall begin, in the first section, by juxtaposing Habermas's account of the structural transformation of the public sphere to an alternative account that can be pieced together from some recent revisionist historiography. Then, I shall identify four assumptions underlying the liberal model of the bourgeois public sphere, as Habermas describes it, which this newer historiography renders suspect. Next, in the following four sections, I shall examine each of these assumptions in turn. Finally, in a brief conclusion, I shall draw together some strands from these critical discussions that point toward an alternative, postbourgeois conception of the public sphere.

Whose History? Which Conception?

Let me begin by sketching some highlights of Habermas's account of the structural transformation of the public sphere. According to Habermas, the idea of a public sphere is that of a body of "private persons" assembled to discuss matters of "public concern" or "common interest." This idea acquired force and reality in early modern Europe in the constitution of "bourgeois public spheres" as counterweights to absolutist states. These publics aimed to mediate between "society" and the state by holding the state accountable to "society" by means of "publicity." At first this meant requiring that information about state functioning be made accessible so that state activities would be subject to critical scrutiny and the force of "public opinion." Later, it meant transmitting the considered "general interest" of "bourgeois society" to the state by means of legally guaranteed free speech, free press, and free assembly, and eventually through the parliamentary institutions of representative government.

Thus, at one level, the idea of the public sphere designated an institutional mechanism for "rationalizing" political domination by rendering states accountable to (some of) the citizenry. At another level, it designated a specific kind of discursive interaction. Here the public sphere connoted an ideal of unrestricted rational discussion of public matters. The discussion was to be open and accessible to all; merely private interests were to be inadmissible; inequalities of status were to be bracketed; power was to be excluded; and discussants were to deliberate as peers. The result of such discussion would be "public opinion" in the strong sense of a rational consensus about the common good.

According to Habermas, the full utopian potential of the liberal model of the bourgeois public sphere was never realized in practice. The claim to open access in particular was not made good. Moreover, the bourgeois public sphere was premised on a social order in which the state was sharply differentiated from the newly privatized market economy; it was this clear separation of "society" and state that was supposed to underpin a form of public discussion that excluded "private interests." But these conditions eventually eroded as nonbourgeois strata gained access to the public sphere. Then, "the social question" came to the fore; society was polarized by class struggle; and the public fragmented into a mass of competing interest groups. Street demonstrations and backroom, brokered compromises among sectional interests replaced reasoned public debate about the common good. Finally, with the emergence of "welfare state mass democracy," society and the state became intertwined; publicity in the sense of critical scrutiny of the state gave way to public relations, mass-mediated staged displays, and the manufacture and manipulation of public opinion.

Now, let me juxtapose to this sketch of Habermas's account an alternative account that I shall piece together from some recent revisionist historiography. Briefly, scholars like Joan Landes, Mary Ryan, Elizabeth Brooks-Higginbotham, and Geoff Eley contend that Habermas's account idealizes the bourgeois public sphere. They argue that, despite the rhetoric of publicity and accessibility, that official public sphere rested on, indeed was importantly constituted by, a number of significant exclusions. For Landes, the key axis of exclusion is gender; she argues that the ethos of the new republican public sphere in France was constructed in deliberate opposition to that of a more woman-friendly salon culture that the republicans anathematized as "artificial," "effeminate," and "aristocratic." Consequently, a new, austere style of public speech and behavior was promoted, a style deemed "rational," "virtuous," and "manly." In this way, masculinist gender constructs were built into the very conception of the republican public sphere, as was a logic that led, at the height of Jacobin rule, to the formal exclusion from political life of women.[4] Here the republicans drew on classical traditions that cast femininity and publicity as oxymorons; the depth of such traditions can be gauged in the etymological connection between "public" and "pubic," a graphic trace of the fact that in the ancient world possession of a penis was a requirement for speaking in public. (A similar link is preserved, incidentally, in the etymological connection between "testimony" and "testicle.")[5]

Extending Landes's argument, Eley contends that exclusionary operations were essential to bourgeois public spheres not only in France but also in England and Germany, and that in all these countries gender exclusions were linked to other exclusions rooted in processes of class formation. In all these countries, he claims, the soil that nourished the bourgeois public sphere was "civil society," the emerging new congeries of voluntary associations that sprung up in what came to be known as "the age of societies." But this network of clubs and associations—philanthropic, civic, professional, and cultural—was anything but accessible to everyone. On the contrary, it was the arena, the training ground, and eventually the power base of a stratum of bourgeois men, who were coming to see themselves as a "universal class" and preparing to assert their fitness to govern. Thus, the elaboration of a distinctive culture of civil society and of an associated public sphere was implicated in the process of bourgeois class formation; its practices and ethos were markers of "distinction" in Pierre Bourdieu's sense,[6] ways of defining an emergent elite, setting it off from the older aristocratic elites it was intent on displacing, on the one hand, and from the various popular and plebeian strata it aspired to rule, on the other. This process of distinction, moreover, helps explain the exacerbation of sexism characteristic of the bourgeois public sphere; new gender norms enjoining feminine domesticity and a sharp separation of public and private spheres functioned as key signifiers of bourgeois difference from both higher and lower social strata. It is a measure of the eventual success of this bourgeois project that these norms later became hegemonic, sometimes imposed on, sometimes embraced by, broader segments of society.[7]

Now, there is a remarkable irony here, one that Habermas's account of the rise of the public sphere fails fully to appreciate.[8] A discourse of publicity touting accessibility, rationality, and the suspension of status hierarchies is itself deployed as a strategy of distinction. Of course, in and of itself, this irony does not fatally compromise the discourse of publicity; that discourse can be, indeed has been, differently deployed in different circumstances and contexts. Nevertheless, it does suggest that the relationship between publicity and status is more complex than Habermas intimates, that declaring a deliberative arena to be a space where extant status distinctions are bracketed and neutralized is not sufficient to make it so.

Moreover, the problem is not only that Habermas idealizes the bourgeois public sphere but also that he fails to examine other, nonliberal, nonbourgeois, competing public spheres. Or rather, it is precisely because he fails to examine these other public spheres that he ends up idealizing the bourgeois public sphere.[9] Mary Ryan documents the variety of ways in which nineteenth-century North American women of various classes and ethnicities constructed access routes to public political life, even despite their exclusion from the official public sphere. In the case of elite bourgeois women, this involved building a counter civil society of alternative women-only voluntary associations, including philanthropic and moral reform societies; in some respects, these associations aped the all-male societies built by these women's fathers and grandfathers, yet in other respects the women were innovating because they creatively used the heretofore quintessentially "private" idioms of domesticity and motherhood precisely as springboards for public activity. Meanwhile, for some less privileged women, access to public life came through participation in supporting roles in male-dominated working-class protest activities. Still other women found public outlets in street protests and parades. Finally, women's rights advocates publicly contested both women's exclusion from the official public sphere and the privatization of gender politics.[10]

Similarly, Brooks-Higginbotham has recently documented the existence of an alternative, parallel black public sphere in the United States in the 1880–1920 period. During this "nadir" in African-American history, blacks were excluded not only from suffrage but also from the full gamut of "whites"-only discursive arenas and institutions of civil society. In this context, they built a public sphere in the one space they had: the black church. From this unlikely location, unimaginable from the perspective of the liberal model of the bourgeois public sphere, with its Kantian secular-Enlightenment norms of publicity, they published national newspapers and held national conventions. In these forums, they denounced U.S. racism, criticized state and federal government policies, and debated antiracist strategy. Creatively adapting their religious institutions, African Americans made a public sphere where the liberal model would have denied there could be one.[11]

Ryan's and Brooks-Higginbotham's studies show that, even in the absence of formal political incorporation through suffrage, there were a variety of ways of accessing public life and a multiplicity of public arenas. Thus, the view that women and blacks were excluded from "the public sphere" turns out to be ideological; it rests on a class- and gender-biased notion of publicity, one that accepts at face value the bourgeois public's claim to be *the* public. In fact, the historiography of Ryan, Brooks-Higginbotham, and others demonstrates that the bourgeois public was never *the* public. On the contrary, virtually contemporaneous with the bourgeois public there arose a host of competing counterpublics, including nationalist publics, popular peasant publics, elite women's publics, black publics, and working-class publics. Thus, there were competing publics from the start, not just from the late-nineteenth and twentieth centuries, as Habermas implies.[12]

Moreover, not only was there always a plurality of competing publics but the relations between bourgeois publics and other publics were always conflictual. Virtually from the beginning, counterpublics contested the exclusionary norms of the bourgeois public, elaborating alternative styles of political behavior and alternative norms of public speech. Bourgeois publics, in turn, excoriated these alternatives and deliberately sought to block broader participation. As Eley puts it, "The emergence of a bourgeois public was never defined solely by the struggle against absolutism and traditional authority, but . . . addressed the problem of popular containment as well. The public sphere was always constituted by conflict."[13]

In general, this revisionist historiography suggests a much darker view of the bourgeois public sphere than the one that emerges from Habermas's study. The exclusions and conflicts that appeared as accidental trappings from his perspective, in the revisionists' view become constitutive. The result is a gestalt switch that alters the very meaning of the public sphere. We can no longer assume that the liberal model of the bourgeois public sphere was simply an unrealized utopian ideal; it was also an ideological notion that functioned to legitimate an emergent form of class (and race) rule. Therefore, Eley draws a Gramscian moral from the story: the official bourgeois public sphere is the institutional vehicle for a major historical transformation in the nature of political domination. This is the shift from a repressive mode of domination to a hegemonic one, from rule based primarily on acquiescence to superior force to rule based primarily on consent supplemented with some measure of repression.[14] The important point is that this new mode of political domination, like the older one, secures the ability of one stratum of society to rule the rest. The official public sphere, then, was—indeed, is—the prime institutional site for the construction of the consent that defines the new, hegemonic mode of domination.[15]

Now, what conclusions should we draw from this conflict of historical interpretations? Should we conclude that the very concept of the public sphere is a piece of bourgeois, masculinist, white-supremacist ideology, so thoroughly compromised that it can shed no genuinely critical light on the limits of actually existing democracy? Or, should we conclude, rather, that the liberal model of the public sphere was a good idea that unfortunately was not realized in practice but that retains some emancipatory force? In short, is the idea of the public sphere an instrument of domination or a utopian ideal?

Well, perhaps both. But actually neither. I contend that both of those conclusions are too extreme and unsupple to do justice the material I have been discussing.[16] Instead of endorsing either one of them, I want to propose a more nuanced alternative. I shall argue that the revisionist historiography neither undermines nor vindicates *"the* concept of the public sphere" *simpliciter,* but that it calls into question four assumptions that are central to a specific—*bourgeois, masculinist, white-supremacist*—conception of the public sphere, at least as Habermas describes it.

1. The assumption that it is possible for interlocutors in a public sphere to bracket status differentials and to deliberate "as if" they were social equals; the assumption, therefore, that social equality is not a necessary condition for political democracy.

2. The assumption that the proliferation of a multiplicity of competing publics is necessarily a step away from, rather than toward, greater democracy, and that a single, comprehensive public sphere is always preferable to a nexus of multiple publics.
3. The assumption that discourse in public spheres should be restricted to deliberation about the common good, and that the appearance of "private interests" and "private issues" is always undesirable.
4. The assumption that a functioning democratic public sphere requires a sharp separation between civil society and the state.

Let me consider each of these in turn.

Open Access, Participatory Parity, and Social Equality

Habermas's account of the liberal model of the bourgeois public sphere stresses its claim to be open and accessible to all. Indeed, this idea of open access is one of the central meanings of the norm of publicity. Of course, we know, both from the revisionist history and from Habermas's account, that the bourgeois public's claim to full accessibility was not in fact realized. Women of all classes and ethnicities were excluded from official political participation precisely on the basis of ascribed gender status, and plebeian men were formally excluded by property qualifications. Moreover, in many cases, women and men of racialized ethnicities of all classes were excluded on racial grounds.

Now, what are we to make of this historical fact of the nonrealization in practice of the bourgeois public sphere's ideal of open access? One approach is to conclude that the ideal itself remains unaffected because it is possible in principle to overcome these exclusions. And, in fact, it was only a matter of time before formal exclusions based on gender, property, and race were eliminated.

This is convincing enough as far as it goes, but it does not go far enough. The question of open access cannot be reduced without remainder to the presence or absence of formal exclusions. It requires us to look also at the process of discursive interaction within formally inclusive public arenas. Here we should recall that the liberal model of the bourgeois public sphere requires bracketing inequalities of status. This public sphere was to be an arena in which interlocutors would set aside such characteristics as differences in birth and fortune and speak to one another as if they were social and economic peers. The operative phrase here is "as if." In fact, the social inequalities among the interlocutors were not eliminated but only bracketed.

But were they really effectively bracketed? The revisionist historiography suggests they were not. Rather, discursive interaction within the bourgeois public sphere was governed by protocols of style and decorum that were themselves correlates and markers of status inequality. These functioned informally to marginalize women, people of color, and members of the plebeian classes and to prevent them from participating as peers.

Here we are talking about informal impediments to participatory parity that can persist even after everyone is formally and legally licensed to participate. That these constitute a more serious challenge to the liberal model of the bourgeois public sphere can be seen from a familiar contemporary example. Feminist research has documented a syndrome that many of us have observed in faculty meetings and other mixed-sex deliberative bodies: men tend to interrupt women more than women interrupt men; men also tend to speak more than women, taking more turns and longer turns; and women's interventions are more often ignored or not responded to than men's. In response to the sorts of experiences documented in this research, an important strand of feminist political theory has claimed that deliberation can serve as a mask for domination. Theorists like Jane Mansbridge have argued that

> the transformation of "I" into "we" brought about through political deliberation can easily mask subtle forms of control. Even the language people use as they reason together usually favors one way of seeing things and discourages others. Subordinate groups sometimes cannot find the right voice or words to express their thoughts, and when they do, they discover they are not heard. [They] are silenced, encouraged to keep their wants inchoate, and heard to say "yes" when what they have said is "no."[17]

Mansbridge rightly notes that many of these feminist insights into ways in which deliberation can serve as a mask for domination extend beyond gender to other kinds of unequal relations, like those based on class or "race." They alert us to the ways in which social inequalities can infect deliberation, even in the absence of any formal exclusions.

Here we encounter a very serious difficulty with the liberal model of the bourgeois public sphere. Insofar as the bracketing of social inequalities in deliberation means proceeding as if they don't exist when they do, this does not foster participatory parity. On the contrary, such bracketing usually works to the advantage of dominant groups in society and to the disadvantage of subordinates. In most cases, it would be more appropriate to *unbracket* inequalities in the sense of explicitly thematizing them—a point that accords with the spirit of Habermas's later "communicative ethics."

The misplaced faith in the efficacy of bracketing suggests another flaw in the liberal model. This conception assumes that a public sphere is or can be a space of zero-degree culture, so utterly bereft of any specific ethos as to accommodate with perfect neutrality and equal ease interventions expressive of any and every cultural ethos. But this assumption is counterfactual, and not for reasons that are merely accidental. In stratified societies, unequally empowered social groups tend to develop unequally valued cultural styles. The result is the development of powerful informal pressures that marginalize the contributions of members of subordinated groups both in everyday life contexts and in official public spheres.[18] Moreover, these pressures are amplified, rather than mitigated, by the peculiar political economy of the bourgeois public sphere. In this public sphere, the media that constitute the material support for the circulation of views are privately owned and operated for profit. Consequently, subordinated social groups usually lack equal access to the material means of equal participation.[19] Thus, political economy enforces structurally what culture accomplishes informally.

If we take these considerations seriously, then we should be led to entertain serious doubts about a conception of the public sphere that purports to bracket, rather than to eliminate, structural social inequalities. We should question whether it is possible even in principle for interlocutors to deliberate *as if* they were social peers in specially designated discursive arenas, when these discursive arenas are situated in a larger societal context that is pervaded by structural relations of dominance and subordination.

What is at stake here is the autonomy of specifically political institutions vis-à-vis the surrounding societal context. One salient feature that distinguishes liberalism from some other political-theoretical orientations is that liberalism assumes the autonomy of the political in a very strong form. Liberal political theory assumes that it is possible to organize a democratic form of political life on the basis of socioeconomic and sociosexual structures that generate systemic inequalities. For liberals, then, the problem of democracy becomes the problem of how to insulate political processes from what are considered to be nonpolitical or prepolitical processes, those characteristic, for example, of the economy, the family, and informal everyday life. The problem for liberals, thus, is how to strengthen the barriers separating political institutions that are supposed to instantiate relations of equality from economic, cultural, and sociosexual institutions that are premised on systemic relations of inequality.[20] Yet the weight of circumstance suggests that in order to have a public sphere in which interlocutors can deliberate as peers, it is not sufficient merely to bracket social inequality. Instead, it is a necessary condition for participatory parity that systemic social inequalities be eliminated. This does not mean that everyone must have exactly the same income, but it does require the sort of rough equality that is inconsistent with systemically generated relations of dominance and subordination. *Pace* liberalism, then, political democracy requires substantive social equality.[21]

So far, I have been arguing that the liberal model of the bourgeois public sphere is inadequate insofar as it supposes that social equality is not a necessary condition for participatory parity in public spheres. What follows from this for the critique of actually existing democracy? One task for critical theory is to render visible the ways in which societal inequality infects formally inclusive existing public spheres and taints discursive interaction within them.

Equality, Diversity, and Multiple Publics

So far I have been discussing what we might call "intrapublic relations," that is, the character and quality of discursive interactions within a given public sphere. Now I want to consider what we might call "interpublic relations," that is, the character of interactions among different publics.

Let me begin by recalling that Habermas's account stresses the singularity of the liberal model of the bourgeois public sphere, its claim to be *the* public arena in the singular. In addition, his narrative tends in this respect to be faithful to that conception because it casts the emergence of additional publics as a late development signaling fragmentation and decline. This narrative, then, like the liberal model itself, is informed by an underlying evaluative assumption, namely, that the institutional confinement of public life to a single, overarching public sphere is a positive and desirable state of affairs, whereas the proliferation of a multiplicity of publics represents a departure from, rather than an advance toward, democracy.[22] It is this normative assumption that I now want to scrutinize. In this section, I shall assess the relative merits of single, comprehensive publics versus multiple publics in two kinds of modern societies—stratified societies and egalitarian multicultural societies.[23]

First, let me consider the case of stratified societies, by which I mean societies whose basic institutional framework generates unequal social groups in structural relations of dominance and subordination. I have already argued that in such societies, full parity of participation in public debate and deliberation is not within the reach of possibility. The question to be addressed here, then, is, What form of public life comes closest to approaching that ideal? What institutional arrangements will best help narrow the gap in participatory parity between dominant and subordinate groups?

I contend that, in stratified societies, arrangements that accommodate contestation among a plurality of competing publics better promote the ideal of participatory parity than does a single, comprehensive, overarching public. This follows from the argument of the previous section. There I argued that it is not possible to insulate special discursive arenas from the effects of societal inequality; and that where societal inequality persists, deliberative processes in public spheres will tend to operate to the advantage of dominant groups and to the disadvantage of subordinates. Now I want to add that these effects will be exacerbated where there is only a single, comprehensive public sphere. In that case, members of subordinated groups would have no arenas for deliberation among themselves about their needs, objectives, and strategies. They would have no venues in which to undertake communicative processes that were not, as it were, under the supervision of dominant groups. In this situation, they would be less likely than otherwise to "find the right voice or words to express their thoughts," and more likely than otherwise "to keep their wants inchoate." This would render them less able than otherwise to articulate and defend their interests in the comprehensive public sphere. They would be less able than otherwise to expose modes of deliberation that mask domination by "absorbing the less powerful into a false 'we' that reflects the more powerful."[24]

This argument gains additional support from the revisionist historiography of the public sphere, up to and including very recent developments. This history records that members of subordinated social groups—women, workers, peoples of color, and gays and lesbians—have repeatedly found it advantageous to constitute alternative publics. I propose to call these *subaltern counterpublics* in order to signal that they are parallel discursive arenas where members of subordinated social groups invent and circulate counterdiscourses, which in turn permit them to formulate oppositional interpretations of their identities, interests, and needs.[25] Perhaps the most striking example is the late-twentieth-century U.S. feminist subaltern counterpublic, with its variegated array of journals, bookstores, publishing companies, film and video distribution networks, lecture series, research centers, academic programs, conferences, conventions, festivals, and local meeting places. In this public sphere, feminist women have invented new terms for describing social reality, including "sexism," "the double shift," "sexual harassment," and "marital, date, and acquaintance rape." Armed with such language, we have recast our needs and identities, thereby reducing, although not eliminating, the extent of our disadvantage in official public spheres.[26]

Let me not be misunderstood. I do not mean to suggest that subaltern counterpublics are always necessarily virtuous; some of them, alas, are explicitly antidemocratic and antiegalitarian; and even those with democratic and egalitarian intentions are not always above practicing their own modes of informal exclusion and marginalization. Still, insofar as these counterpublics emerge in response to exclusions within dominant publics, they help expand discursive space. In principle, assumptions that were previously exempt from contestation will now have to be publicly argued out. In general, the proliferation of subaltern counterpublics means a widening of discursive contestation, and that is a good thing in stratified societies.

I am emphasizing the contestatory function of subaltern counterpublics in stratified societies in part in order to complicate the issue of separatism. In my view, the concept of a counterpublic militates in the long run against separatism because it assumes an orientation that is *publicist*. Insofar as these arenas are *publics* they are by definition not enclaves—which is not to deny that they are often involuntarily enclav*ed*. After all, to interact discursively as a member of a public—subaltern or otherwise—is to aspire to disseminate one's discourse into ever-widening arenas. Habermas captures well this aspect of the meaning of publicity when he notes that however limited a public may be in its empirical manifestation at any given time, its members understand themselves as part of a potentially wider public, that indeterminate, empirically counterfactual body we call "the public-at-large." The point is that, in stratified societies, subaltern counterpublics have a dual character. On the one hand, they function as spaces of withdrawal and regroupment; on the other hand, they also function as bases and training grounds for agitational activities directed toward wider publics. It is precisely in the dialectic between these two functions that their emancipatory potential resides. This dialectic enables subaltern counterpublics partially to offset, although not wholly to eradicate, the unjust participatory privileges enjoyed by members of dominant social groups in stratified societies.

So far, I have been arguing that, although in stratified societies the ideal of participatory parity is not fully realizable, it is more closely approximated by arrangements that permit contestation among a plurality of competing publics than by a single, comprehensive public sphere. Of course, contestation among competing publics supposes interpublic discursive interaction. How, then, should we understand such interaction? Geoff Eley suggests we think of the public sphere (in stratified societies) as "the structured setting where cultural and ideological contest or negotiation among a variety of publics takes place."[27] This formulation does justice to the multiplicity of public arenas in stratified societies by expressly acknowledging the presence and activity of "a variety of publics." At the same time, it also does justice to the fact that these various publics are situated in a single "structured setting" that advantages some and disadvantages others. Finally, Eley's formulation does justice to the fact that, in stratified societies, the discursive relations among differentially empowered publics are as likely to take the form of contestation as that of deliberation.

Let me now consider the relative merits of multiple publics versus a singular public for egalitarian, multicultural societies. By egalitarian societies I mean nonstratified societies, societies whose basic framework does not generate unequal social groups in structural relations of dominance and subordination. Egalitarian societies, therefore, are classless societies without gender or racial divisions of labor. However, they need not be culturally homogeneous. On the contrary, provided such societies permit free expression and association, they are likely to be inhabited by social groups with diverse values, identities, and cultural styles, hence to be multicultural. My question is, Under conditions of cultural diversity in the absence of structural inequality, would a single, comprehensive public sphere be preferable to multiple publics?

To answer this question we need to take a closer look at the relationship between public discourse and social identities. *Pace* the liberal model, public spheres are not arenas only for the formation of discursive opinion; in addition, they are arenas for the formation and enactment of social identities.[28] This means that participation is not simply a matter of being able to state propositional contents that are neutral with respect to form of expression. Rather, as I argued in the previous section, participation means being able to speak "in one's own voice," thereby simultaneously constructing and expressing one's cultural identity through idiom and style.[29] Moreover, as I also suggested, public spheres themselves are not spaces of zero-degree culture, equally hospitable to any possible form of cultural expression. Rather, they consist in culturally specific institutions—for example, the fora of textual exchange, including various journals and the Internet; and social geographies of urban space, including cafes, public parks, and shopping malls. These institutions may be understood as culturally specific rhetorical lenses that filter and alter the utterances they frame; they can accommodate some expressive modes and not others.[30]

It follows that public life in egalitarian, multicultural societies cannot consist exclusively in a single, comprehensive public sphere. That would be tantamount to filtering diverse rhetorical and stylistic norms through a single, overarching lens. Moreover, because there can be no such lens that is genuinely culturally neutral, it would effectively privilege the expressive norms of one cultural group over those of others, thereby making discursive assimilation a condition for participation in public debate. The result would be the demise of multiculturalism (and the likely demise of social equality). In general, then, we can conclude that the idea of an egalitarian, multicultural society makes sense only if we suppose a plurality of public arenas in which groups with diverse values and rhetorics participate. By definition, such a society must contain a multiplicity of publics.

However, this need not preclude the possibility of an additional, more comprehensive arena in which members of different, more limited publics talk across lines of cultural diversity. On the contrary, our hypothetical egalitarian, multicultural society would surely have to entertain debates over policies and issues affecting everyone.[31] The question is, Would participants in such debates share enough in the way of values, expressive norms, and, therefore, protocols of persuasion to lend their talk the quality of deliberations aimed at reaching agreement through giving reasons?

In my view, this is better treated as an empirical question than as a conceptual question. I see no reason to rule out in principle the possibility of a society in which social equality and cultural diversity coexist with participatory democracy. I certainly hope there can be such a society. That hope gains some plausibility if we consider that, however difficult it may be, communication across lines of cultural difference is not in principle impossible—although it will certainly become impossible if one imagines that it requires bracketing of differences. Granted such communication requires multicultural literacy, but that, I believe, can be acquired through practice. In fact, the possibilities expand once we acknowledge the complexity of cultural identities. *Pace* reductive, essentialist conceptions, cultural identities are woven of many different strands, and some of these strands may be common to people whose identities otherwise diverge, even when it is the divergences that are most salient.[32] Likewise, under conditions of social equality, the porousness, outer-directedness, and open-endedness of publics could promote intercultural communication. After all, the concept of a public presupposes a plurality of perspectives among those who participate within it, thereby allowing for internal differences and antagonisms, and likewise discouraging reified blocs.[33] In addition, the unbounded character and publicist orientation of publics allows for the fact that people participate in more than one public, and that the memberships of different publics may partially overlap. This in turn makes intercultural communication conceivable in principle. All told, then, there do not seem to be any conceptual (as opposed to empirical) barriers to the possibility of a socially egalitarian, multicultural society that is also a participatory democracy.[34] But this will necessarily be a society with many different publics, including at least one public in which participants can deliberate as peers across lines of difference about policy that concerns them all.

In general, I have been arguing that the ideal of participatory parity is better achieved by a multiplicity of publics than by a single public. This is true both for stratified societies and for egalitarian, multicultural societies, albeit for different reasons. In neither case is my argument intended as a simple postmodern celebration of multiplicity. Rather, in the case of stratified societies, I am defending subaltern counterpublics formed under conditions of dominance and subordination. In the other case, by contrast, I am defending the possibility of combining social equality, cultural diversity, and participatory democracy.

What are the implications of this discussion for a critical theory of the public sphere in actually existing democracy? Briefly, we need a critical political sociology of a form of public life in which multiple but unequal publics participate. This means theorizing the contestatory interaction of different publics and identifying the mechanisms that render some of them subordinate to others.

Public Spheres, Common Concerns, and Private Interests

I have argued that in stratified societies, like it or not, subaltern counterpublics stand in a contestatory relationship to dominant publics. One important object of such interpublic contestation is the appropriate boundaries of the public sphere. Here the central questions are, What counts as a public matter and what, in contrast, is private? This brings me to a third set of problematic assumptions underlying the liberal conception of the bourgeois public sphere, namely, assumptions concerning the appropriate scope of publicity in relation to privacy.

Recall that it is central to Habermas's account that the bourgeois public sphere was to be a discursive arena in which "private persons" deliberated about "public matters." There are several different senses of privacy and publicity in play here. "Publicity," for example, can mean (1) state-related; (2) accessible to everyone; (3) of concern to everyone; and (4) pertaining to a common good or shared interest. Each of these corresponds to a contrasting sense of "privacy." In addition, there are two other senses of "privacy" hovering just below the surface here: (5) pertaining to private property in a market economy; and (6) pertaining to intimate domestic or personal life, including sexual life.

I have already discussed at length the sense of "publicity" as open or accessible to all. Now I want to examine some of the other senses, beginning with (3) of concern to everyone.[35] This is ambiguous between what objectively affects or has an impact on everyone, as seen from an outsider's perspective, on the one hand, and what is recognized as a matter of common concern by participants, on the other hand. The idea of a public sphere as an arena of collective self-determination does not sit well with approaches that would appeal to an outsider perspective to delimit its proper boundaries. Thus, it is the second, participant's perspective that is relevant here. Only participants themselves can decide what is and what is not of common concern to them. However, there is no guarantee that all of them will agree. For example, until quite recently, feminists were in the minority in thinking that domestic violence against women was a matter of common concern and thus a legitimate topic of public discourse. The great majority of people considered this issue to be a private matter between what was assumed to be a fairly small number of heterosexual couples (and perhaps the social and legal professionals who were supposed to deal with them). Then, feminists formed a subaltern counterpublic from which we disseminated a view of domestic violence as a widespread systemic feature of male-dominated societies. Eventually, after sustained discursive contestation, we succeeded in making it a common concern.

The point is that there are no naturally given, a priori boundaries here. What will count as a matter of common concern will be decided precisely through discursive contestation. It follows that no topics should be ruled off-limits in advance of such contestation. On the contrary, democratic publicity requires positive guarantees of opportunities for minorities to convince others that what in the past was not public in the sense of being a matter of common concern should now become so.[36]

What, then, of the sense of "publicity" as pertaining to a common good or shared interest? This is the sense that is in play when Habermas characterizes the bourgeois public sphere as an arena in which the topic of discussion is restricted to the "common good" and in which discussion of "private interests" is ruled out.

This is a view of the public sphere that we would today call civic republican, as opposed to liberal-individualist. Briefly, the civic-republican model stresses a view of politics as people reasoning together to promote a common good that transcends the mere sum of individual preferences. The idea is that through deliberation the members of the public can come to discover or create such a common good. In the process of their deliberations, participants are transformed from a collection of self-seeking, private individuals into a public-spirited collectivity, capable of acting together in the common interest. On this view, private interests have no proper place in the political public sphere. At best, they are the prepolitical starting point of deliberation, to be transformed and transcended in the course of debate.[37]

Now, this civic-republican view of the public sphere is in one respect an improvement over the liberal-individualist alternative. Unlike the latter, it does not assume that people's preferences, interests, and identities are given exogenously in advance of public discourse and deliberation. It appreciates, rather, that preferences, interests, and identities are as much outcomes as antecedents of public deliberation, indeed are discursively constituted in and through it. However, as Jane Mansbridge has argued, the civic-republican view contains a very serious confusion, one that blunts its critical edge. This view conflates the ideas of deliberation and the common good by assuming that deliberation must be deliberation *about* the common good. Consequently, it limits deliberation to talk framed from the standpoint of a single, all-encompassing "we," thereby ruling claims of self-interest and group interest out of order. Yet this works against one of the principal aims of deliberation, namely, helping participants clarify their interests, even when those interests turn out to conflict. "Ruling self-interest [and group interest] out of order makes it harder for any participant to sort out what is going on. In particular, the less powerful may not find ways to discover that the prevailing sense of 'we' does not adequately include them."[38]

In general, there is no way to know in advance whether the outcome of a deliberative process will be the discovery of a common good in which conflicts of interest evaporate as merely apparent or, rather, the discovery that conflicts of interests are real and the common good is chimerical. But if the existence of a common good cannot be presumed in advance, then there is no warrant for putting any strictures on what sorts of topics, interests, and views are admissible in deliberation.[39]

This argument holds even in the best-case scenario of societies whose basic institutional frameworks do not generate systemic inequalities; even in such relatively egalitarian societies, we cannot assume in advance that there will be no real conflicts of interest. How much more pertinent, then, is the argument to stratified societies, which are traversed with pervasive relations of dominance and subordination. After all, when social arrangements operate to the systemic profit of some groups of people and to the systemic detriment of others, there are prima facie reasons for thinking that the postulation of a common good shared by exploiters and exploited may well be a mystification. Moreover, any consensus that purports to represent the common good in this social context should be regarded with suspicion, since this consensus will have been reached through deliberative processes tainted by the effects of dominance and subordination.

In general, critical theory needs to take a harder, more critical look at the terms "private" and "public." These terms, after all, are not simply straightforward designations of societal spheres; they are cultural classifications and rhetorical labels. In political discourse, they are powerful terms that are frequently deployed to delegitimate some interests, views, and topics and to valorize others.

This brings me to two other senses of "privacy," which often function ideologically to delimit the boundaries of the public sphere in ways that disadvantage subordinate social groups. These are sense (5) pertaining to private property in a market economy, and sense (6) pertaining to intimate domestic or personal life, including sexual life. Each of these senses is at the center of a rhetoric of privacy that has historically been used to restrict the universe of legitimate public contestation.

The rhetoric of domestic privacy seeks to exclude some issues and interests from public debate by personalizing and/or familializing them; it casts these as private-domestic or personal-familial matters in contradistinction to public, political matters. The rhetoric of economic privacy, in contrast, seeks to exclude some issues and interests from public debate by economizing them; the issues in question here are cast as impersonal market imperatives or as "private" ownership prerogatives or as technical problems for managers and planners, all in contradistinction to public, political matters. In both cases, the result is to enclave certain matters in specialized discursive arenas and thereby to shield them from broad-based debate and contestation. This usually works to the advantage of dominant groups and individuals and to the disadvantage of their subordinates.[40] If wife battering, for example, is labeled a "personal" or "domestic" matter and if public discourse about this phenomenon is canalized into specialized institutions associated with, say, family law, social work, and the sociology and psychology of "deviance," then this serves to reproduce gender dominance and subordination. Similarly, if questions of workplace democracy are labeled "economic" or "managerial" problems and if discourse about these questions is shunted into specialized institutions associated with, say, "industrial-relations" sociology, labor law, and "management science," then this serves to perpetuate class (and usually also gender and race) dominance and subordination.

This shows once again that the lifting of formal restrictions on public sphere participation does not suffice to ensure inclusion in practice. On the contrary, even after women, people of color, and workers have been formally licensed to participate, their participation may be hedged by conceptions of economic privacy and domestic privacy that delimit the scope of debate. These notions, therefore, are vehicles through which gender, "race," and class disadvantages may continue to operate subtextually and informally, even after explicit, formal restrictions have been rescinded.

Strong Publics, Weak Publics: On Civil Society and the State

Let me turn now to my fourth and last assumption underlying the liberal model of the bourgeois public sphere, namely, the assumption that a functioning democratic public sphere requires a sharp separation of civil society and the state. This assumption is susceptible to two different interpretations, depending on how one understands the expression "civil society." If one takes that expression to mean a privately ordered, capitalist economy, then to insist on its separation from the state is to defend classical liberalism. The claim would be that a system of limited government and laissez-faire capitalism is a necessary precondition for a well-functioning public sphere.

We can dispose of this (relatively uninteresting) claim fairly quickly by drawing on some arguments of the previous sections. I have already shown that participatory parity is essential to a democratic public sphere and that rough socioeconomic equality is a precondition of participatory parity. Now I need only add that laissez-faire capitalism does not foster socioeconomic equality and that some form of politically regulated economic reorganization and redistribution is needed to achieve that end. Likewise, I have also shown that efforts to "privatize" economic issues and to cast them as off-limits with respect to state activity impede, rather than promote, the sort of full and free discussion that is built into the idea of a public sphere. It follows from these considerations that a sharp separation of (economic) civil society and the state is not a necessary condition for a well-functioning public sphere. On the contrary, and *pace* the liberal model, it is precisely some sort of interimbrication of these institutions that is needed.[41]

However, there is also a second, more interesting, interpretation of the liberal assumption that a sharp separation of civil society and the state is necessary to a working public sphere, one that warrants more extended examination. In this interpretation, "civil society" means the nexus of nongovernmental or "secondary" associations that are neither economic nor administrative. We can best appreciate the force of the claim that civil society in this sense should be separate from the state if we recall Habermas's definition of the liberal public sphere as a "body of private persons assembled to form a public." The emphasis here on "private persons" signals (among other things) that the members of the bourgeois public are not state officials and that their participation in the public sphere is not undertaken in any official capacity. Accordingly, their discourse does not eventuate in binding, sovereign decisions authorizing the use of state power; on the contrary, it eventuates in "public opinion," critical commentary on authorized decision making that takes place elsewhere. The public sphere, in short, is not the state; it is rather the informally mobilized body of nongovernmental discursive opinion that can serve as a counterweight to the state. Indeed, in the liberal model, it is precisely this extragovernmental character of the public sphere that confers an aura of independence, autonomy, and legitimacy on the "public opinion" generated in it.

Thus, the liberal model of the bourgeois public sphere supposes the desirability of a sharp separation of (associational) civil society and the state. As a result, it promotes what I shall call *weak publics,* publics whose deliberative practice consists exclusively in opinion formation and does not also encompass decision making. Moreover, the liberal model seems to imply that an expansion of such publics' discursive authority to encompass decision making as well as opinion making would threaten the autonomy of public opinion—for then the public would effectively become the state, and the possibility of a critical discursive check on the state would be lost.

That, at least, is suggested by Habermas's initial formulation of the liberal model. In fact, the issue becomes more complicated as soon as we consider the emergence of parliamentary sovereignty. With that landmark development in the history of the public sphere, we encounter a major structural transformation, since a sovereign parliament functions as a public sphere *within* the state. Moreover, sovereign parliaments are what I shall call *strong publics,* publics whose discourse encompasses both opinion formation and decision making. As a locus of public deliberation culminating in legally binding decisions (or laws), parliament was to be the site for the discursive authorization of the use of state power. With the achievement of parliamentary sovereignty, therefore, the line separating (associational) civil society and the state is blurred.

Clearly, the emergence of parliamentary sovereignty and the consequent blurring of the (associational) civil society/state separation represents a democratic advance over earlier political arrangements. This is because, as the terms "strong public" and "weak public" suggest, the "force of public opinion" is strengthened when a body representing it is empowered to translate such "opinion" into authoritative decisions. At the same time, there remain important questions about the relation between parliamentary strong publics and the weak publics to which they are supposed to be accountable. In general, these developments raise some interesting and important questions about the relative merits of weak and strong publics and about the respective roles that institutions of both kinds might play in a democratic and egalitarian society.

One set of questions concerns the possible proliferation of strong publics in the form of self-managing institutions. In self-managed workplaces, child-care centers, or residential communities, for example, internal institutional public spheres could be arenas both of opinion formation and decision making. This would be tantamount to constituting sites of direct or quasi-direct democracy wherein all those engaged in a collective undertaking would participate in deliberations to determine its design and operation.[42] However, this would still leave open the relationship between such internal public spheres-cum-decision-making-bodies and those external publics to which they might also be deemed accountable. The question of that relationship becomes important when we consider that people who are affected by an undertaking in which they do not directly participate as agents may nonetheless have a stake in its modus operandi; they therefore also have a legitimate claim to a say, through some other (weaker or stronger) public sphere, in its institutional design and operation.

Here we are again broaching the issue of accountability. What institutional arrangements best ensure the accountability of democratic decision-making bodies (strong publics) to *their* (external, weak or, given the possibility of hybrid cases, weak*er*) publics?[43] Where in society are direct-democracy arrangements called for and where are representative forms more appropriate? How are the former best articulated with the latter? More generally, what democratic arrangements best institutionalize coordination among different institutions, including among their various coimplicated publics? Should we think of central parliament as a strong superpublic with authoritative discursive sovereignty over basic societal ground rules and coordination arrangements? If so, does that require the assumption of a single weak(er) external superpublic (in addition to, not instead of, various other smaller publics)? In any event, given the inescapable global interdependence manifest in the international division of labor within a single shared planetary biosphere, does it make sense to understand the nation-state as the appropriate unit of sovereignty?

I do not know the answers to most of these questions and I am unable to explore them further in this essay. However, the possibility of posing them, even in the absence of full, persuasive answers, enables us to draw one salient conclusion: any conception of the public sphere that requires a sharp separation between (associational) civil society and the state will be unable to imagine the forms of self-management, interpublic coordination, and political accountability that are essential to a democratic and egalitarian society. The liberal model of the bourgeois public sphere, therefore, is not adequate for contemporary critical theory. What is needed, rather, is a post-bourgeois conception that can permit us to envision a greater role for (at least some) public spheres than mere autonomous opinion formation removed from authoritative decision making. Such a postbourgeois conception would enable us to think about strong *and* weak publics, as well as about various hybrid forms. In addition, it would allow us to theorize the range of possible relations among such publics, thereby expanding our capacity to envision democratic possibilities beyond the limits of actually existing democracy.

Conclusion: Rethinking the Public Sphere

Let me conclude by recapitulating what I believe I have accomplished in this chapter. I have shown that the liberal model of the bourgeois public sphere, as described by Habermas, is not adequate for the critique of the limits of actually existing democracy in late-capitalist societies. At one level, my argument undermines the liberal model as a normative ideal. I have shown, first, that an adequate conception of the public sphere requires not merely the bracketing but, rather, the elimination, of social inequality. Second, I have shown that a multiplicity of publics is preferable to a single public sphere in both stratified societies and egalitarian societies. Third, I have shown that a tenable conception of the public sphere must countenance not the exclusion but the inclusion of interests and issues that bourgeois masculinist ideology labels "private" and treats as inadmissible. Finally, I have shown that a defensible conception must allow both for strong publics and for weak publics and that it should help theorize the relations among them. In sum, I have argued against four constitutive assumptions of the liberal model of the bourgeois public sphere; at the same time, I have identified some corresponding elements of a new, postbourgeois conception.

At another level, my argument enjoins four corresponding tasks on the critical theory of actually existing democracy. First, this theory should render visible the ways in which social inequality taints deliberation within publics in late-capitalist societies. Second, it should show how inequality affects relations among publics in late-capitalist societies, how publics are differentially empowered or segmented, and how some are involuntarily enclaved and subordinated to others. Next, a critical theory should expose ways in which the labeling of some issues and interests as "private" limits the range of problems, and of approaches to problems, that can be widely contested in contemporary societies. Finally, our theory should show how the overly weak character of some public spheres in late-capitalist societies denudes "public opinion" of practical force.

In all these ways, the theory should expose the limits of the specific form of democracy we enjoy in late-capitalist societies. Perhaps it can thereby help inspire us to try to push back those limits, while also cautioning people in other parts of the world against heeding the call to install them.

Notes

1. Research for this chapter was supported by the Center for Urban Affairs and Policy Research, Northwestern University. I am grateful for helpful comments from Craig Calhoun, Joshua Cohen, Tom McCarthy, Moishe Postone, Baukje Prins, David Schweikart, and Rian Voet. I also benefited from the inspiration and stimulation of participants in the conference "Habermas and the Public Sphere," University of North Carolina, Chapel Hill, September 1989.

2. Jürgen Habermas, *The Structural Transformation of the Public Sphere: An Inquiry into a Category of Bourgeois Society,* trans. Thomas Burger with Frederick Lawrence (Cambridge: MIT Press, 1989). For Habermas's later use of the category of the public sphere, see Jürgen Habermas, *The Theory of Communicative Action,* vol. 2, *Lifeworld and System: A Critique of Functionalist Reason,* trans. Thomas McCarthy (Boston: Beacon Press, 1987). For a critical secondary discussion of Habermas's later use of the concept, see Nancy Fraser, "What's Critical about Critical Theory? The Case of Habermas and Gender," in Fraser, *Unruly Practices: Power, Discourse and Gender in Contemporary Social Theory* (Minneapolis: University of Minnesota Press, 1989).

3. Throughout this book, I refer to paid workplaces, markets, credit systems, and so on as "*official-*economic system institutions" so as to avoid the androcentric implication that domestic institutions are not also "economic." For a discussion of this issue, see my "What's Critical about Critical Theory?"

4. Joan Landes, *Women and the Public Sphere in the Age of the French Revolution* (Ithaca: Cornell University Press, 1988). For a critique of Landes, see Keith Michael Baker, "Defining the Public Sphere in Eighteenth-Century France: Variations on a Theme by Habermas," in *Habermas and the Public Sphere,* ed. Craig Calhoun (Cambridge: MIT Press, 1992). Baker claims that Landes conflates the "essentially masculinist" Rousseauian republican model of the public sphere with the "contingently masculinist" and potentially feminist liberal model of Condorcet. I believe there is some merit in this criticism, for Landes does fail to distinguish the two variants sufficiently. Nevertheless, Baker himself fails to interrogate the liberal model with sufficient depth and rigor to establish the "merely contingent" character of its masculinism. Interestingly, Habermas's own subsequent (1992) discussion of this issue goes further and concedes more, although he vacillates inconsistently on whether the gender exclusion of the model was/is "radical"

and "constitutive." See his "Further Reflections on the Public Sphere," in *Habermas and the Public Sphere,* ed. Craig Calhoun (Cambridge: MIT Press, 1992), esp. pp. 425–29.

5. For the "public"/"pubic" connection, see the *Oxford English Dictionary* (2d ed., 1989) entry for "public." For the "testimony"/"testicle" connection, see Lucie White, "Subordination, Rhetorical Survival Skills and Sunday Shoes: Notes on the Hearing of Mrs. G.," *Buffalo Law Review* 38, no. 1 (winter 1990): 6.

6. Pierre Bourdieu, *Distinction: A Social Critique of the Judgment of Pure Taste* (Cambridge: Harvard University Press, 1979).

7. Geoff Eley, "Nations, Publics, and Political Cultures: Placing Habermas in the Nineteenth Century," in *Habermas and the Public Sphere,* ed. Craig Calhoun (Cambridge: MIT Press, 1992). See also Leonore Davidoff and Catherine Hall, *Family Fortunes: Men and Women of the English Middle Class, 1780–1850* (Chicago: University of Chicago Press, 1987). For Habermas's response to Eley, see his "Further Reflections on the Public Sphere."

8. Habermas does recognize that the self-understanding of the bourgeois public sphere was "ideological" in that its professed openness was belied by its class exclusivity. He also recognizes that the issue of gender exclusion is connected to a shift from aristocratic to bourgeois public spheres. Nevertheless, as I argue below, he fails to grasp the full implications of both points.

9. I do not mean to suggest that Habermas is unaware of the existence of public spheres other than the bourgeois one; on the contrary, in the preface to *Structural Transformation* (p. xviii), he explicitly states that his object is the liberal model of the bourgeois public sphere and that therefore he will discuss neither "the plebeian public sphere" (which he understands as an ephemeral phenomenon that existed "for just one moment" during the French Revolution) nor "the plebiscitary-acclamatory form of regimented public sphere characterizing dictatorships in highly developed industrial societies." My point is that, although Habermas acknowledges that there were alternative public spheres, he assumes that it is possible to understand the character of the bourgeois public by looking at it alone, in isolation from its relations to other, competing publics. This assumption is problematic. In fact, as I shall demonstrate, an examination of the bourgeois public's relations to alternative counterpublics challenges the liberal model of the bourgeois public sphere.

10. Mary P. Ryan, *Women in Public: Between Banners and Ballots, 1825–1880* (Baltimore: Johns Hopkins University Press, 1990), and "Gender and Public Access: Women's Politics in Nineteenth Century America," in *Habermas and the Public Sphere,* ed. Craig Calhoun (Cambridge: MIT Press, 1992).

11. Elizabeth Brooks-Higginbotham, *Righteous Discontent: The Women's Movement in the Black Baptist Church, 1880–1920* (Cambridge: Harvard University Press, 1993). For an account of the "white" subtext of the eighteenth-century U.S. public sphere, see Michael Warner, *The Letters of the Republic: Publication and the Public Sphere in Eighteenth Century America* (Cambridge: Harvard University Press, 1990).

12. Eley, "Nations, Publics, and Political Cultures."

13. Ibid.

14. This Gramscian notion clearly does not apply to the case of African Americans in the period treated by Brooks-Higginbotham. Far from being based on black consent, white supremacy was based on brute repression. Given this indisputable "exception," one might question whether the term "consent" is appropriate in other cases as well. One might wonder whether one should speak here not of consent *tout court* but rather of "some-

thing approaching consent," or "something appearing as consent," or "something constructed as consent" in order to leave open the possibility of degrees of consent or different balances of consent and repression.

15. According to the Gramscian view, the public sphere produces consent by means of circulation of discourses that construct the "common sense" of the day and represent the existing order as natural and/or just, but not simply as a ruse that is imposed. Rather, the public sphere in its mature form includes sufficient participation and sufficient representation of multiple interests and perspectives to permit most people most of the time to recognize themselves in its discourses. People who are ultimately disadvantaged by the social construction of consent nonetheless manage to find in the discourses of the public sphere representations of their interests, aspirations, life-problems, and anxieties that are close enough to resonate with their own lived self-representations, identities, and feelings. Their consent to hegemonic rule is secured when their culturally constructed perspectives are taken up and articulated with other culturally constructed perspectives in hegemonic sociopolitical projects. Given the reservations expressed in the preceding note, this account is probably best treated as applicable only in contexts that postdate women's suffrage and black civil rights. In the United States, this means post-1964!

16. Here I want to distance myself from a certain overly facile line of argument that is sometimes made against Habermas. This is the line that ideological functions of the public spheres in class societies simply undermine the normative notion as an ideal. This I take to be a non sequitur, since it is always possible to reply that under other conditions, say, the abolition of classes, genders, and other pervasive axes of inequality, the public sphere would no longer have this function but would instead be an institutionalization of democratic interaction. Moreover, as Habermas has often pointed out, even in existing class societies, the significance of the public sphere is not entirely exhausted by its class function. On the contrary, the idea of the public sphere also functions here and now as a norm of democratic interaction we use to criticize the limitations of actually existing public spheres. The point here is that even the revisionist story and the Gramscian theory that cause us to doubt the value of the public sphere are themselves possible only because of it. It is the idea of the public sphere that provides the conceptual condition of possibility for the revisionist critique of its imperfect realization.

17. Jane Mansbridge, "Feminism and Democracy," *American Prospect,* spring 1990, no. 1: 127.

18. In *Distinction* Bourdieu has theorized these processes in an illuminating way in terms of the concept of "class habitus."

19. As Habermas notes, this tendency is exacerbated with the concentration of media ownership in late-capitalist societies. For the steep increase in concentration in the United States in the late twentieth century, see Ben H. Bagdikian, *The Media Monopoly* (Boston: Beacon Press, 1983) and "Lords of the Global Village," *Nation,* 12 June 1989. This situation contrasts in some respects with countries with state-owned and -operated television. But even there it is doubtful that subordinated groups have equal access. Moreover, political-economic pressures have recently encouraged privatization of media in several of these countries. In part, this reflects the problems of state networks having to compete for "market share" with private channels airing U.S.-produced mass entertainment. For a fascinating, if somewhat dated, public-sphere-oriented discussion of public television in the former Federal Republic of Germany, see Oskar Negt and Alexander Kluge, *Public Sphere and Experience: Toward an Analysis of the Bourgeois and Proletarian Public Sphere,* trans. Peter Labanyi, Jamie Owen Daniel, and Assenka Oksiloff (Minneapolis: University of Minnesota Press, 1993).

20. This is the spirit behind, for example, proposals for electoral campaign financing reforms aimed at preventing the intrusion of economic dominance into the public sphere. Needless to say, within a context of massive societal inequality, it is far better to have such reforms than not to have them. However, in light of the sorts of informal effects of dominance and inequality discussed above, one ought not to expect too much from them. The most thoughtful recent defense of the liberal view comes from someone who in other respects is not a liberal. See Michael Walzer, *Spheres of Justice: A Defense of Pluralism and Equality* (New York: Basic Books, 1983). Another very interesting approach has been suggested by Joshua Cohen. In response to an earlier draft of this chapter, he argued that policies designed to facilitate the formation of social movements, secondary associations, and political parties would better foster participatory parity than would policies designed to achieve social equality, since the latter would require redistributive efforts that carry "deadweight losses." I certainly support the sort of policies that Cohen recommends, as well as his more general aim of an "associative democracy"—the sections of this chapter on multiple publics and strong publics make a case for related arrangements. However, I am not persuaded by the claim that these policies can achieve participatory parity under conditions of social inequality. That seems to me to be another variant of the liberal view of the autonomy of the political, which Cohen otherwise says he rejects. See Joshua Cohen, "Comments on Nancy Fraser's 'Rethinking the Public Sphere'" (paper presented at the meetings of the American Philosophical Association, Central Division, New Orleans, April 1990).

21. My argument draws on Karl Marx's still unsurpassed critique of liberalism in Part I of "On the Jewish Question." Hence, the allusion to Marx in the title of this essay.

22. Habermas has subsequently distanced himself from this view. See his "Further Reflections on the Public Sphere."

23. My argument in this section is deeply indebted to Joshua Cohen's perceptive comments on an earlier draft of this chapter in "Comments on Nancy Fraser's 'Rethinking the Public Sphere.'"

24. Mansbridge, "Feminism and Democracy."

25. I have coined this expression by combining two terms that other theorists have recently used with very good effects for purposes that are consonant with my own. I take the term "subaltern" from Gayatri Spivak, "Can the Subaltern Speak?" in *Marxism and the Interpretation of Culture,* ed. Cary Nelson and Larry Grossberg (Chicago: University of Illinois Press, 1988), pp. 271–313. I take the term "counterpublic" from Rita Felski, *Beyond Feminist Aesthetics* (Cambridge: Harvard University Press, 1989).

26. For an analysis of the political import of oppositional feminist discourses about needs, see Nancy Fraser, "Struggle over Needs: Outline of a Socialist-Feminist Critical Theory of Late-Capitalist Political Culture," in Fraser, *Unruly Practices* (Minneapolis: University of Minnesota Press, 1989). For an important effort to analyze the contemporary African-American subaltern counterpublic, see the Black Public Sphere Collective, *The Black Public Sphere* (Chicago: University of Chicago Press, 1995).

27. Eley, "Nations, Publics, and Political Cultures." Eley goes on to explain that this is tantamount to "extend[ing] Habermas's idea of the public sphere toward the wider public domain where authority is not only constituted as rational and legitimate, but where its terms are contested, modified, and occasionally overthrown by subaltern groups."

28. It seems to me that public discursive arenas are among the most important and under-recognized sites in which social identities are constructed, deconstructed, and reconstructed. My view stands in contrast to various psychoanalytic accounts of identity formation, which neglect the formative importance of post-Oedipal discursive interaction

outside the nuclear family and which therefore cannot explain identity shifts over time. It strikes me as unfortunate that so much of contemporary feminist theory has taken its understanding of social identity from psychoanalytic models, while neglecting to study identity construction in relation to public spheres. The revisionist historiography of the public sphere discussed earlier can help redress the balance by identifying public spheres as loci of identity reconstruction. For an account of the discursive character of social identity and a critique of Lacanian psychoanalytic approaches to identity, see Nancy Fraser, "Structuralism or Pragmatics? On Discourse Theory and Feminist Politics," in this volume.

29. For another statement of this position, see Nancy Fraser, "Toward a Discourse Ethic of Solidarity," *Praxis International* 5, no. 4 (January 1986): 425–29. See also Iris Young, "Impartiality and the Civic Public: Some Implications of Feminist Critiques of Moral and Political Theory," in *Feminism as Critique,* ed. Seyla Benhabib and Drucilla Cornell (Minneapolis: University of Minnesota Press, 1987), pp. 56–76.

30. For an analysis of the rhetorical specificity of one historical public sphere, see Warner, *The Letters of the Republic.*

31. For a thoughtful discussion of this point, see Miriam Hansen, foreword to Negt and Kluge, *Public Sphere and Experience.*

32. One could say that at the deepest level, everyone is *mestizo.* The best metaphor here may be Wittgenstein's idea of family resemblances, or networks of crisscrossing, overlapping differences and similarities, no single thread of which runs continuously throughout the whole. For an account that stresses the complexity of cultural identities and the salience of discourse in their construction, see my "Structuralism or Pragmatics? On Discourse Theory and Feminist Politics," in this volume. For accounts that draw on concepts of *métissage,* see Gloria Anzaldua, *Borderlands/La Frontera: The New Mestiza* (San Francisco: Spinsters/Aunt Lute Press, 1987); and Françoise Lionnet, *Autobiographical Voices: Race, Gender, Self-Portraiture* (Ithaca: Cornell University Press, 1989).

33. In these respects, the concept of a public differs from that of a community. "Community" suggests a bounded and fairly homogeneous group, and it often connotes consensus. "Public," in contrast, emphasizes discursive interaction that is in principle unbounded and open-ended, and this in turn implies a plurality of perspectives. Thus, the idea of a public, better than that of a community, can accommodate internal differences, antagonisms, and debates. For an account of the connection between publicity and plurality, see Hannah Arendt, *The Human Condition* (Chicago: University of Chicago Press, 1958). For a critique of the concept of community, see Iris Young, "The Ideal of Community and the Politics of Difference," in *Feminism and Postmodernism,* ed. Linda J. Nicholson (New York: Routledge, Chapman & Hall, 1989), pp. 300–323.

34. For a counterargument, see Jeffrey Spinner-Halev, "Difference and Diversity in an Egalitarian Democracy," *Journal of Political Philosophy* 3, no. 3 (September 1995): 259–279.

35. In this chapter, I do not directly discuss sense (1) state-related. However, in the next section of this chapter, I consider some issues that touch on that sense.

36. This is the equivalent in democratic theory of a point that Paul Feyerabend has argued in the philosophy of science. See Feyerabend, *Against Method* (New York: Verso, 1988).

37. In contrast, the liberal-individualist model stresses a view of politics as the aggregation of self-interested, individual preferences. Deliberation in the strict sense drops out altogether. Instead, political discourse consists in registering individual preferences and in bargaining, looking for formulas that satisfy as many private interests as possible. It is assumed that there is no such thing as the common good over and above the sum of all

the various individual goods, and so private interests are the legitimate stuff of political discourse.

38. Mansbridge, "Feminism and Democracy," p. 131.

39. This point, incidentally, is in the spirit of a strand of Habermas's recent normative thought, which stresses the procedural, as opposed to the substantive, definition of a democratic public sphere; here, the public sphere is defined as an arena for a certain type of discursive interaction, not as an arena for dealing with certain types of topics and problems. There are no restrictions, therefore, on what may become a topic of deliberation. See Seyla Benhabib's account of this radical proceduralist strand of Habermas's thought and her defense of it as the strand that renders his view of the public sphere superior to alternative views. Benhabib, "Models of Public Space: Hannah Arendt, the Liberal Tradition, and Jürgen Habermas," in *Habermas and the Public Sphere,* ed. Craig Calhoun (Cambridge: MIT Press, 1992).

40. Usually, but not always. As Josh Cohen has argued, exceptions are the uses of privacy in *Roe v. Wade,* the U.S. Supreme Court decision legalizing abortion, and in Justice Blackmun's dissent in *Bowers,* the decision upholding state antisodomy laws. These examples show that the privacy rhetoric is multivalent rather than univocally and necessarily harmful. On the other hand, there is no question but that the weightier tradition of privacy argument has buttressed inequality by restricting debate. Moreover, many feminists have argued that even the "good" privacy uses have some serious negative consequences in the current context and that gender domination is better challenged in this context on other discursive grounds. For a defense of "privacy" talk, see Cohen, "Comments on Nancy Fraser's 'Rethinking the Public Sphere.'"

41. There are many possibilities here, including such mixed forms as market socialism.

42. I use the expression "quasi-direct democracy" in order to signal the possibility of hybrid forms of self-management involving the democratic designation of representatives, managers, or planners held to strict standards of accountability through, for example, recall.

43. By hybrid possibilities I mean arrangements involving very strict accountability of representative decision-making bodies to their external publics through veto and recall rights. Such hybrid forms might in some, though certainly not all, circumstances be desirable.

4

Sex, Lies, and the Public Sphere

Reflections on the Confirmation
of Clarence Thomas

The making of mainstream public opinion is mainly a routinized affair, the business of pundits as opposed to lay citizens. Occasionally, however, something happens that explodes the circuits of professional opinion-making-as-usual and calls forth widespread and intense public debate. In such moments, something approximating mass participation crystallizes, and for a brief instant, at least, we sense the possibility of a robust political public sphere. Yet the experience is characteristically mixed. Intimations of democracy are laced with demagoguery and exclusion, which the bright light of hyperpublicity casts into sharp relief. These moments can accordingly have great diagnostic value. They make starkly visible the structures of inequality and practices of power that deform public-opinion-making in ordinary times, less obtrusively but more systematically.[1]

One such moment was the 1991 struggle over the confirmation of Clarence Thomas as an associate justice of the U.S. Supreme Court. Combining flashes of democratic participation with practices of strategic containment, this struggle raised in a dramatic and pointed way key questions about the nature of contemporary publicity. It was not simply a battle for public opinion within an already constituted public sphere. What was at stake was, on the contrary, the very meaning and boundaries of publicity. The way the struggle unfolded, moreover, depended at every point on who

99

had the power to draw the line between the public and the private. As a result, the "Clarence Thomas affair" exposed crucial obstacles to democratic publicity in our society. At the same time, it exposed the inadequacies of the classical liberal model of the public sphere, revealing that standard understandings of publicity are ideological.

Whose Privacy? Which Publicity?

Recall the circumstances. Clarence Thomas, a black conservative, was nominated to the Supreme Court by George Bush in 1991. As former head of the federal Equal Employment Opportunity Commission, Thomas had presided over the transition to the "post-civil-rights era," downsizing the agency's efforts to enforce laws outlawing discrimination. Predictably, his Supreme Court nomination was opposed in liberal, feminist, and civil-rights circles. Black organizations were divided, however, with many hesitating to take a stand against a man who was poised to become only the second African American on the Court in U.S. history. During the regularly scheduled Senate Judiciary Committee confirmation hearings, Thomas played down his record, his "race," and his constitutional and political views, stressing instead his humble origins and subsequent triumph over adversity. When these hearings were concluded and a Senate vote was set, he appeared certain to win confirmation—until he was publicly accused of sexually harassing a former EEOC subordinate.

Then, for several weeks, the country was riveted as the Judiciary Committee investigated the allegations by Anita F. Hill, a black female law professor who had served as Thomas's assistant at the Equal Employment Opportunity Commission in the 1980s. Hill charged that Thomas had repeatedly sexually harassed her at work during this period, pressuring her for dates despite her consistent refusals, graphically describing—over her repeated objections—pornographic films he had seen, and bragging to her about the size of his penis and his talents as a lover despite her requests that he stop. She filed no complaint at the time. The government agency that handles such complaints is the Equal Employment Opportunity Commission, then headed by Thomas, the very site where Hill claimed the harassment occurred. By the time her charges were publicly aired in 1991, the U.S. Supreme Court had ruled that sexual harassment is a form of sex discrimination and is illegal under the U.S. civil rights laws.

Thomas categorically denied Hill's charges. The cat, however, was out of the bag. Bowing to intense public pressure, the Senate delayed its scheduled confirmation vote to hold an unprecedented second round of televised Judiciary Committee hearings on the sexual-harassment accusations. Following these hearings, the Senate, by the narrowest margin ever in such votes, confirmed the appointment of Thomas to the Supreme Court.

Few dramas have so gripped the country as this one. Everywhere people put their ordinary activities aside to watch the hearings and to debate the issues. Everywhere, people argued passionately over whether Thomas or Hill was telling the truth. Radio talk shows were bombarded with callers, including women who claimed that they themselves had been sexually harassed in the past but until now had been too ashamed to tell anyone. The press was filled with opinion articles representing all sides of the issue. It was hard to find a corner of life where the talk was not about Clarence Thomas and Anita Hill.

In short, this was a rare moment in American life in which a lively contentious public sphere was in evidence. I mean a public sphere in Habermas's sense of an arena in which public opinion is constituted through discourse; where members of the public debate matters of common concern, seeking to persuade one another through giving reasons; and where the force of public opinion is brought to bear on government decision making.[2]

Indeed, the Clarence Thomas affair seems at first glance to provide a textbook example of the public sphere in action. The Senate Judiciary Committee hearings on Hill's accusations seemed to constitute an exercise in democratic publicity, as understood in the classical liberal model of the public sphere. The hearings opened to public scrutiny an aspect of government functioning, namely, the nomination and confirmation of a Supreme Court justice. They thus subjected a decision of state officials to the force of public opinion. Through the hearings, in fact, public opinion was constituted and brought to bear directly on the decision, affecting the process by which it was made as well as its substantive outcome. As a result, state officials were held accountable to the public by means of a discursive process of opinion and will formation.

On closer examination, however, these events belie the classical liberal model of the public sphere. That model treats the meaning and boundaries of publicity and privacy as simply given and self-evident. But the Thomas/Hill confrontation was largely a struggle over the meaning and boundaries of those categories. The antagonists vied over where precisely the line between the public and the private would be drawn. And the outcome depended on who had the power to enforce and defend that line.

Those issues underlay many of the questions that were explicitly debated: How should one view the initial public disclosure on 6 October 1991 of

Hill's accusations, which had been communicated confidentially to Judiciary Committee staff? Was this a leak to the press aimed at torpedoing the Thomas nomination, hence an egregious breach of proper procedure and confidentiality? Or was it a heroic act of whistle-blowing that properly blew the lid off an outrageous cover-up? Was Hill's failure to go public with her accusations prior to 6 October grounds for doubting her account or was it consistent with her story? Should the behavior Hill ascribed to Thomas be considered innocent camaraderie or abuse of power? Is such behavior "normal" or "pathological"?

Moreover, do men and women have different views of these issues and are they positioned differently with respect to privacy and publicity? Did the efforts of Thomas's supporters to undermine the credibility of Hill constitute an unconscionable invasion of her privacy or a proper and vigorous exercise of public scrutiny? Were there significant differences in the ability of Thomas and Hill respectively to define and defend their privacy?

Was the subsequent injection of the issue of "race" by Thomas a mere smokescreen or did the convening of an all-white public tribunal to adjudicate on television a dispute between two African Americans signal the existence of real racial-ethnic differences in relation to privacy and publicity? Is "sexual harassment" a figment of the fevered imagination of puritanical, sexually repressed, elite white feminists or an instrument of gender, "race," and class power? Does the vindication in this case of a black man's ability to defend his privacy against a white-dominated public represent an advance for his "race" or a setback for black women?

Did the hearings themselves constitute an unseemly circus that degraded the democratic process or were they a rare exercise in democratic publicity, a "national teach-in on sexual harassment"? Was the airing in public hearings of the charge of sexual harassment another sorry case of the American obsession with the private lives of public figures, an obsession that displaces real politics onto questions of "character"? Or was it instead a historic breakthrough in an ongoing struggle to achieve a more equitable balance in the social relations of privacy and publicity?

Finally, is democratic publicity best understood as a check on the public power of the state or should it be understood more broadly as a check against illegitimate private power as well? And what is the relationship between various different publics that emerged here: for example, the official public sphere within the state (the hearings); the extragovernmental public sphere constituted by the mass media; various counterpublics associated with oppositional social movements like feminism and with ethnic enclaves like the African-American community (the feminist press, the black press); various secondary associations active in forming public opinion ("interest groups," lobbies); the ephemeral but intense constitution of informal public spheres at various sites in everyday life—at workplaces, restaurants, campuses, street corners, shopping centers, private homes, wherever people gathered to discuss the events? In each of those public arenas, whose words counted in the conflict of interpretations that determines the official public story of "what really happened"? And why?

Underlying all these questions are two more general problems that are centered on power and inequality: Who has the power to decide where to draw the line between public and private? What structures of inequality underlie the hegemonic understandings of these categories as well as the struggles that contest them?

Gender Struggle

The first phase of the struggle was played out as a gender struggle, and it laid bare important gender asymmetries concerning privacy and publicity. These were not the familiar orthodoxies of an earlier stage of feminist theory, which protested women's alleged confinement to the private sphere and lack of public sphere participation. Rather, the asymmetries here concerned women's greater vulnerability to unwanted, intrusive publicity and lesser ability to define and defend their privacy.

These issues first emerged when the public-at-large learned of a struggle that had been waged behind closed doors for several weeks between Hill and members of the Senate Judiciary Committee over the handling of her accusations against Thomas. We learned that Hill had been approached by committee staff and asked to confirm a report that Thomas had harassed her; that she did so, but asked that the matter be pursued in a way that would protect her privacy by keeping her identity secret; that the committee had dropped the matter after only a very cursory investigation, although Hill had several times urged the committee to pursue it, finally agreeing that her name could be used; and that the committee had elected not to publicize the matter. A reporter broke the story, however.

In her first public news conference after her charges had been publicly reported, Hill put great stress on what she called her lack of "control" over the routing, timing, and dissemination of her information. She was already having to defend herself against two apparently contradictory charges: first, that she had failed to make public her allegations in a timely fashion, as any bona-fide victim of sexual harassment supposedly would have; but second, that in making these charges she was seeking publicity and self-aggrandizement. Hill sought to explain her actions, first, by insisting that "control" over these disclosures "never rested with me," and second, by acknowledging her difficulty in balancing her need for privacy against her duty to disclose information in response to the committee's inquiry.[3] As it turned out, she never succeeded in fully dispelling many Americans' doubts on these points.

For its part, the committee's decision not to publicize Hill's sexual harassment charges against Thomas represented an effort to delimit the scope of the first round of public hearings in September and to contain public debate about the nomination. Once the charges were made public, however, the committee lost control of the process. Instead, its members became embroiled in a public struggle with feminists who objected to the privatization of an important gender issue and accused the senators of "sexism" and "insensitivity."

This gender struggle was widely reported in the media in counterpoint with a counterdiscourse of outrage over "the leak." These two themes of "sexism in the Senate" and "leaks" were for a time the two principal contenders in the battle for preeminence in interpreting the events, as a struggle was being waged over whether or not to delay the confirmation vote.[4] The vote *was* of course delayed, and feminists succeeded in broadening the space of the official national political public sphere to encompass, for the first time, the subject of sexual harassment.

Getting an issue on the public sphere agenda, however, does not guarantee success in controlling the discussion of it. Even as it was being decided that the vote on Thomas's nomination would be delayed and that public hearings on the sexual harassment charges would be held, there began a fierce backstage contest to shape the public debate over the issues. While public debate focused on the question of the Senate's "insensitivity," White House strategists worked behind the scenes to shape the focus of the hearings and the interpretation of events.

As it turned out, the administration plan to shape public debate and limit the scope of the hearings had three crucial features. First, the White House sought to construct the hearings as a "he said, she said" affair by preventing or marginalizing any new allegations of sexual harassment by other victims. Second, it sought to rule off-limits any interrogation of what was defined as Thomas's private life, including what the *New York Times* called his "well-documented taste for watching and discussing pornographic movies while he was at Yale Law School."[5] Third, and last, it sought to exclude expert testimony about the nature of sexual harassment and the characteristic responses of victims, so that, in the words of one administration spin doctor, it could "prevent this from turning into a referendum on 2000 years of male dominance and sexual harassment."[6]

Together these three moves cast Thomas and Hill in very different relations to privacy and publicity. Thomas was enabled to declare key areas of his life "private" and therefore off-limits. Hill, in contrast, was cast as someone whose motives and character would be subjects of intense scrutiny and intrusive speculation, since her credibility was to be evaluated in a conceptual vacuum. When the Senate Judiciary Committee adopted these ground rules for the hearings, it sealed in place a structural differential in relation to publicity and privacy that worked overwhelmingly to Thomas's advantage and to Hill's disadvantage.

Once these ground rules were in place, the administration concentrated on undermining Hill. It sought to ensure, as Republican Senator Alan K. Simpson presciently predicted in a speech on the Senate floor, that "Anita Hill will be sucked right into the maw, the very thing she wanted to avoid most. She will be injured and destroyed and belittled and hounded and harassed, real harassment, different from the sexual kind."[7]

Meanwhile, Thomas attempted to define and defend his privacy. His attempts had a certain ironic flavor, to be sure, given his insistence in the earlier, routine round of hearings on substituting his personal life story—or at least his version thereof—for discussion of his political, legal, and constitutional views. Having first tried to make his private character the public issue, he was nearly undone by the focus on his character when Hill's accusation was made public.

In the extraordinary, second round of hearings, Thomas responded to Hill's charges by trying to define what he thought was or should be his private life. He refused to accept questions that breached his privacy as he defined it. And he objected to "reporters and interest groups . . . looking for dirt" as un-American and Kafkaesque.

> I am not here . . . to put my private life on display for prurient interests or other reasons. I will not allow this committee or anyone else to probe into my private life . . . I will not provide the rope for my own lynching or for further humiliation. I am not going to engage in discussions nor will I submit to roving questions of what goes on in the most intimate parts of my private life, or the sanctity of my bedroom. These are the most intimate parts of my privacy, and they will remain just that, private.[8]

As it turned out, Thomas was relatively successful in enforcing his definitions of privacy and publicity. His questioners on the committee generally accepted his definition of privacy, and their questions did not trespass on that space as he had defined it. They didn't inquire into his sexual history or his fantasy life, and he was not in fact questioned about his practice of viewing and discussing pornographic films. On the one time when this subject was broached by Democratic Senator Patrick Leahy, at the session of 12 October 1991, Thomas successfully repulsed the inquiry:

> [Senator Leahy]: Did you ever have a discussion of pornographic films with . . . any other women [than Professor Hill]?
> [Thomas]: Senator, I will not get into any discussions that I might have about my personal life or my sex life with any person outside of the workplace.[9]

The question was not pursued. Later, after the Senate confirmed the nomination, Democratic members of the Judiciary Committee defended their failure to cross-examine Thomas vigorously by saying that he had put up a "wall" and refused to answer questions about his private life.[10]

So successful, in fact, was Thomas in defending his privacy that while the country was awash in speculation concerning the character, motives, and psychology of Hill, there was no comparable speculation about him. No one wondered, it seemed, what sort of anxieties and hurts could lead a powerful and successful self-made black man from a very poor background to sexually harass a black female subordinate from a similar background.

Hill also sought to define and defend her privacy but was far less successful than Thomas. Although she sought to keep the focus on her complaint and on the evidence that corroborated it, the principal focus soon became *her* character. During the course of the struggle, it was variously suggested that Hill was a lesbian, a heterosexual erotomaniac, a delusional schizophrenic, a fantasist, a vengeful spurned woman, a perjurer, and a malleable tool of liberal interest groups. Not only the Republican hit men, Senators Arlen Specter, Orrin Hatch, and Alan Simpson, but even her female coworkers from the Equal Employment Opportunity Commission tarred her with many of the classical sexist stereotypes: "stridently aggressive," "arrogant," "ambitious," "hard," "tough," "scorned," "opinionated." Nor did any of the Democratic committee members succeed, or for that matter even try, to limit the scope of inquiry into her privacy.[11]

Hill's lesser success in drawing the line between public and private testifies to the gendered character of these categories and to the way their constitution reflects an asymmetry or hierarchy of power along gender lines. That asymmetry is reflected in the phenomenon of sexual harassment as well.

Consider the following account by Hill in response to the questioning of Democratic Senator Howell Heflin, who first read portions of her own opening statement:

> "I sense[d] that my discomfort with [Thomas's] discussions [of pornography] only urged him on as though my reaction of feeling ill at ease and vulnerable was what he wanted."

Then, in response to Heflin's request for elaboration, Hill replied:

> It was almost as though he wanted me at a disadvantage . . . so that I would have to concede to whatever his wishes were . . . I would be under his control. I think it was the fact that I had said no to him that caused him to want to do this.[12]

As Hill saw it, then, Thomas's behavior had been an assertion (or reassertion) of power, aimed simultaneously at compensating himself and punishing her for rejection. She herself had lacked the power to define their interaction as professional, not sexual. He, in contrast, had had the power to inject what liberals consider private sexual elements into the public sphere of the workplace against her wishes and over her objections.

Given the gender differential in ability to define and protect one's privacy, we can understand some of the deeper issues at stake in Thomas's insistence on avoiding the "humiliation" of a "public probe" into his "privacy." This insistence can be understood in part as a defense of his masculinity. To be subject to having one's privacy publicly probed is to be feminized.

Women's difficulty in defining and defending their privacy was also attested by an extremely important absence from the hearings: the last-minute nonappearance of Angela Wright, a second black woman who claimed to have been sexually harassed by Thomas and whose scheduled testimony to that effect was to have been corroborated by yet another witness, Rose Jordain, in whom Wright had confided at the time. Given that disbelief of Hill was often rationalized by the assertion that there were no other complainants, the nonappearance of Wright was significant. We can speculate that had she testified and proved a credible witness, the momentum of the struggle might have shifted decisively. Why then did Angela Wright suddenly not appear? Both sides had reasons to privatize her story. Fearing that a second accusation would be extremely damaging, Thomas's supporters threatened to discredit Wright by introducing information concerning her personal history. Meanwhile, Hill's supporters may have feared that a woman described in the press as presenting "a more complex picture than Professor Hill"[13] would appear to lack credibility and undermine Hill's as well. Thus, the silencing of a complainant who lacked Hill's respectability was a crucial and possibly even decisive factor in the dynamics and outcome of the struggle.

The Struggle over "Race"

During the first, gender-dominated, phase of the struggle, the issue of "race" was barely discussed, despite repeated but unelaborated references to the Senate as an all-white body.[14] The relative silence about "race" was soon shattered, however, when Thomas himself broached the issue. Moving quickly to occupy an otherwise vacant discursive terrain, he and his supporters managed to establish a near-monopoly on "race" talk, and the result proved disastrous for Hill.

Thomas declared that the hearings were a "high tech lynching" designed to stop "uppity Blacks who in any way deign to think for themselves."[15] He also spoke repeatedly about his defenselessness before charges that played into racial stereotypes of black men as having large penises and unusual sexual prowess.[16] Here it is important to note that by combining references to lynching with references to stereotypes about black men's sexual prowess, Thomas artfully conflated two stereotypes that, although related, are by no means identical. The first is the stereotype of the black man as sexual stud, highly desired by women and capable of providing them great sexual pleasure. This was the figure that emerged from Hill's testimony, according to which Thomas bragged about his (hetero)sexual virtuosity. The second stereotype is that of the black man as rapist, a lust-driven animal, whose sexuality is criminal and out of control. There was no hint of that stereotype in Hill's testimony.

It is possible that at an unconscious level there are affinities between these two stereotypes, but they differ importantly in at least one crucial respect. Although both have been embraced by white racists, the first, but not the second, has also been embraced by some black men.[17] Thus, while it may be inconceivable that Thomas would have elected to affect the persona of the black man as rapist, it is not inconceivable that he would have affected the persona of the black male sexual stud. Yet by conflating these two stereotypes, Thomas was able to suggest that Hill's reports of his behavior as a would-be stud were equivalent to southern white racist fabrications of criminal sexuality and rape. This turned out to be a rhetorical masterstroke. The

Democrats on the committee were too cowed by Thomas's charge of racism to question the nominee's logic. Many leading black liberals seemed caught off guard and unable to respond effectively; most simply denied that "race" had any relevance in the case at all.

The mainstream press contributed to the confusion. The *New York Times*, for example, printed solemn quotations from Harvard psychologist Alvin Poussaint about the effects of Hill's charges on black men:

> "Black men will feel [her allegations] reinforce negative stereotypes about them as sexual animals out of control. . . . It will increase their level of tension and vulnerability around charges of this type. . . . There's a high level of anger among black men . . . that black women will betray them; that black women are given preference over them; that white men will like to put black women in between them to use them. Black men feel that white men are using this black woman to get another black man."[18]

I have no way of knowing whether or to what extent Poussaint was accurately reporting the views and feelings of black men. What is clear, however, was the lack of any comparable discussion of the effects of the case on black women. In the absence of such discussion, moreover, the fears ascribed to black men seemed to acquire legitimacy. They were not contextualized or counterpointed by any other perspective. The press coverage of the racial dimensions of the struggle generally slighted black women. It focused chiefly on questions such as whether or not all black men would be tarred in the eyes of white America, and whether or not another black man would get a shot at a seat on the Supreme Court.

One of the most important features of the entire struggle was the absence from the hearings and from the mainstream public sphere debate of a black feminist analysis. No one who was in a position to be heard in the hearings or in the mass media spoke about the historic vulnerability of black women to sexual harassment in the United States and about the use of racist-misogynist stereotypes to justify such abuse and to malign black women who protest.

The lone exception was Ellen Wells, a witness who corroborated Hill's version of events by testifying that Hill had told her that Thomas was harassing her at the time. In the course of her testimony, Wells explained why Hill might have nonetheless maintained contact with Thomas:

> "My mother told me, and I'm sure Anita's mother told her. When you leave, make sure you leave friends behind, because you don't know who

you may need later on. And so you do at least want to be cordial. I know I get Christmas cards from people that I . . . quite frankly do not wish to [see]. And I also return their cards and will return their calls. And these are people who have insulted me and done things which have degraded me at times. But these are things you have to put up with. And being a black woman you know you have to put up with a lot. And so you grit your teeth and you do it."[19]

Wells's voice was, however, the exception that proved the rule. Absent from the mainstream public sphere was the sort of black feminist analysis that could have corroborated and contextualized Hill's experience. As a result, African-American women were in effect "asked to choose . . . whether to stand against the indignities done to them as women, sometimes by men of their own race, or to remember that black men take enough of a beating from the white world and to hold their peace."[20]

In other words, there was no widely disseminated perspective that persuasively integrated a critique of sexual harassment with a critique of racism. The struggle was cast as *either* a gender struggle *or* a "race" struggle. It could not, apparently, be both at once.

The result was that it became difficult to see Anita Hill as a black woman. She became, in effect, functionally white. Certainly, Thomas's references to lynching had the effect of calling into question her blackness. The lynching story requires a white woman as "victim" and pretext. To my knowledge, no black man has ever been lynched for the sexual exploitation of a black woman. Thomas's charge thus implied that Hill might not really be black. Perhaps because she was a tool of white interest groups. Or perhaps because she had internalized the uptight, puritanical sexual morality of elite white feminists and had mistaken Thomas's lower-class African-American courting style for abuse, a view propounded by Harvard sociologist Orlando Patterson in an op-ed piece in the *New York Times*.[21] Or perhaps most ingeniously of all because, like Adela Quested, the white female protagonist of E. M. Forster's *A Passage to India*, Hill was an erotomaniacal spinster who fantasized abuse at the hands of a dark-skinned man out of the depths of her experiences of rejection and sexual frustration. This view was apparently originated by a witness named John Doggett, who declared that Hill had once been obsessed with him. But it was more effectively—because less self-servingly—presented by Senator Orrin Hatch and other Thomas supporters.

Whichever of these scenarios one chose to believe, the net effect was the same: Hill became functionally white. She was treated, consequently, very differently from the way that Angela Wright would probably have been treated had *she* testified. Wright might very well have been cast as Jezebel, opposite Hill's Adela Quested, in a bizarre melodramatic pastiche of traditional and nontraditional casting.

The "whitening" of Anita Hill had much broader implications, however, since it cast black women who seek to defend themselves against abuse at the hands of black men as traitors or enemies of the "race." Consequently, when the struggle was cast exclusively as a racial struggle, the sole black protagonist became the black man. He was made to stand synechdochically for the entire "race," and the black woman was erased from view.

The dynamics of black female erasure during the hearings did not pass uncontested by black feminists. In the heat of the struggle, a group called African American Women in Defense of Ourselves formed, seeking to redress their erasure. Although the group developed a highly sophisticated analysis, it was unable to attract media coverage. Eventually, having raised sufficient funds to purchase space, it published a statement in the *New York Times* on 17 November 1991, a full month after Thomas was confirmed. Although this statement appeared too late to influence events, it is worth quoting at some length:

> Many have erroneously portrayed the allegations against Clarence Thomas as an issue of either gender or race. As women of African descent, we understand sexual harassment as both. We further understand that Clarence Thomas outrageously manipulated the legacy of lynching in order to shelter himself from Anita Hill's allegations. To deflect attention away from the reality of sexual abuse in African American women's lives, he trivialized and misrepresented this painful part of African American people's history. This country, which has a long legacy of racism and sexism, has never taken the sexual abuse of Black women seriously. Throughout U.S. history, Black women have been sexually stereotyped as immoral, insatiable, perverse; the initiators in all sexual contact—abusive or otherwise. The common assumption in legal proceedings as well as in the larger society has been that Black women cannot be raped or otherwise sexually abused. As Anita Hill's experience demonstrates, Black women who speak of these matters are not likely to be believed.
>
> In 1991 we cannot tolerate this type of dismissal of any one Black woman's experience or this attack upon our collective character without protest, outrage, and resistance. . . . No one will speak for us but ourselves.[22]

What is so important about this statement is its rejection of the view, held by many supporters of Hill, that "race" was simply irrelevant to this struggle, apart from Thomas's manipulation of it. Instead, the statement implies that the categories of privacy and publicity are not simply gendered categories; they are racialized categories as well. Historically, African Americans have been denied privacy in the sense of domesticity. As a result, black women have been highly vulnerable to sexual harassment at the hands of masters, overseers, bosses, and supervisors. At the same time, they have lacked the public standing to claim state protection against abuse, whether suffered at work or at home. Black men, meanwhile, have lacked the rights and preroga-tives enjoyed by white men, including the right to exclude white men from "their" women and the right to exclude the state from their "private" sphere.

Perhaps, then, it is worth exploring the hypothesis that in making his case before the white tribunal, Thomas was trying to claim the same rights and immunities of masculinity that white men have historically enjoyed, especial-ly the right to maintain open season on black women. Or perhaps he was not claiming *exactly* the same rights and immunities as white men. Perhaps he was not seeking these privileges vis-à-vis all women. After all, no white woman claimed to have been sexually harassed by him. Is that because in fact he never sexually harassed a white woman, although he married one? And if so, is *that* because he felt less of a sense of entitlement in his interac-tions with his white female subordinates at work? If so, then perhaps his references to lynching were not *merely* a smokescreen, as many liberals and feminists assumed. Perhaps they were also traces of the racialization of his masculinity. In any event, we need more work that theorizes the racial sub-text of the categories of privacy and publicity and its intersection with the gender subtext.[23]

Class Struggle?

Sexual harassment is not only a matter of gender and racial domination but one of status and class domination as well. The scene of harassment is the workplace or educational institution. The protagonists are superordinate bosses, supervisors, or teachers, on the one hand, and subordinate employ-ees or students, on the other. The effect of the practice is to maintain the class or status control of the former over the latter.[24] Sexual harassment, therefore, raises the classic issues of workers' power in the workplace and students' power in the school. It should be high on the agenda of every trade union, labor organization, and student association.

Yet the class and status dimensions of the struggle over Thomas's confir-mation were not aired in the public sphere debates. No trade unionist or workers' or students' representative testified in the hearings. Nor did any publish an op-ed piece in the *New York Times*. In general, no one in a position to be widely heard articulated support for Hill grounded in class or status solidarity. No one foregrounded the accents of class to rally workers and students to her side.

The absence of a discourse of class conflict in the United States is no surprise. What is surprising perhaps was the deployment in the final phase of the struggle of a counterdiscourse of class resentment to mobilize support for Thomas. On the day before the Senate confirmation vote, the *New York Times* printed an op-ed piece by someone purporting to be a friend of labor. Peggy Noonan, former speechwriter for Presidents Reagan and Bush, predicted victory for Thomas based on a "class division" between the "chattering classes" supporting Hill and the "normal humans," who believed Thomas. She also glossed this as a division between the "clever people who talk loudly in restaurants and those who seat them":

> You could see it in the witnesses. For Anita Hill, the professional, move-ment-y, and intellectualish Susan Hoerchner, who spoke with a sincere, unmakedupped face of inherent power imbalances in the workplace. For Clarence Thomas, the straight-shooting Maybellined J. C. Alvarez, who once broke up a mugging because she hates bullies and who paid $900 she doesn't have to get there because she still hates 'em. . . . Ms. Alvarez was the voice of the real, as opposed to the abstract America: she was like a person who if a boss ever sexually abused her would kick him in the gajoobies and haul him straight to court.[25]

Noonan appealed to the "real American" workers (tough and macho, even if wearing eyeliner) to resist the effeminate (albeit makeup-free) intellectuals who impersonate them and feign concern for their interests, but whose American-ness is suspect (shades of communism). The scenario thus appeared to oppose "the real worker," J. C. Alvarez, to "the intellectual," Susan Hoerchner. Yet Alvarez here actually represented Thomas, the boss, while the aggrieved subordinate, Hill, disappeared altogether. Moreover, by painting "the worker" as a Maybellined tough guy, Noonan simultaneously updated and perpetuated masculinist stereotypes. The result was that it became hard to see most women, who do not repay sexual harassment with a kick to the groin, as workers.

Noonan's rhetoric mobilized class resentment in support of Thomas by disappearing Hill as a worker. A similar tack was taken by Orlando Patterson, whose own *New York Times* op-ed piece appeared the following week in the guise of an analytical postmortem. Although Patterson acknowledged Hill's lower-class origins, he nonetheless treated her as an instrument of "elitist" forces. In his scenario she was a tool not simply of whites or of feminists but of *elite, upper-class* white feminists bent on using the law to impose a class-specific sexual morality on poor and working-class populations with different, less repressive norms. Workers were in effect called to defend their class culture—by siding with the boss against his assistant.[26]

Both Noonan and Patterson in effect bourgeoisified Hill, just as Thomas had earlier whitened her. Her actual social origins in rural poverty, which she had stressed in her opening statement to the committee, had by the end of the affair become so clouded by the rhetoric of class resentment that to many she was just another yuppie. The way, once again, was paved by Thomas. Very early on, even before the sexual harassment story broke, he staked out a strong claim to the discourse of impoverished origins. And as in the case of "race," here too he retained a near-monopoly.

The "class struggle" in this affair, then, was largely a matter of manipulating the signifiers of class to mobilize resentment in the interests of management. But was class not relevant in any other sense? Were there no class differences in the way Americans viewed these events and in the way they chose sides?

Some news reports following closely upon Thomas's confirmation portrayed white working-class women and women of color of all classes as unsympathetic to Hill. For example, in an article titled "Women See Hearing from a Perspective of Their Own Jobs," the *New York Times* reported that blue-collar women were put off by her softspokenness and what they construed as her inability to take care of herself. The story contrasted this "blue-collar" view with the views of female "lawyers, human service professionals, and politicians," who strongly sympathized with and believed Hill.[27] Despite the title of article, the *Times* did not consider the possibility that these putative class differences could be rooted in different class work structures. It could be the case, for example, that working-class people who felt that Hill should simply have told Thomas off, quit, and found another job were not attuned to professional career structures, which require cultivation of one's reputation in the profession by means of networking and long-term maintenance of relationships.

There was another sense in which class affected this struggle, but it remained largely unspoken and implicit. Polls taken on the last night of the hearings showed that party affiliation was the most statistically significant factor distinguishing Thomas's supporters from Hill's.[28] This suggests that a large part of what was at stake in the confirmation struggles over this and other Republican Supreme Court nominees, that of Robert Bork, for exam-

ple, was the continuation—or not—of the Reagan-Bush agenda, broadly
conceived. For a moment, the question of sexual harassment became the
condensation point for a host of anxieties, resentments, and hopes about
who gets what and who deserves what in the United States. In our current
political culture, those anxieties, resentments, and hopes are often articulated in discourses of gender and "race," but they are also necessarily about
status and class. Noonan and Patterson notwithstanding, class remains the
great unarticulated American secret. As such, it remains highly susceptible to
manipulation and abuse.

Morals of the Story

The extraordinary struggle over Clarence Thomas's nomination proved the
continuing importance of the public sphere in relation to state power.
However, it also showed the need to revise the standard liberal view of the
public sphere, which takes the categories of public and private as self-evident. This struggle showed, in contrast, that these categories are multivalent
and contested. Not all understandings of them promote democracy. For
example, male-supremacist constructions enshrine gender hierarchy by pri-
vatizing practices of domination like sexual harassment. They enforce men's
privacy rights to harass women with impunity in part by smearing in public
any woman who dares to protest. As Alan Simpson understood so well,
women are effectively asked to choose between quiet abuse in private and
noisy discursive abuse in public.

However, the gendered character of the categories publicity and privacy
cannot today be understood in terms of Victorian separate-spheres ideology,
as some feminists have assumed. It is not the case now, and never was, that
women are simply excluded from public life; nor that the private sphere is
women's sphere and the pubic sphere is men's; nor that the feminist project
is to collapse the boundaries between public and private. Rather, feminist
analysis shows the political, ideological, gender-coded character of these categories. And the feminist project aims in part to overcome the gender
hierarchy that gives men more power than women to draw the line between
public and private.

Yet even that more complicated view is still too simple because the categories of public and private also have a racial-ethnic dimension. The legacy
of American slavery and racism has denied black women even the minimal
protections from abuse that white women have occasionally managed to
claim, even as their disadvantaged economic position has rendered them

more vulnerable to sexual harassment. That same legacy has left black men without white men's privacy rights; and they have sometimes tried to claim those rights in ways that endanger black women. That suggests the need to develop an antiracist project that does not succeed at black women's expense, one that simultaneously attacks the racial and gender hierarchy embedded in hegemonic understandings of privacy and publicity.

Recognizing how the categories of publicity and privacy have become coded by gender and "race" points up several inadequacies of the liberal theory of the public sphere. For one thing, it is not adequate to analyze these categories as supports for and challenges to state power exclusively. Rather, we need also to understand the ways in which discursive privatization supports the "private" power of bosses over workers, husbands over wives, and whites over blacks. Publicity, then, is not only a weapon against state tyranny, as its bourgeois originators and current Eastern European exponents assume. It is also potentially a weapon against the extrastate power of capital, employers, supervisors, husbands, and fathers, among others. There was no more dramatic proof of the emancipatory side of publicity in relation to private power than the way in which these events momentarily empowered many women to speak openly for the first time of heretofore privately suffered humiliations of sexual harassment.

Nevertheless, it is not correct to view publicity as always and unambiguously an instrument of empowerment and emancipation. For members of subordinate groups, it will always be a matter of balancing the potential political uses of publicity against the dangers of loss of privacy.

These events also show that even emancipatory uses of publicity cannot be understood simply in terms of making public what was previously private. They demonstrate that merely publicizing some action or practice is not always sufficient to discredit it. That is the case only when the view that the practice is wrong is already widely held and uncontroversial. When, in contrast, the practice is widely approved or contested, publicity means staging a discursive struggle over its interpretation. Certainly, a key feature of the Thomas-Hill confrontation was the wider struggle it sparked over the meaning and moral status of sexual harassment.

The way that struggle played out, moreover, reflected the then-current state of American political culture. The drama unfolded at a point at which a feminist vocabulary for naming and interpreting the behavior ascribed to Thomas had already been created in the feminist counterpublic sphere and disseminated to a broader public. Not only was that vocabulary thus available and ready to hand, but it was also even encoded in the law. However, the feminist interpretation of sexual harassment was neither deeply rooted in

5

A Genealogy of 'Dependency'

Tracing a Keyword of the U.S. Welfare State

Nancy Fraser and Linda Gordon

'Dependency' has become a keyword of U.S. politics.[1] Politicians of diverse views regularly criticize what they term "welfare dependency." Supreme Court Justice Clarence Thomas spoke for many conservatives in 1980 when he vilified his sister: "She gets mad when the mailman is late with her welfare check. That's how dependent she is. What's worse is that now her kids feel entitled to the check, too. They have no motivation for doing better or getting out of that situation."[2] Liberals usually blame the victim less, but they, too, decry welfare dependency. Democratic Senator Daniel P. Moynihan prefigured today's discourse when he began his 1973 book by declaring that

> the issue of welfare is the issue of dependency. It is different from poverty. To be poor is an objective condition; to be dependent, a subjective one as well. . . . Being poor is often associated with considerable personal qualities; being dependent rarely so. [Dependency] is an incomplete state in life: normal in the child, abnormal in the adult. In a world where completed men and women stand on their own feet, persons who are dependent—as the buried imagery of the word denotes—hang.[3]

Today, "policy experts" from both major parties agree "that [welfare] dependency is bad for people, that it undermines their motivation to sup-

121

port themselves, and isolates and stigmatizes welfare recipients in a way that over a long period feeds into and accentuates the underclass mindset and condition."[4]

If we can step back from this discourse, however, we can interrogate some of its underlying presuppositions. Why are debates about poverty and inequality in the United States now being framed in terms of welfare dependency? How did the receipt of public assistance become associated with dependency, and why are the connotations of that word in this context so negative? What are the gender and racial subtexts of this discourse, and what tacit assumptions underlie it?

We propose to shed some light on these issues by examining welfare-related meanings of the word 'dependency'.[5] We will analyze 'dependency' as a keyword of the U.S. welfare state and reconstruct its genealogy.[6] By charting some major historical shifts in the usage of this term, we will excavate some of the tacit assumptions and connotations that it still carries today but that usually go without saying.

Our approach is inspired in part by the English cultural-materialist critic Raymond Williams.[7] Following Williams and others, we assume that the terms that are used to describe social life are also active forces shaping it.[8] A crucial element of politics, then, is the struggle to define social reality and to interpret people's inchoate aspirations and needs.[9] Particular words and expressions often become focal in such struggles, functioning as keywords, sites at which the meaning of social experience is negotiated and contested.[10] Keywords typically carry unspoken assumptions and connotations that can powerfully influence the discourses they permeate—in part by constituting a body of *doxa*, or taken-for-granted commonsense belief that escapes critical scrutiny.[11]

We seek to dispel the doxa surrounding current U.S. discussions of dependency by reconstructing that term's genealogy. Modifying an approach associated with Michel Foucault,[12] we will excavate broad historical shifts in linguistic usage that can rarely be attributed to specific agents. We do *not* present a causal analysis. Rather, by contrasting present meanings of 'dependency' with past meanings, we aim to defamiliarize taken-for-granted beliefs in order to render them susceptible to critique and to illuminate present-day conflicts.

Our approach differs from Foucault's, however, in two crucial respects: first, we seek to contextualize discursive shifts in relation to broad institutional and social-structural shifts, and second, we welcome normative political reflection.[13] Our article is a collaboration between a philosopher and an historian. We combine historical analysis of linguistic and social-structural changes with conceptual analysis of the discursive construction of social problems, and we leaven the mix with a feminist interest in envisioning emancipatory alternatives.

In what follows, then, we provide a genealogy of 'dependency'. We sketch the history of this term and explicate the assumptions and connotations it carries today in U.S. debates about welfare—especially assumptions about human nature, gender roles, the causes of poverty, the nature of citizenship, the sources of entitlement, and what counts as work and as a contribution to society. We contend that unreflective uses of this keyword serve to enshrine certain interpretations of social life as authoritative and to delegitimate or obscure others, generally to the advantage of dominant groups in society and to the disadvantage of subordinate ones. All told, we provide a critique of ideology in the form of a critical political semantics.

'Dependency', we argue, is an ideological term. In current U.S. policy discourse it usually refers to the condition of poor women with children who maintain their families with neither a male breadwinner nor an adequate wage and who rely for economic support on a stingy and politically unpopular government program called Aid to Families with Dependent Children (AFDC). Participation in this highly stigmatized program may be demoralizing in many cases, even though it may enable women to leave abusive or unsatisfying relationships without having to give up their children. Still, naming the problems of poor, solo-mother families as 'dependency' tends to make them appear to be individual problems, as much moral or psychological as economic. The term carries strong emotive and visual associations and a powerful pejorative charge. In current debates, the expression 'welfare dependency' evokes the image of "the welfare mother," often figured as a young, unmarried black woman (perhaps even a teenager) of uncontrolled sexuality. The power of this image is overdetermined, we contend, in that it condenses multiple and often contradictory meanings of dependency. Only by disaggregating those different strands, by unpacking the tacit assumptions and evaluative connotations that underlie them, can we begin to understand, and to dislodge, the force of the stereotype.

Registers of Meaning

In its root meaning, the verb 'to depend' refers to a physical relationship in which one thing hangs from another. The more abstract meanings—social, economic, psychological, and political—were originally metaphorical. In current usage, we find four registers in which the meanings of 'dependency' reverberate. The first is an economic register, in which one depends on some other person(s) or institution for subsistence. In a second register, the term denotes a sociolegal status, the lack of a separate legal or public identity, as in the status of married women created by coverture. The third register is political: here 'dependency' means subjection to an external ruling power and may be predicated of a colony or of a subject caste of noncitizen residents. The fourth register we call the moral/psychological; dependency in this sense is an individual character trait like lack of will power or excessive emotional neediness.

To be sure, not every use of 'dependency' fits neatly into one and only one of these registers. Still, by distinguishing them analytically, we present a matrix on which to plot the historical adventures of the term. In what follows, we shall trace the shift from a patriarchal preindustrial usage in which women, however subordinate, shared a condition of dependency with many men to a modern, industrial, male-supremacist usage that constructed a specifically feminine sense of dependency. That usage is now giving way, we contend, to a postindustrial usage in which growing numbers of relatively prosperous women claim the same kind of independence that men do while a more stigmatized but still feminized sense of dependency attaches to groups considered deviant and superfluous. Not just gender but also racializing practices play a major role in these shifts, as do changes in the organization and meaning of labor.

Preindustrial 'Dependency'

In preindustrial English usage, the most common meaning of 'dependency' was subordination. The economic, sociolegal, and political registers were relatively undifferentiated, reflecting the fusion of various forms of hierarchy in state and society, and the moral/psychological use of the term barely existed. The earliest social definition of the verb 'to depend (on)' in the *Oxford English Dictionary* (OED) is "to be connected with in a relation of subordination." A 'dependent', from at least 1588, was one "who depends on another for support, position, etc.; a retainer, attendant, subordinate, servant." A 'dependency' was either a retinue or body of servants or a foreign territorial possession or colony. This family of terms applied widely in an hierarchical social context in which nearly everyone was subordinate to someone else but did not thereby incur individual stigma.[14]

We can appreciate just how common dependency was in preindustrial society by examining its opposite. The term 'independence' at first applied primarily to aggregate entities, not to individuals; thus in the seventeenth century a nation or a church congregation could be independent. By the eighteenth century, however, an individual could be said to have an 'independency', meaning an ownership of property, a fortune that made it possible to live without laboring. (This sense of the term, which we would today call economic, survives in our expressions 'to be independently wealthy' and 'a person of independent means'.) To be dependent, in contrast, was to gain one's livelihood by working for someone else. This of course was the condition of most people, of wage laborers as well as serfs and slaves, of most men as well as most women.[15]

Dependency, therefore, was a normal, as opposed to a deviant, condition, a social relation, as opposed to an individual trait. Thus, it did not carry any moral opprobrium. Neither English nor U.S. dictionaries report any pejorative uses of the term before the early twentieth century. In fact, some leading preindustrial definitions were explicitly positive, implying trusting, relying on, counting on another, the predecessors of today's 'dependable'.

Nevertheless, 'dependency' did mean status inferiority and legal coverture, being a part of a unit headed by someone else who had legal standing. In a world of status hierarchies dominated by great landowners and their retainers, all members of a household other than its "head" were dependents, as were free or servile peasants on an estate. They were, as Peter Laslett put it, "caught up, so to speak, 'subsumed' . . . into the personalities of their fathers and masters."[16]

Dependency also had what we would today call political consequences. While the term did not mean precisely 'unfree', its context was a social order in which subjection, not citizenship, was the norm. 'Independence' connoted unusual privilege and superiority, as in freedom from labor. Thus, throughout most of the European development of representative government, independence in the sense of property ownership was a prerequisite for political rights. When dependents began to claim rights and liberty, they perforce became revolutionaries.

'Dependency' was not then applied uniquely to characterize the relation of a wife to her husband. Women's dependency, like children's, meant being on a lower rung in a long social ladder; their husbands and fathers were above them but below others. For the agrarian majority, moreover, there was no implication of unilateral economic dependency because women's and children's labor was recognized as essential to the family economy; the women were economic dependents only in the sense that the men of their class were as well. In general, women's dependency in preindustrial society was less gender-specific than it later became; it was similar in kind to that of subordinate men, only multiplied. But so too were the lives of children, servants, and the elderly overlaid with multiple layers of dependency.

In practice, of course, these preindustrial arrangements did not always provide satisfactorily for the poor. In the fourteenth century new, stronger states began to limit the freedom of movement of the destitute and to codify older informal distinctions between those worthy and unworthy of assistance. When the English Poor Law of 1601 confirmed this latter distinction, it was already shameful to ask for public help. But the culture neither disapproved of dependency nor valorized individual independence. Rather, the aim of the statutes was to return the mobile, uprooted, and excessively "independent" poor to their local parishes or communities, and hence to enforce their traditional dependencies.

Nevertheless, dependency was not universally approved or uncontested. It was subject, rather, to principled challenges from at least the seventeenth century on, when liberal-individualist political arguments became common. The terms 'dependence' and 'independence' often figured centrally in political debates in this period, as they did, for example, in the Putney Debates of the English Civil War. Sometimes they even became key signifiers of social crisis, as in the seventeenth-century English controversy about "out-of-doors" servants, hired help who did not reside in the homes of their masters and who were not bound by indentures or similar legal understandings. In the discourse of the time, the anomalous "independence" of these men served as a general figure for social disorder, a lightning rod focusing diffuse cultural anxieties—much as the anomalous "dependence" of "welfare mothers" does today.

Industrial 'Dependency': The Worker and His Negatives

With the rise of industrial capitalism, the semantic geography of dependency shifted significantly. In the eighteenth and nineteenth centuries 'independence', not 'dependence', figured centrally in political and economic discourse; and its meanings were radically democratized. But if we read the discourse about independence carefully, we see the shadow of a powerful anxiety about dependency.

What in preindustrial society had been a normal and unstigmatized condition became deviant and stigmatized. More precisely, certain dependencies became shameful while others were deemed natural and proper. In particular, as eighteenth- and nineteenth-century political culture intensified gender difference, new, specifically feminine senses of dependency appeared—states considered proper for women but degrading for men. Likewise, emergent racial constructions made some forms of dependency appropriate for the "dark races" but intolerable for "whites." Such differentiated valuations became possible as the term's preindustrial unity fractured. No longer designating only generalized subordination, 'dependency' in the industrial era could be sociolegal or political or economic. With these distinctions came another major semantic shift: now 'dependency' need not always refer to a social relation; it could also designate an individual character trait. Thus, the moral/psychological register was born.

These redefinitions were greatly influenced by Radical Protestantism. It elaborated a new positive image of individual independence and a critique of sociolegal and political dependency. In the Catholic and the early Protestant traditions, dependence on a master had been modeled on dependence on God. In contrast, to the radicals of the English Civil War, or to Puritans, Quakers, and Congregationalists in the United States, rejecting dependence on a master was akin to rejecting blasphemy and false gods.[17] From this perspective, status hierarchies no longer appeared natural or just. Political subjection and sociolegal subsumption were offenses against human dignity, defensible only under special conditions, if supportable at all. These beliefs informed a variety of radical movements throughout the industrial era, including abolitionism, feminism, and labor organizing, with substantial successes. In the nineteenth century these movements abolished slavery and some of the legal disabilities of women. More thoroughgoing victories were won by white male workers who, in the eighteenth and nineteenth centuries, threw off their sociolegal and political dependency and won civil and electoral rights. In the age of democratic revolutions, the developing new concept of citizenship rested on independence; dependency was deemed antithetical to citizenship.

Changes in the civil and political landscape of dependence and independence were accompanied by even more dramatic changes in the economic register. When white workingmen demanded civil and electoral rights, they claimed to be independent. This entailed reinterpreting the meaning of wage labor so as to divest it of the association with dependency. That in turn required a shift in focus—from the experience or means of labor (for example, ownership of tools or land, control of skills and of the organization of work) to its remuneration and how that was spent. Radical workingmen, who had earlier rejected wage labor as "wage slavery," claimed a new form of manly independence within it. Their collective pride drew on another aspect of Protestantism, its work ethic, that valorized discipline and labor. Workers sought to reclaim these values within the victorious wage labor system; many of them—women as well as men—created and exercised a new kind of independence in their militancy and boldness toward employers. Through their struggles, economic independence came eventually to encompass the ideal of earning a family wage, a wage sufficient to maintain a household and to support a dependent wife and children. Thus, working-men expanded the meaning of economic independence to include a form of wage labor in addition to property ownership and self-employment.[18]

This shift in the meaning of independence also transformed the meanings of dependency. As wage labor became increasingly normative—and increasingly definitive of independence—it was precisely those excluded from wage labor who appeared to personify dependency. In the new industrial semantics, there emerged three principal icons of dependency, all effectively negatives of the dominant image of "the worker," and each embodying a different aspect of nonindependence.

The first icon of industrial dependency was "the pauper," who lived not on wages but on poor relief.[19] In the strenuous new culture of emergent capitalism, the figure of the pauper was like a bad double of the upstanding workingman, threatening the latter should he lag. The image of the pauper was elaborated largely in an emerging new register of dependency discourse—the moral/psychological register. Paupers were not simply poor but degraded, their character corrupted and their will sapped through reliance on charity. To be sure, the moral/psychological condition of pauperism was related to the economic condition of poverty, but the relationship was complex, not simple. Although nineteenth-century charity experts acknowledged that poverty could contribute to pauperization, they also held that character defects could cause poverty.[20] Toward the end of the century, as hereditarian (eugenic) thought caught on, the pauper's character defects were given a basis in biology. The pauper's dependency was figured as unlike the serf's in that it was unilateral, not reciprocal. To be a pauper was not to be subordinate within a system of productive labor; it was to be outside such a system altogether.

A second icon of industrial dependency was embodied alternately in the figures of "the colonial native" and "the slave." They, of course, were very much inside the economic system, their labor often fundamental to the development of capital and industry. Whereas the pauper represented the characterological distillation of economic dependency, natives and slaves personified political subjection.[21] Their images as "savage," "childlike," and "submissive" became salient as the old, territorial sense of dependency as a colony became intertwined with a new, racist discourse developed to justify colonialism and slavery.[22] There emerged a drift from an older sense of dependency as a relation of subjection imposed by an imperial power on an indigenous population to a newer sense of dependency as an inherent property or character trait of the people so subjected. In earlier usage, colonials were dependent because they had been conquered; in nineteenth-century imperialist culture, they were conquered because they were dependent. In this new conception, it was the intrinsic, essential dependency of natives and slaves that justified their colonization and enslavement.

The dependency of the native and the slave, like that of the pauper, was elaborated largely in the moral/psychological register. The character traits adduced to justify imperialism and slavery, however, arose less from individual temperament than from the supposed nature of human groups. Racialist thought was the linchpin for this reasoning. By licensing a view of "the Negro" as fundamentally *other,* it provided the extraordinary justificatory power required to rationalize subjection at a time when liberty and equality were being proclaimed inalienable "rights of man"—for example, in that classic rejection of colonial status, the United States' Declaration of Independence. Thus racism helped transform dependency as political subjection into dependency as psychology and forged enduring links between the discourse of dependency and racial oppression.

Like the pauper, the native and the slave were excluded from wage labor and thus were negatives of the image of the worker. They shared that characteristic, if little else, with the third major icon of dependency in the industrial era: the newly invented figure of "the housewife." As we saw, the independence of the white workingman presupposed the ideal of the family wage, a wage sufficient to maintain a household and to support a nonemployed wife and children. Thus, for wage labor to create (white-male) independence, (white) female economic dependence was required. Women were thus transformed "from partners to parasites."[23] But this transformation was by no means universal. In the United States, for example, the family wage ideal held greater sway among whites than among blacks, and was at variance with actual practice for all of the poor and the working class. Moreover, both employed and nonemployed wives continued to perform work once considered crucial to a family economy. Because few husbands actually were able to support a family single-handedly, most families continued to depend on the labor of women and children. Nevertheless, the family wage norm commanded great loyalty in the United States, partly because it was used by the organized working class as an argument for higher wages.[24]

Several different registers of dependency converged in the figure of the housewife. This figure melded woman's traditional sociolegal and political dependency with her more recent economic dependency in the industrial order. Continuing from preindustrial usage was the assumption that fathers headed households and that other household members were represented by them, as codified in the legal doctrine of coverture. The sociolegal and political dependency of wives enforced their new economic dependency, for under coverture even married women who were wage workers could not legally control their wages. But the connotations of female dependency were altered. Although erstwhile dependent white men gained political rights, most white women remained legally and politically dependent. The result was to feminize—and stigmatize—sociolegal and political dependency, making coverture appear increasingly obnoxious and stimulating agitation for the statutes and court decisions that eventually dismantled it.

Together, then, a series of new personifications of dependency combined to constitute the underside of the workingman's independence. Henceforth, those who aspired to full membership in society would have to distinguish themselves from the pauper, the native, the slave, and the housewife in order to construct their independence. In a social order in which wage labor was becoming hegemonic, it was possible to encapsulate all these distinctions simultaneously in the ideal of the family wage. On the one hand, and most overtly, the ideal of the family wage premised the white workingman's independence on his wife's subordination and economic dependence. But on the other hand, it simultaneously contrasted with counterimages of dependent men—first with degraded male paupers on poor relief and later with racist stereotypes of Negro men unable to dominate Negro women. The family wage, therefore, was a vehicle for elaborating meanings of dependence and independence that were deeply inflected by gender, race, and class.

In this new industrial semantics, white workingmen appeared to be economically independent, but their independence was largely illusory and ideological. Because few actually earned enough to support a family single-handedly, most depended in fact—if not in word—on their wives' and children's contributions. Equally important, the language of wage labor in capitalism denied workers' dependence on their employers, thereby veiling their status as subordinates in a unit headed by someone else. Thus, hierarchy that had been relatively explicit and visible in the peasant-landlord relation was mystified in the relationship of factory operative to factory owner. There was a sense, then, in which the economic dependency of the white workingman was spirited away through linguistic sleight of hand—somewhat like reducing the number of poor people by lowering the official poverty demarcating line.

By definition, then, economic inequality among white men no longer created dependency. But noneconomic hierarchy among white men was considered unacceptable in the United States. Thus, 'dependency' was redefined to refer exclusively to those noneconomic relations of subordination deemed suitable only for people of color and for white women. The result was to differentiate dimensions of dependency that had been fused in preindustrial usage. Whereas all relations of subordination had previously counted as dependency relations, now capital-labor relations were exempted. Sociolegal and political hierarchy appeared to diverge from economic hierarchy, and only the former seemed incompatible with hegemonic views of society. It seemed to follow, moreover, that were sociolegal dependency and political dependency ever to be formally abolished, no social-structural dependency would remain. Any dependency that did persist could only be moral or psychological.

The Rise of American 'Welfare Dependency': 1890–1945

Informed by these general features of industrial-era semantics, a distinctive welfare-related use of 'dependency' developed in the United States. Originating in the late-nineteenth-century discourse of pauperism, modified in the Progressive Era and stabilized in the period of the New Deal, this use of the term was fundamentally ambiguous, slipping easily, and repeatedly, from an economic meaning to a moral/psychological meaning.

The United States was especially hospitable to elaborating dependency as a defect of individual character. Because the country lacked a strong legacy of feudalism or aristocracy and thus a strong popular sense of reciprocal obligations between lord and man, the older, preindustrial meanings of dependency—as an ordinary, majority condition—were weak, and the pejorative meanings were stronger. In the colonial period, dependency was seen mainly as a voluntary condition, as in indentured servitude. But the American Revolution so valorized independence that it stripped dependency of its voluntarism, emphasized its powerlessness, and imbued it with stigma. One result was to change the meaning of women's social and legal dependency, making it distinctly inferior.[25]

The long American love affair with independence was politically double-edged. On the one hand, it helped nurture powerful labor and women's movements. On the other hand, the absence of a hierarchical social tradition in which subordination was understood to be structural, not characterological, facilitated hostility to public support for the poor. Also influential was the very nature of the American state, weak and decentralized in comparison to European states throughout the nineteenth century. All told, the United States proved fertile soil for the moral/psychological discourse of dependency.

As discussed earlier, the most general definition of economic dependency in this era was simply non-wage-earning. By the end of the nineteenth century, however, that definition had divided into two: a "good" household dependency, predicated of children and wives, and an increasingly "bad" (or at least dubious) charity dependency, predicated of recipients of relief. Both senses had as their reference point the ideal of the family wage, and both were eventually incorporated into the discourse of the national state. The good, household sense was elaborated by means of the census[26] and by the Internal Revenue Service, which installed the category of dependent as the norm for wives. The already problematic charity sense became even more pejorative with the development of public assistance. The old distinction between the deserving and the undeserving poor intensified in the late-nineteenth-century's Gilded Age. Theoretically, the undeserving should not be receiving aid, but constant vigilance was required to ensure they did not slip in by disguising themselves as deserving. Dependence on assistance became increasingly stigmatized, and it was harder and harder to rely on relief without being branded a pauper.

Ironically, reformers in the 1890s introduced the word 'dependent' into relief discourse as a substitute for 'pauper' precisely in order to destigmatize the receipt of help. They first applied the word to children, the paradigmatic "innocent" victims of poverty.[27] Then, in the early twentieth century, Progressive-era reformers began to apply the term to adults, again to rid them of stigma. Only after World War II did 'dependent' become the hegemonic word for a recipient of aid.[28] By then, however, the term's pejorative connotations were fixed.

The attempt to get rid of stigma by replacing 'pauperism' with 'dependency' failed. Talk about economic dependency repeatedly slid into condemnation of moral/psychological dependency. Even during the Great Depression of the 1930s, experts worried that receipt of relief would create "habits of dependence" or, as one charity leader put it, "a belligerent dependency, an attitude of having a right and title to relief."[29] Because the hard times lasted so long and created so many newly poor people, there was a slight improvement in the status of recipients of aid. But attacks on "chiseling" and "corruption" continued to embarrass those receiving assistance, and many of the neediest welfare beneficiaries accepted public aid only after much hesitation and with great shame, so strong was the stigma of dependency.[30]

Most important, the New Deal intensified the dishonor of receiving help by consolidating a two-track welfare system. First-track programs like unemployment and old-age insurance offered aid as an entitlement, without stigma or supervision and hence without dependency. Such programs were constructed to create the misleading appearance that beneficiaries merely got back what they put in. They constructed an honorable status for recipients and are not called 'welfare' even today. Intended to replace the white workingman's family wage, at least partially, first-track programs excluded most minorities and white women. In contrast, second-track public assistance programs, among which Aid to Dependent Children (ADC), later Aid to Families with Dependent Children (AFDC), became the biggest and most well known, continued the private charity tradition of searching out the deserving few among the many chiselers. Funded from general tax revenues instead of from earmarked wage deductions, these programs created the appearance that claimants were getting something for nothing.[31] They established entirely different conditions for receiving aid: means testing; morals testing; moral supervision; home visits; extremely low stipends—in short, all the conditions associated with welfare dependency today.[32]

The racial and sexual exclusions of the first-track programs were not accidental. They were designed to win the support of southern legislators who wanted to keep blacks dependent in another sense, namely, on low wages or sharecropping.[33] Equally deliberate was the construction of the differential in legitimacy between the two tracks of the welfare system. The Social Security Board propagandized for Social Security Old Age Insurance (the program today called just "Social Security") precisely because, at first, it did not seem more earned or more dignified than public assistance. To make Social Security more acceptable, the Board worked to stigmatize public assistance, even pressuring states to keep stipends low.[34]

Most Americans today still distinguish between "welfare" and "nonwelfare" forms of public provision and see only the former as creating dependency. The assumptions underlying these distinctions, however, had to be constructed politically. Old people became privileged (nonwelfare) recipients only through decades of militant organization and lobbying. All programs of public provision, whether they are called 'welfare' or not, shore up some dependencies and discourage others. Social Security subverted adults' sense of responsibility for their parents, for example. Public assistance programs, by contrast, aimed to buttress the dependence of minorities on low-wage labor, of wives on husbands, of children on their parents.

The conditions of second-track assistance made recipients view their dependence on public assistance as inferior to the supposed independence of wage labor.[35] Wage labor, meanwhile, had become so naturalized that its own inherent supervision could be overlooked; thus, one ADC recipient complained, "Welfare life is a difficult experience. . . . When you work, you don't have to report to anyone."[36] Yet the designers of ADC did not initially intend to drive white solo mothers into paid employment. Rather, they wanted to protect the norm of the family wage by making dependence on a male breadwinner continue to seem preferable to dependence on the state.[37] ADC occupied the strategic semantic space where the good, household sense of dependency and the bad, relief sense of dependency intersected. It enforced at once the positive connotations of the first and the negative connotations of the second.

Thus, the poor solo mother was enshrined as the quintessential 'welfare dependent'.[38] That designation has thus become significant not only for what it includes but also for what it excludes and occludes. Although it appears to mean relying on the government for economic support, not all recipients of public funds are considered equally dependent. Hardly anyone today calls recipients of Social Security retirement insurance 'dependents'. Similarly, persons receiving unemployment insurance, agricultural loans, and home mortgage assistance are excluded from that categorization, as indeed are defense contractors and the beneficiaries of corporate bailouts and regressive taxation.

Postindustrial Society and the Disappearance of "Good" Dependency

With the transition to a postindustrial phase of capitalism, the semantic map of dependency is being redrawn yet again. Whereas industrial usage had cast some forms of dependency as natural and proper, postindustrial usage figures all forms as avoidable and blameworthy. No longer moderated by any positive countercurrents, the term's pejorative connotations are being strengthened. Industrial usage had recognized some forms of dependency to be rooted in relations of subordination; postindustrial usage, in contrast, focuses more intensely on the traits of individuals. The moral/psychological register is expanding, therefore, and its qualitative character is changing, with new psychological and therapeutic idioms displacing the explicitly racist and misogynous idioms of the industrial era. Yet dependency nonetheless remains feminized and racialized; the new psychological meanings have strong feminine associations, and currents once associated with the native and the slave are increasingly inflecting the discourse about welfare.

One major influence here is the formal abolition of much of the legal and political dependency that was endemic to industrial society. Housewives, paupers, natives, and the descendants of slaves are no longer formally excluded from most civil and political rights; neither their subsumption nor their subjection is viewed as legitimate. Thus, major forms of dependency deemed proper in industrial usage are now considered objectionable, and postindustrial uses of the term carry a stronger negative charge.

A second major shift in the geography of postindustrial dependency is affecting the economic register. This is the decentering of the ideal of the family wage, which had been the gravitational center of industrial usage. The relative deindustrialization of the United States is restructuring the political economy, making the single-earner family far less viable. The loss of higher-paid "male" manufacturing jobs and the extensive entry of women into low-wage service work are meanwhile altering the gender composition of employment.[39] At the same time, divorce is common and, thanks in large part to the feminist and gay and lesbian liberation movements, changing gender norms are helping to proliferate new family forms, making the male breadwinner/female homemaker model less attractive to many.[40] Thus, the family wage ideal is no longer hegemonic but competes with alternative gender norms, family forms, and economic arrangements. It no longer goes without saying that a woman should rely on a man for economic support, nor that mothers should not also be "workers." Thus, another major form of dependency that was positively inflected in industrial semantics has become contested if not simply negative.

The combined result of these developments is to increase the stigma of dependency. With all legal and political dependency now illegitimate, and with wives' economic dependency now contested, there is no longer any self-evidently "good" adult dependency in postindustrial society. Rather, all dependency is suspect, and independence is enjoined upon everyone. Independence, however, remains identified with wage labor. That identification seems even to increase in a context where there is no longer any "good" adult personification of dependency who can be counterposed to "the worker." In this context, the worker tends to become the universal social subject: everyone is expected to "work" and to be "self-supporting." Any adult not perceived as a worker shoulders a heavier burden of self-justification. Thus, a norm previously restricted to white workingmen applies increasingly to everyone. Yet this norm still carries a racial and gender subtext, for it supposes that the worker has access to a job paying a decent wage and is not also a primary parent.

If one result of these developments is an increase in dependency's negative connotations, another is its increased individualization. As we saw, talk of dependency as a character trait of individuals was already widespread in the industrial period, diminishing the preindustrial emphasis on relations of subordination. The importance of individualized dependency tends to be heightened, however, now that sociolegal and political dependency are officially ended. Absent coverture and Jim Crow, it has become possible to declare that equality of opportunity exists and that individual merit determines outcomes. As we saw, the groundwork for that view was laid by industrial usage, which redefined dependency so as to exclude capitalist relations of subordination. With capitalist economic dependency already abolished by definition, and with legal and political dependency now abolished by law, postindustrial society appears to some conservatives and liberals to have eliminated every social-structural basis of dependency. Whatever dependency remains, therefore, can be interpreted as the fault of individuals. That interpretation does not go uncontested, to be sure, but the burden of argument has shifted. Now those who would deny that the fault lies in themselves must swim upstream against the prevailing semantic currents. Postindustrial dependency, thus, is increasingly individualized.

Welfare Dependency as Postindustrial Pathology

The worsening connotations of 'welfare dependency' have been nourished by several streams from outside the field of welfare. New postindustrial medical and psychological discourses have associated dependency with pathology. In articles with titles such as "Pharmacist Involvement in a Chemical-Dependency Rehabilitation Program," social scientists began in the 1980s to write about 'chemical', 'alcohol', and 'drug dependency', all euphemisms for addiction.[41] Because welfare claimants are often—falsely—assumed to be addicts, the pathological connotations of 'drug dependency' tend also to infect 'welfare dependency', increasing stigmatization.

A second important postindustrial current is the rise of new psychological meanings of dependency with very strong feminine associations. In the 1950s, social workers influenced by psychiatry began to diagnose dependence as a form of immaturity common among women, particularly among solo mothers (who were often, of course, welfare claimants). "Dependent, irresponsible, and unstable, they respond like small children to the immediate moment," declared the author of a 1954 discussion of out-of-wedlock pregnancy.[42] The problem was that women were supposed to be just dependent enough, and it was easy to tip over into excess in either direction. The norm, moreover, was racially marked: white women were usually portrayed as erring on the side of excessive dependence, while black women were typically charged with excessive independence.

Psychologized dependency became the target of some of the earliest second-wave feminism. Betty Friedan's 1963 classic, *The Feminine Mystique,* provided a phenomenological account of the housewife's psychological dependency and drew from it a political critique of her social subordination.[43] More recently, however, a burgeoning cultural-feminist, postfeminist, and antifeminist self-help and pop-psychology literature has obfuscated the link between the psychological and the political. In Colette Dowling's 1981 book, *The Cinderella Complex,* women's dependency was hypostatized as a depth-psychological gender structure: "women's hidden fear of independence" or the "wish to be saved."[44] The late 1980s saw a spate of books about "co-dependency," a supposedly prototypically female syndrome of supporting or "enabling" the dependency of someone else. In a metaphor that reflects the drug hysteria of the period, dependency here, too, is an addiction. Apparently, even if a woman manages herself to escape her gender's predilection to dependency, she is still liable to incur the blame for facilitating the dependency of her husband or children. This completes the vicious circle: the increased stigmatizing of dependency in the culture at large has also deepened contempt for those who care for dependents, reinforcing the traditionally low status of the female helping professions, such as nursing and social work.[45]

The 1980s saw a cultural panic about dependency. In 1980 the American Psychiatric Association codified "Dependent Personality Disorder" (DPD) as an official psychopathology. According to the 1987 edition of the *Diagnostic and Statistical Manual of Mental Disorders* (DSM-III-R),

> the essential feature of this disorder is a pervasive pattern of dependent and submissive behavior beginning by early childhood. . . . People with this disorder are unable to make everyday decisions without an excessive amount of advice and reassurance from others, and will even allow others to make most of their important decisions. . . . The disorder is apparently common and is diagnosed more frequently in females.[46]

The codification of DPD as an official psychopathology represents a new stage in the history of the moral/psychological register. Here the social relations of dependency disappear entirely into the personality of the dependent. Overt moralism also disappears in the apparently neutral, scientific, medicalized formulation. Thus, although the defining traits of the dependent personality match point for point the traits traditionally ascribed to housewives, paupers, natives, and slaves, all links to subordination have vanished. The only remaining trace of those themes is the flat, categorical, and uninterpreted observation that DPD is "diagnosed more frequently in females."

If psychological discourse has further feminized and individualized dependency, other postindustrial developments have further racialized it. The increased stigmatization of welfare dependency followed a general increase in public provision in the United States, the removal of some discriminatory practices that had previously excluded minority women from participation in AFDC, especially in the South, and the transfer of many white women to first-track programs as social-insurance coverage expanded. By the 1970s the figure of the black solo mother had come to epitomize welfare dependency. As a result, the new discourse about welfare draws on older symbolic currents that linked dependency with racist ideologies.

The ground was laid by a long, somewhat contradictory stream of discourse about "the black family," in which African-American gender and kinship relations were measured against white middle-class norms and deemed pathological. One supposedly pathological element was "the excessive independence" of black women, an ideologically distorted allusion to long traditions of wage work, educational achievement, and community activism. The 1960s and 1970s discourse about poverty recapitulated traditions of misogyny toward African-American women; in Daniel Moynihan's diagnosis, for example, "matriarchal" families had "emasculated" black men and created a "culture of poverty" based on a "tangle of [family] pathology."[47] This discourse placed black AFDC claimants in a double bind: they were pathologically independent with respect to men and pathologically dependent with respect to government.

By the 1980s, however, the racial imagery of dependency had shifted. The black welfare mother who haunted the white imagination ceased to be the powerful matriarch. Now the preeminent stereotype is the unmarried teenage mother caught in the "welfare trap" and rendered dronelike and passive. This new icon of welfare dependency is younger and weaker than the matriarch. She is often evoked in the phrase "children having children," which can express feminist sympathy or antifeminist contempt, black appeals for parental control or white-racist eugenic anxieties.

Many of these postindustrial discourses coalesced in the early 1990s. Vice President Dan Quayle brought together the pathologized, feminized, and racialized currents in his comment on the May 1992 Los Angeles riot: "Our inner cities are filled with children having children . . . with people who are dependent on drugs and on the narcotic of welfare."[48]

Thus postindustrial culture has called up a new personification of dependency: the black, unmarried, teenaged, welfare-dependent mother. This image has usurped the symbolic space previously occupied by the housewife, the pauper, the native, and the slave, while absorbing and condensing their connotations. Black, female, a pauper, not a worker, a housewife and mother, yet practically a child herself—the new stereotype partakes of virtually every quality that has been coded historically as antithetical to independence. Condensing multiple, often contradictory meanings of dependency, it is a powerful ideological trope that simultaneously organizes diffuse cultural anxieties and dissimulates their social bases.

Postindustrial Policy and the Politics of Dependency

Despite the worsening economic outlook for many Americans in the past few decades, there has been no cultural revaluation of welfare. Families working harder for less often resent those who appear to them not to be working at all. Apparently lost, at least for now, are the struggles of the 1960s that aimed to recast AFDC as an entitlement in order to promote recipients' independence. Instead, the honorific term 'independent' remains firmly centered on wage labor, no matter how impoverished the worker. 'Welfare dependency', in contrast, has been inflated into a behavioral syndrome and made to seem more contemptible.

Contemporary policy discourse about welfare dependency is thoroughly inflected by these assumptions. It divides into two major streams. The first continues the rhetoric of pauperism and the culture of poverty. It is used in both conservative and liberal, victim-blaming or non-victim-blaming ways, depending on the causal structure of the argument. The contention is that poor, dependent people have something more than lack of money wrong with them. The flaws can be located in biology, psychology, upbringing, neighborhood influence; they can be cast as cause or as effect of poverty, or even as both simultaneously. Conservatives, such as George Gilder and Lawrence Mead, argue that welfare causes moral/psychological dependency.[49] Liberals, such as William Julius Wilson and Christopher Jencks, blame social and economic influences but agree that claimants' culture and behavior are problematic.[50]

A second stream of thought begins from neoclassical economic premises. It assumes a "rational man" facing choices in which welfare and work are both options. For these policy analysts, the moral/psychological meanings of dependency are present but uninterrogated, assumed to be undesirable. Liberals of this school, such as many of the social scientists associated with the Institute for Research on Poverty at the University of Wisconsin, grant that welfare inevitably has some bad, dependency-creating effects, but claim that these are outweighed by other, good effects like improved conditions for children, increased societal stability, and relief of suffering. Conservatives of this school, such as Charles Murray, disagree.[51] The two camps argue above all about the question of incentives. Do AFDC stipends encourage women to have more out-of-wedlock children? Do they discourage them from accepting jobs? Can reducing or withholding stipends serve as a stick to encourage recipients to stay in school, keep their children in school, get married?

Certainly, there are real and significant differences here, but there are also important similarities. Liberals and conservatives of both schools rarely situate the notion of dependency in its historical or economic context, nor do they interrogate its presuppositions. Neither group questions the assumption that independence is an unmitigated good or its identification with wage labor. Many poverty and welfare analysts equivocate between an official position that 'dependency' is a value-neutral term for receipt of (or need for) welfare and a usage that makes it a synonym for 'pauperism'.

These assumptions permeate the public sphere. In the current round of alarms about welfare dependency, it is increasingly stated that "welfare mothers ought to work," a usage that tacitly defines work as wage earning and child rearing as nonwork. Here we run up against contradictions in the discourse of dependency: when the subject under consideration is teenage pregnancy, these mothers are cast as children; when the subject is welfare, they become adults who should be self-supporting. It is only in the past decade that welfare experts have reached consensus on the view that AFDC recipients should be employed. The older view, which underlay the original passage of ADC, was that children need a mother at home—although in practice there was always a class double standard because full-time maternal domesticity was a privilege that had to be purchased, not an entitlement poor women could claim. However, as wage work among mothers of young children has become more widespread and normative, the last defenders of a welfare program that permitted recipients to concentrate full-time on child rearing were silenced.

None of the negative imagery about welfare dependency has gone uncontested, of course. From the 1950s through the 1970s, many of these presuppositions were challenged, most directly in the mid-1960s by an organization of women welfare claimants, the National Welfare Rights Organization. NWRO women cast their relation with the welfare system as active rather than passive, a matter of claiming rights rather than receiving charity. They also insisted that their domestic labor was socially necessary and praiseworthy. Their perspective helped reconstruct the arguments for welfare, spurring poverty lawyers and radical intellectuals to develop a legal and political-theoretical basis for welfare as an entitlement and right. Edward Sparer, a legal strategist for the welfare rights movement, challenged the usual understanding of dependency:

> The charge of antiwelfare politicians is that welfare makes the recipient "dependent." What this means is that the recipient is dependent upon the welfare check for his [*sic*] material subsistence rather than upon some other source . . . whether that is good or bad depends on whether some better source of income is available. . . . The real problem . . . is something entirely different. The recipient and the applicant traditionally have been dependent on the whim of the caseworker.[52]

The cure for welfare dependency, then, was welfare rights. Had the NWRO not been greatly weakened by the late 1970s, the revived discourse of pauperism in the 1980s could not have become hegemonic.

Even in the absence of a powerful National Welfare Rights Organization, many AFDC recipients maintained their own oppositional interpretation of welfare dependency. They complained not only of stingy allowances but also of infantilization due to supervision, loss of privacy, and a maze of bureaucratic rules that constrained their decisions about housing, jobs, and even (until the 1960s) sexual relations. In the claimants' view, welfare dependency is a social condition, not a psychological state, a condition they analyze in terms of power relations. It is what a left-wing English dictionary of social welfare calls 'enforced dependency', "the creation of a dependent class" as a result of "enforced reliance . . . for necessary psychological or material resources."[53]

This idea of enforced dependency was central to another, related challenge to the dominant discourse. During the period in which NWRO activism was at its height, New Left revisionist historians developed an interpretation of the welfare state as an apparatus of social control. They argued that what apologists portrayed as helping practices were actually modes of domination that created enforced dependency. The New Left critique bore some resemblance to the NWRO critique, but the overlap was only partial. The historians of social control told their story mainly from the perspective of the "helpers" and cast recipients as almost entirely passive. They thereby occluded the agency of actual or potential welfare claimants in articulating needs, demanding rights, and making claims.[54]

Still another contemporary challenge to mainstream uses of 'dependency' arose from a New Left school of international political economy. The context was the realization, after the first heady days of postwar decolonization, that politically independent former colonies remained economically dependent. In "dependency theory," radical theorists of "underdevelopment" used the concept of dependency to analyze the global neocolonial economic order from an antiracist and anti-imperialist perspective. In so doing, they resurrected the old preindustrial meaning of dependency as a subjected territory, seeking thereby to divest the term of its newer moral/psychological accretions and to retrieve the occluded dimensions of subjection and subordination. This usage remains strong in Latin America as well as in U.S. social-scientific literature, where we find articles such as "Institutionalizing Dependency: The Impact of Two Decades of Planned Agricultural Modernization."[55]

What all these oppositional discourses share is a rejection of the dominant emphasis on dependency as an individual trait. They seek to shift the focus back to the social relations of subordination, but they do not have much impact on mainstream talk about welfare in the United States today. On the contrary, with economic dependency now a synonym for poverty, and with moral/psychological dependency now a personality disorder, talk of dependency as a social relation of subordination has become increasingly rare. Power and domination tend to disappear.[56]

Conclusion

'Dependency', once a general-purpose term for all social relations of subordination, is now differentiated into several analytically distinct registers. In the economic register, its meaning has shifted from gaining one's livelihood by working for someone else to relying for support on charity or welfare; wage labor now confers independence. In the sociolegal register, the meaning of dependency as subsumption is unchanged, but its scope of reference and connotations have altered: once a socially approved majority condition, it first became a group-based status deemed proper for some classes of persons but not others and then shifted again to designate (except in the case of children) an anomalous, highly stigmatized status of deviant and incompetent individuals. Likewise, in the political register, dependency's meaning as subjection to an external governing power has remained relatively constant, but its evaluative connotations worsened as individual political rights and national sovereignty became normative. Meanwhile, with the emergence of a newer moral/psychological register, properties once ascribed to social relations came to be posited instead as inherent character traits of individuals or groups, and the connotations here, too, have worsened. This last register now claims an increasingly large proportion of the discourse, as if the social relations of dependency were being absorbed into personality. Symptomatically, erstwhile relational understandings have been hypostatized in a veritable portrait gallery of dependent personalities: first, housewives, paupers, natives, and slaves; then poor black teenage solo mothers.

These shifts in the semantics of dependency reflect some major sociohistorical developments. One is the progressive differentiation of the official economy—that which is counted in the gross domestic product—as a seemingly autonomous system that dominates social life. Before the rise of capitalism, all forms of work were woven into a net of dependencies, which constituted a single, continuous fabric of social hierarchies. The whole set of relations was constrained by moral understandings, as in the preindustrial idea of a moral economy. In the patriarchal families and communities that characterized the preindustrial period, women were subordinated and their labor often controlled by others, but their labor was visible, understood, and valued. With the emergence of religious and secular individualism, on the one hand, and of industrial capitalism, on the other, a sharp, new dichotomy was constructed in which economic dependence and economic independence were unalterably opposed to each other. A crucial corollary of this dependence/independence dichotomy, and of the hegemony of wage labor in general, was the occlusion and devaluation of women's unwaged domestic and parenting labor.

The genealogy of dependency also expresses the modern emphasis on individual personality. This is the deepest meaning of the spectacular rise of the moral/psychological register, which constructs yet another version of the independence/dependence dichotomy. In the moral/psychological version, social relations are hypostatized as properties of individuals or groups. Fear of dependency, both explicit and implicit, posits an ideal, independent personality in contrast to which those considered dependent are deviant. This contrast bears traces of a sexual division of labor that assigns men primary responsibility as providers or breadwinners and women primary responsibility as caretakers and nurturers and then treats the derivative personality patterns as fundamental. It is as if male breadwinners absorbed into their personalities the independence associated with their ideologically interpreted economic role, whereas the persons of female nurturers became satu-rated with the dependency of those for whom they care. In this way, the opposition between the independent personality and the dependent person-ality maps onto a whole series of hierarchical oppositions and dichotomies that are central in modern capitalist culture: masculine/feminine, public/private, work/care, success/love, individual/community, economy/family, and competitive/self-sacrificing.

A genealogy cannot tell us how to respond politically to today's discourse about welfare dependency. It does suggest, however, the limits of any response that presupposes rather than challenges the definition of the prob-lem that is implicit in that expression. An adequate response would need to question our received valuations and definitions of dependence and inde-pendence in order to allow new, emancipatory social visions to emerge. Some contemporary welfare-rights activists adopt this strategy, continuing the NWRO tradition. Pat Gowens, for example, elaborates a feminist rein-terpretation of dependency:

> The vast majority of mothers of *all classes and all educational levels* "depends" on another income. It may come from child support . . . or from a husband who earns $20,000 while she averages $7,000. But "dependence" more accurately defines dads who count on women's unwaged labor to raise children and care for the home. Surely, "depen-dence" doesn't define the single mom who does it all: child-rearing, homemaking, and bringing in the money (one way or another). When caregiving is valued and paid, when dependence is not a dirty word, and interdependence is the norm—only then will we make a dent in poverty.[57]

Notes

1. Nancy Fraser is grateful for research support from the Center for Urban Affairs, Northwestern University; the Newberry Library; the National Endowment for the Humanities; and the American Council of Learned Societies. Linda Gordon thanks the University of Wisconsin Graduate School, Vilas Trust, and the Institute for Research on Poverty. We both thank the Rockefeller Foundation Research and Study Center, Bellagio, Italy. We are also grateful for helpful comments from Lisa Brush, Robert Entman, Joel Handler, Dirk Hartog, Barbara Hobson, Allen Hunter, Eva Kittay, Felicia Kornbluh, Jenny Mansbridge, Linda Nicholson, Erik Wright, Eli Zaretsky, and the reviewers and editors of *Signs*.

2. Clarence Thomas, quoted by Karen Tumulty, "Sister of High Court Nominee Traveled Different Road," *Los Angeles Times*, 5 July 1991, p. A4.

3. Daniel P. Moynihan, *The Politics of a Guaranteed Income: The Nixon Administration and the Family Assistance Plan* (New York: Random House, 1973), p. 17.

4. Richard P. Nathan, quoted by William Julius Wilson, "Social Policy and Minority Groups: What Might Have Been and What Might We See in the Future," in *Divided Opportunities: Minorities, Poverty, and Social Policy,* ed. Gary D. Sandefur and Marta Tienda (New York: Plenum Press, 1986), p. 248.

5. Another part of the story, of course, concerns the word 'welfare', but we do not have space to consider it fully here. For a fuller discussion, see Nancy Fraser and Linda Gordon, "Contract Versus Charity: Why Is There No Social Citizenship in the United States?" *Socialist Review* 22, no. 3 (1992): 45–68.

6. Our focus is U.S. political culture and thus North American English usage. Our findings should be of more general interest, however, because some other languages have similar meanings embedded in analogous words. In this essay we have of necessity used British sources for the early stages of our genealogy, which spans the sixteenth and seventeenth centuries. We assume that these meanings of 'dependency' were brought to "the New World" and were formative for the early stages of U.S. political culture.

7. Raymond Williams, *Keywords: A Vocabulary of Culture and Society* (Oxford: Oxford University Press, 1976).

8. This stress on the performative, as opposed to the representational, dimension of language is a hallmark of the pragmatics tradition in the philosophy of language. It has been fruitfully adapted for sociocultural analysis by several writers in addition to Williams. See, for example, Pierre Bourdieu, *Outline of a Theory of Practice* (Cambridge: Cambridge University Press, 1977); Judith Butler, *Gender Trouble: Feminism and the Subversion of Identity* (New York: Routledge, 1990); and Joan Wallach Scott, *Gender and the Politics of History* (New York: Columbia University Press, 1988). For fuller discussion of the advantages of the pragmatics approach, see Fraser, "Structuralism or Pragmatics?" in this volume.

9. Nancy Fraser, "Struggle over Needs: Outline of a Socialist-Feminist Critical Theory of Late-Capitalist Political Culture," in Fraser, *Unruly Practices: Power, Discourse and Gender in Contemporary Social Theory* (Minneapolis: University of Minnesota Press, 1989).

10. Williams, *Keywords*.

11. Bourdieu, *Outline of a Theory of Practice*.

12. Michel Foucault, "Nietzsche, Genealogy, History," in *The Foucault Reader,* ed. Paul Rabinow (New York: Pantheon, 1984), pp. 76–100.

13. The critical literature on Foucault is enormous. For feminist assessments, see Linda Alcoff, "Feminist Politics and Foucault: The Limits to a Collaboration," in *Crisis in Continental Philosophy,* ed. Arlene Dallery and Charles Scott (Albany: SUNY Press, 1990); Judith Butler, "Variations on Sex and Gender: Beauvoir, Wittig and Foucault," in *Feminism as Critique,* ed. Seyla Benhabib and Drucilla Cornell (Minneapolis: University of Minnesota Press, 1987), pp. 128–42; Nancy Hartsock, "Foucault on Power: A Theory for Women?" in *Feminism/Postmodernism,* ed. Linda J. Nicholson (New York: Routledge, 1990), pp. 157–75; Chris Weedon, *Feminist Practice and Poststructuralist Theory* (Oxford: Basil Blackwell, 1987); and the essays in *Foucault and Feminism: Reflections on Resistance,* ed. Irene Diamond and Lee Quinby (Boston: Northeastern University Press, 1988). For balanced discussions of Foucault's strengths and weaknesses, see Fraser, *Unruly Practices;* Axel Honneth, *The Critique of Power: Reflective Stages in a Critical Social Theory* (Cambridge: MIT Press, 1992); and Thomas McCarthy, *Ideals and Illusions: On Reconstruction and Deconstruction in Contemporary Critical Theory* (Cambridge: MIT Press, 1991).

14. Joan R. Gundersen, "Independence, Citizenship, and the American Revolution," *Signs* 13, no. 1 (1987): 59–77.

15. In preindustrial society, moreover, the reverse dependence of the master upon his men was widely recognized. The historian Christopher Hill evoked that understanding when he characterized the "essence" of feudal society as "the bond of loyalty and dependence between lord and man." Here 'dependence' means interdependence. Hill, *The World Turned Upside Down: Radical Ideas During the English Revolution* (New York: Viking, 1972), p. 32.

16. Peter Laslett, *The World We Have Lost: England Before the Industrial Age* (New York: Scribner, 1971), p. 21.

17. Christopher Hill, *The Century of Revolution, 1603–1714* (New York: Norton, 1961).

18. One might say that this redefinition foregrounded wage labor *as* a new form of property, namely, property in one's own labor power. This conception was premised on what C. B. Macpherson called "possessive individualism," the assumption of an individual's property in his (*sic*) own person. See Macpherson, *The Political Theory of Possessive Individualism: Hobbes to Locke* (Oxford: Oxford University Press, 1962). Leading to the construction of wages as an entitlement, this approach was overwhelmingly male. Allen Hunter (personal communication) describes it as a loss of systemic critique, a sense of independence gained by narrowing the focus to the individual worker and leaving behind aspirations for collective independence from capital.

19. In the sixteenth century the term 'pauper' had meant simply a poor person and, in law, one who was allowed to sue or defend in a court without paying costs (OED). Two centuries later, it took on a more restricted definition, denoting a new class of persons who subsisted on poor relief instead of wages and who were held to be deviant and blameworthy.

20. Linda Gordon, "Social Insurance and Public Assistance: The Influence of Gender in Welfare Thought in the United States, 1890–1935," *American Historical Review* 97, no. 1 (1992): 19–54.

21. Actually, there are many variants within the family of images that personify subjection in the industrial era. Among these are related but not identical stereotypes of the Russian serf, the Caribbean slave, the slave in the United States, and the American Indian. Moreover, there are distinct male and female stereotypes within each of those categories. We simplify here in order to highlight the features that are common to all these images, notably the idea of natural subjection rooted in race. We focus especially on stereotypes that portray African Americans as personifications of dependency because of their historic importance and contemporary resonance in the U.S. language of social welfare.

22. The evolution of the term 'native' neatly encapsulates this process. Its original meaning in English, dating from about 1450, was tied to dependency: "one born in bondage; a born thrall," but without racial meaning. Two centuries later it carried the additional meaning of colored or black (OED).

23. Hilary Land, "The Family Wage," *Feminist Review* 6 (1980): 57. Jeanne Boydston, *Home and Work: Housework, Wages, and the Ideology of Labor in the Early Republic* (New York: Oxford University Press, 1991).

24. Gwendolyn S. Hughes, *Mothers in Industry* (New York: New Republic, 1925); Sophonisba P. Breckinridge, "The Home Responsibilities of Women Workers and the 'Equal Wage,'" *Journal of Political Economy* 31 (1928): 521–43; Lorine Pruette, ed., *Women Workers Through the Depression: A Study of White Collar Employment Made by the American Woman's Association* (New York: Macmillan, 1934); and Gordon, "Social Insurance and Public Assistance."

25. Gundersen, "Independence, Citizenship, and the American Revolution."

26. Nancy Folbre, "The Unproductive Housewife: Her Evolution in Nineteenth-century Economic Thought," *Signs* 16, no. 3 (1991): 463–84.

27. For example, Amos Griswold Warner uses 'dependent' only for children in *American Charities and Social Work* (New York: Thomas Y. Crowell, 1894 through 1930). The same is true of Edith Abbott and Sophonisba P. Breckinridge in *The Administration of the Aid-to-Mothers Law in Illinois,* Publication 82 (Washington, D.C.: U.S. Children's Bureau, 1921), p. 7; and the *Proceedings* of the National Conference of Charities and Correction (1890s through 1920s). This usage produced some curious effects because of its intersection with the dependency produced by the normative family. For example, charity experts debated the propriety of "keeping dependent children in their own homes." The children in question were considered dependent because their parent(s) could not support them; yet other children were deemed dependent precisely because their parents did support them.

28. Studies of welfare done in the 1940s still used the word 'dependents' only in the sense of those supported by family heads; see, e.g., Josephine Chapin Brown, *Public Relief, 1929–1939* (New York: Holt, 1940); Donald S. Howard, *The WPA and Federal Relief Policy* (New York: Russell Sage, 1943); and Frank J. Bruno, *Trends in Social Work* (New York: Columbia University Press, 1948).

29. Lilian Brandt, *An Impressionistic View of the Winter of 1930–31 in New York City* (New York: Welfare Council of New York City, 1932), pp. 23–24; Gertrude Vaile, untitled, in *College Women and the Social Sciences,* ed. Herbert Elmer Mills (New York: John Day, 1934), p. 26; and Mary L. Gibbons, "Family Life Today and Tomorrow," *Proceedings, National Conference of Catholic Charities* 19 (1933): 133–68.

30. E. Wight Bakke, *Citizens without Work: A Study of the Effects of Unemployment upon Workers' Social Relations and Practices* (New Haven: Yale University Press, 1940); and *The Unemployed Worker: A Study of the Task of Making a Living without a Job* (New Haven: Yale University Press, 1940).

31. Fraser and Gordon, "Contract Versus Charity."

32. Nancy Fraser, "Women, Welfare, and the Politics of Need Interpretation," in Fraser, *Unruly Practices* (Minneapolis: University of Minnesota Press, 1989); Linda Gordon, "The New Feminist Scholarship on the Welfare State," and Barbara J. Nelson, "The Origins of the Two-Channel Welfare State: Workmen's Compensation and Mothers' Aid," both in *Women, the State, and Welfare,* ed. Linda Gordon (Madison: University of Wisconsin Press, 1990), pp. 9–35, and pp. 123–51. Starting in the 1960s increasing numbers of black women were able to claim AFDC, but prior to that they were largely excluded. At first, the language of the New Deal followed the precedent of earlier programs in applying the term 'dependent' to children. De facto, however, the recipients of ADC were virtually exclusively solo mothers. Between the 1940s and 1960s the term's reference gradually shifted from the children to their mothers.

33. Jill Quadagno, "From Old-Age Assistance to Supplemental Social Security Income: The Political Economy of Relief in the South, 1935–1972," in *The Politics of Social Policy in the United States,* ed. Margaret Weir, Ann Shola Orloff, and Theda Skocpol (Princeton: Princeton University Press, 1988), pp. 235–63.

34. Jerry R. Cates, *Insuring Inequality: Administrative Leadership in Social Security, 1935–54* (Ann Arbor: University of Michigan Press, 1983).

35. Jacqueline Pope, *Biting the Hand That Feeds Them: Organizing Women on Welfare at the Grass Roots Level* (New York: Praeger, 1989), pp. 73, 144; Guida West, *The National*

Welfare Rights Movement: The Social Protest of Poor Women (New York: Praeger, 1981); and Milwaukee County Welfare Rights Organization, *Welfare Mothers Speak Out* (New York: Norton, 1972).

36. Annie S. Barnes, *Single Parents in Black America: A Study in Culture and Legitimacy* (Bristol, Conn.: Wyndham Hall Press, 1987), p. vi.

37. Gordon, "Social Insurance and Public Assistance."

38. Men on "general relief" are sometimes also included in that designation; their treatment by the welfare system is usually as bad or worse.

39. Joan Smith, "The Paradox of Women's Poverty: Wage-earning Women and Economic Transformation," *Signs* 10, no. 2 (1984): 291–310.

40. Judith Stacey, "Sexism by a Subtler Name? Postindustrial Conditions and Postfeminist Consciousness in the Silicon Valley," *Socialist Review* 96 (1987): 7–28; and Kath Weston, *Families We Choose: Lesbians, Gays, Kinship* (New York: Columbia University Press, 1991).

41. M. Haynes, "Pharmacist Involvement in a Chemical-Dependency Rehabilitation Program," *American Journal of Hospital Pharmacy* 45, no. 10 (1988): 2099–2101.

42. Leontine Young, *Out of Wedlock* (New York: McGraw-Hill, 1954), p. 87.

43. Betty Friedan, *The Feminine Mystique* (New York: Norton, 1963).

44. Colette Dowling, *The Cinderella Complex: Women's Hidden Fear of Independence* (New York: Summit Books, 1981).

45. Virginia Sapiro, "The Gender Basis of American Social Policy," in *Women, the State, and Welfare,* ed. Linda Gordon (Madison: University of Wisconsin Press, 1990), pp. 36–54.

46. American Psychiatric Association, *Diagnostic and Statistical Manual of Mental Disorders,* 3d ed. rev. (Washington, D.C.: American Psychiatric Association, 1987), pp. 353–54.

47. Lee Rainwater and William L. Yancey, *The Moynihan Report and the Politics of Controversy* (Cambridge: MIT Press, 1967).

48. Dan Quayle, "Excerpts from Vice President's Speech on Cities and Poverty," *New York Times,* 20 May 1992, p. A11.

49. George Gilder, *Wealth and Poverty* (New York: Basic Books, 1981); and Lawrence Mead, *Beyond Entitlement: The Social Obligations of Citizenship* (New York: Free Press, 1986).

50. William Julius Wilson, *The Truly Disadvantaged: The Inner City, the Underclass, and Public Policy* (Chicago: University of Chicago Press, 1987); and Christopher Jencks, *Rethinking Social Policy: Race, Poverty, and the Underclass* (Cambridge: Harvard University Press, 1992).

51. Charles Murray, *Losing Ground: American Social Policy, 1950–1980* (New York: Basic Books, 1984).

52. Edward V. Sparer, "The Right to Welfare," in *The Rights of Americans: What They Are— What They Should Be,* ed. Norman Dorsen (New York: Pantheon, 1971), p. 71.

53. Noel and Rita Timms, *Dictionary of Social Welfare* (London: Routledge & Kegan Paul, 1982), pp. 55–56.

54. For a fuller discussion of the social-control critique, see Gordon, "The New Feminist Scholarship on the Welfare State." On needs claims, see Fraser, "Struggle over Needs"; and Nelson, "The Origins of the Two-Channel Welfare State."

55. M. Gates, "Institutionalizing Dependency: The Impact of Two Decades of Planned Agricultural Modernization," *Journal of Developing Areas* 22, no. 3 (1988): 293–320.

56. For an argument that Clinton's neoliberal policies continue to individualize dependency, see Nancy Fraser, "Clintonism, Welfare and the Antisocial Wage: The Emergence of a Neoliberal Political Imaginary," *Rethinking Marxism* 6, no. 1 (1993): 1–15.

57. Pat Gowens, "Welfare, Learnfare—Unfair! A Letter to My Governor," *Ms.,* September–October 1991, pp. 90–91.

6

Structuralism or Pragmatics?

On Discourse Theory and Feminist Politics

This chapter grew out of an experience of severe puzzlement.[1] For several years I watched with growing incomprehension as a large and influential body of feminist scholars created an interpretation of Jacques Lacan's theory of discourse, which they sought to use for feminist purposes. I myself had felt (and still feel) a deep disaffinity with Lacan, a disaffinity as much intellectual as political. So while many of my fellow feminists were adapting quasi-Lacanian ideas to theorize the discursive construction of subjectivity in film and literature, I was relying on alternative models to develop an account of language that could inform a feminist social theory.[2] For a long while, I avoided any explicit, metatheoretical discussion of these matters. I explained neither to myself nor to my colleagues why it is that I looked to the discourse models of writers like Foucault, Bourdieu, Bakhtin, Habermas, and Gramsci instead of to those of Lacan, Kristeva, Saussure, and Derrida.[3] In this chapter, I begin to provide such an explanation. I will try to explain why I think feminists should have no truck with the versions of discourse theory that they attribute to Lacan and why we should have only the most minimal truck with related theories attributed to Julia Kristeva. I will also try to identify some places where I think we can find more satisfactory alternatives.

What Do Feminists Want in a Discourse Theory?

Let me begin by posing two questions, What might a theory of discourse contribute to feminism? and What, therefore, do feminists want in a discourse theory? I suggest that a conception of discourse can help us understand at least four things, all of which are interrelated. First, it can help us understand how people's social identities are fashioned and altered over time. Second, it can help us understand how, under conditions of inequality, social groups in the sense of collective agents are formed and unformed. Third, a conception of discourse can illuminate how the cultural hegemony of dominant groups in society is secured and contested. Fourth and finally, it can shed light on the prospects for emancipatory social change and political practice. Let me elaborate.

First, consider the uses of a conception of discourse for understanding social identities. The basic idea here is that people's social identities are complexes of meanings, networks of interpretation. To have a social identity, to be a woman or a man, for example, just is to live and to act under a set of descriptions. These descriptions, of course, are not simply secreted by people's bodies, nor are they simply exuded by people's psyches. Rather, they are drawn from the fund of interpretive possibilities available to agents in specific societies. It follows that in order to understand the gender dimension of social identity, it does not suffice to study biology or psychology. Instead, one must study the historically specific social practices through which cultural descriptions of gender are produced and circulated.[4]

Moreover, social identities are exceedingly complex. They are knit from a plurality of different descriptions arising from a plurality of different signifying practices. Thus, no one is simply a woman; one is rather, for example, a white, Jewish, middle-class woman, a philosopher, a lesbian, a socialist, and a mother.[5] Moreover, since everyone acts in a plurality of social contexts, the different descriptions comprising any individual's social identity fade in and out of focus. Thus, one is not always a woman in the same degree; in some contexts, one's womanhood figures centrally in the set of descriptions under which one acts; in others, it is peripheral or latent.[6] Finally, it is not the case that people's social identities are constructed once and for all and definitively fixed. Rather, they alter over time, shifting with shifts in agents' practices and affiliations. Thus, even the *way* in which one is a woman will shift, as it does, to take a dramatic example, when one becomes a feminist. In short, social identities are discursively constructed in historically specific social contexts; they are complex and plural; and they shift over time. One use of a conception of discourse for feminist theorizing, then, is in understanding social identities in their full sociocultural complexity, thus in demystifying static, single-variable, essentialist views of gender identity.

A second use of a conception of discourse for feminist theorizing is in understanding the formation of social groups. How does it happen, under conditions of inequality, that people come together, arrange themselves under the banner of *collective* identities, and constitute themselves as collective social agents? How do class formation and, by analogy, gender formation occur?

Clearly, group formation involves shifts in people's social identities and therefore also in their relation to discourse. One thing that happens here is that preexisting strands of identities acquire a new sort of salience and centrality. These strands, previously submerged among many others, are reinscribed as the nub of new self-definitions and affiliations.[7] For example, in the current wave of feminist ferment, many of us who had previously been "women" in some taken-for-granted way have now become "women" in the very different sense of a discursively self-constituted political collectivity. In the process, we have remade entire regions of social discourse. We have invented new terms for describing social reality, for example, "sexism," "sexual harassment," "marital, date, and acquaintance rape," "labor-force sex segregation," "the double shift," and "wife-battery." We have also invented new language games such as consciousness-raising and new, institutionalized public spheres such as the Society for Women in Philosophy.[8] The point is that the formation of social groups proceeds by struggles over social discourse. Thus, a conception of discourse is useful here, both for understanding social groups and for coming to grips with the closely related issue of sociocultural hegemony.

"Hegemony" is the Italian Marxist Antonio Gramsci's term for the discursive face of power. It is the power to establish the "common sense" or "doxa" of a society, the fund of self-evident descriptions of social reality that normally go without saying.[9] This includes the power to establish authoritative definitions of social situations and social needs, the power to define the universe of legitimate disagreement, and the power to shape the political agenda. Hegemony, then, expresses the advantaged position of dominant social groups with respect to discourse. It is a concept that allows us to recast the issues of social identity and social groups in the light of societal inequality. How do pervasive axes of dominance and subordination affect the production and circulation of social meanings? How does stratification along lines of gender, "race," and class affect the discursive construction of social identities and the formation of social groups?

The notion of hegemony points to the intersection of power, inequality, and discourse. However, it does not entail that the ensemble of descriptions that circulate in society constitute a monolithic and seamless web, nor that dominant groups exercise an absolute, top-down control of meaning. On the contrary, "hegemony" designates a process wherein cultural authority is negotiated and contested. It presupposes that societies contain a plurality of discourses and discursive sites, a plurality of positions and perspectives from which to speak. Of course, not all of these have equal authority. Yet conflict and contestation are part of the story. Thus, one use of a conception of discourse for feminist theorizing is to shed light on the processes by which the sociocultural hegemony of dominant groups is achieved and contested. What are the processes by which definitions and interpretations inimical to women's interests acquire cultural authority? What are the prospects for mobilizing counterhegemonic feminist definitions and interpretations to create broad oppositional groups and alliances?

The link between these questions and emancipatory political practice is, I believe, fairly obvious. A conception of discourse that lets us examine identities, groups, and hegemony in the ways I have been describing would be a great aid to feminist practice. It would valorize the empowering dimensions of discursive struggles without leading to "culturalist" retreats from political engagement.[10] In addition, the right kind of conception would counter the disabling assumption that women are just passive victims of male dominance. That assumption overtotalizes male dominance, treating men as the only social agents and rendering inconceivable our own existence as feminist theorists and activists. In contrast, the sort of conception I have been proposing would help us understand how, even under conditions of subordination, women participate in the making of culture.

"Lacanianism" and the Limits of Structuralism

In light of the foregoing, what sort of conception of discourse will be useful for feminist theorizing? What sort of conception can best meet our needs to understand identities, groups, hegemony, and emancipatory practice?

In the postwar period, two general models for theorizing language emerged in France (and elsewhere). The first of these is the structuralist model, which studies language as a symbolic system or code. This model is derived from Saussure, presupposed in the version of Lacanian theory I shall be concerned with here, and abstractly negated but not entirely superseded in deconstruction and in related forms of French "women's writing." The second model, by contrast, I shall call the pragmatics model; it studies language at the level of discourses, as historically specific social practices of communication. This model is operative in the work of Mikhail Bakhtin, Michel Foucault, Pierre Bourdieu, and in some but not all dimensions of the work of Julia Kristeva and Luce Irigaray. In this section, I shall argue that the first, structuralist model is of only limited usefulness for feminist theorizing.

Let me begin by noting that there are good prima facie reasons for feminists to be wary of the structuralist model. This model constructs its object of study by abstracting from exactly what we need to focus on, namely, the social practice and social context of communication. Indeed, the abstraction from practice and context are among the founding gestures of Saussurean linguistics. Saussure began by splitting signification into *langue,* the symbolic system or code, and *parole,* speakers' uses of language in communicative practice or speech. He then made the first of these, *langue,* the proper object of the new science of linguistics, and relegated the second, *parole,* to the status of a devalued remainder.[11] At the same time, Saussure insisted that the study of *langue* be synchronic rather than diachronic; he thereby posited his object of study as static and atemporal, abstracting it from historical change. Finally, the founder of structuralist linguistics posited that *langue* was indeed a single system; he made its unity and systematicity consist in the putative fact that every signifier, every material, signifying element of the code, derives its meaning positionally by way of its difference from all of the others.

Together, these founding operations render the structuralist approach of limited utility for feminist theorizing.[12] Because it abstracts from *parole,* the structuralist model brackets questions of practice, agency, and the speaking subject. Thus, it does not engage with the discursive practices through which social identities and social groups are formed. Because this approach brackets the diachronic, moreover, it is not attuned to shifts in identities and affiliations over time. Similarly, because it abstracts from the social context of communication, the model brackets issues of power and inequality. Thus, it cannot illuminate the processes by which cultural hegemony is secured and contested. Finally, because the model theorizes the fund of available linguistic meanings as a single symbolic system, it lends itself to a monolithic view of signification that denies tensions and contradictions among social meanings. In short, by reducing discourse to a "symbolic system," the structuralist model evacuates social agency, social conflict, and social practice.[13]

Let me now try to illustrate these problems by means of a brief discussion of "Lacanianism." By "Lacanianism" I do not mean the actual thought of

Jacques Lacan, which is far too complex to tackle here. I mean, rather, an ideal-typical neostructuralist reading of Lacan that is widely credited among English-speaking feminists.[14] In discussing "Lacanianism," I shall bracket the question of the fidelity of this reading, which could be faulted for overemphasizing the influence of Saussure at the expense of other, countervailing influences, such as Hegel.[15] For my purposes, however, this ideal-typical, Saussurean reading of Lacan is useful precisely because it evinces with unusual clarity difficulties that beset many conceptions of discourse that are widely considered "poststructuralist" but that remain wedded in important respects to structuralism. Because their attempts to break free of structuralism remain abstract, such conceptions tend finally to recapitulate it. "Lacanianism," as discussed here, is a paradigm case of "neostructuralism."[16]

At first sight, neostructuralist "Lacanianism" seems to promise some advantages for feminist theorizing. By conjoining the Freudian problematic of the construction of gendered subjectivity to the Saussurean model of structural linguistics, it seems to provide each with its needed corrective. The introduction of the Freudian problematic promises to supply the speaking subject that is missing in Saussure and thereby to reopen the excluded questions about identity, speech, and social practice. Conversely, the use of the Saussurean model promises to remedy some of Freud's deficiencies. By insisting that gender identity is *discursively* constructed, "Lacanianism" appears to eliminate lingering vestiges of biologism in Freud, to treat gender as sociocultural all the way down, and to render it in principle more open to change.

Upon closer inspection, however, these apparent advantages fail to materialize. Instead, "Lacanianism" begins to look suspiciously circular. On the one hand, it purports to describe the process by which individuals acquire gendered subjectivity through their painful conscription as young children into a preexisting phallocentric symbolic order. Here the structure of the symbolic order is presumed to constrain the development of individual subjectivity. But on the other hand, and at the same time, the theory purports to show that the symbolic order must necessarily be phallocentric because the attainment of subjectivity requires submission to "the Father's Law." Here, conversely, the nature of individual subjectivity, as dictated by an autonomous psychology, is presumed to determine the character of the symbolic order.

One result of this circularity is an apparently ironclad determinism. As Dorothy Leland has noted, the theory casts the developments it describes as necessary, invariant, and unalterable.[17] Phallocentrism, woman's disadvantaged place in the symbolic order, the encoding of cultural authority as masculine, the putative impossibility of describing a nonphallic sexuality, in short, any number of historically contingent trappings of male dominance now appear as invariable features of the human condition. Women's subordination, then, is inscribed as the inevitable destiny of civilization.

I can spot several spurious steps in this reasoning, some of which have their roots in the presupposition of the structuralist model. First, to the degree "Lacanianism" has succeeded in eliminating biologism, and that is dubious for reasons I shall not go into here,[18] it has replaced it with psychologism, the untenable view that autonomous psychological imperatives given independently of culture and history can dictate the way they are interpreted and acted on within culture and history. "Lacanianism" falls prey to psychologism to the extent that it claims that the phallocentricity of the symbolic order is required by the demands of an enculturation process that is itself independent of culture.[19]

If one half of "Lacanianism's" circular argument is vitiated by psychologism, then the other half is vitiated by what I should like to call "symbolicism." By symbolicism, I mean, first, the homogenizing reification of diverse signifying practices into a monolithic and all-pervasive "symbolic order," and, second, the endowing of that order with an exclusive causal power to fix people's subjectivities once and for all. Symbolicism, then, is an operation whereby the structuralist abstraction *langue* is troped into a quasi divinity, a normative "symbolic order" whose power to shape identities dwarfs to the point of extinction that of mere historical institutions and practices.

Actually, as Deborah Cameron has noted, Lacan himself equivocated on the expression "the symbolic order."[20] Sometimes he used this expression relatively narrowly to refer to Saussurean *langue,* the structure of language as a system of signs. If it followed this narrow usage, "Lacanianism" would be committed to the implausible view that the sign system itself determines individual's subjectivities independently of the social context and social practice of its uses. At other times, by contrast, Lacan used the expression "the symbolic order" far more broadly to refer to an amalgam that includes not only linguistic structures but also cultural traditions and kinship structures, the latter mistakenly equated with social structure in general.[21] If it followed this broad usage, "Lacanianism" would conflate the ahistorical structural abstraction *langue* with variable historical phenomena like family forms and child-rearing practices; cultural representations of love and authority in art, literature, and philosophy; the gender division of labor; forms of political organization and of other institutional sources of power and status. The result would be a conception of "the symbolic order" that essentializes and homogenizes contingent historical practices and traditions, erasing tensions, contradictions, and possibilities for change. This would be a conception, moreover, that is so broad that the claim that *it* determines the structure of subjectivity risks collapsing into an empty tautology.[22]

The combination of psychologism and symbolicism in "Lacanianism" results in a conception of discourse that is of limited usefulness for feminist theorizing. To be sure, this conception offers an account of the discursive construction of social identity. However, it is not an account that can make sense of the complexity and multiplicity of social identities, the ways they are woven from a plurality of discursive strands. Granted, "Lacanianism" stresses that the apparent unity and simplicity of ego identity is imaginary, that the subject is irreparably split both by language and drives. But this insistence on fracture does not lead to an appreciation of the diversity of the sociocultural discursive practices from which identities are woven. It leads, rather, to a unitary view of the human condition as inherently tragic.

In fact, "Lacanianism" differentiates identities only in binary terms, along the single axis of having or lacking the phallus. Now, as Luce Irigaray has shown, this phallic conception of sexual difference is not an adequate basis for understanding femininity[23]—nor, I would add, masculinity. Still less, then, is it able to shed light on other dimensions of social identities, including ethnicity, color, and social class. Nor could the theory be emended to incorporate these manifestly historical phenomena, given its postulation of an ahistorical, tension-free "symbolic order" equated with kinship.[24]

Moreover, "Lacanianism's" account of identity construction cannot account for identity shifts over time. It is committed to the general psychoanalytic proposition that gender identity (the only kind of identity it considers) is basically fixed once and for all with the resolution of the Oedipus complex. "Lacanianism" equates this resolution with the child's entry into a fixed, monolithic, and all-powerful symbolic order. Thus, it actually increases the degree of identity fixity found in classical Freudian theory. It is true, as Jacqueline Rose points out, that the theory stresses that gender identity is always precarious, that its apparent unity and stability are always threatened by repressed libidinal drives.[25] But this emphasis on precariousness is not an opening onto genuine historical thinking about shifts in people's social identities. On the contrary, it is an insistence on a permanent, ahistorical condition because, for "Lacanianism," the only alternative to conventional gender identity is psychosis.

If "Lacanianism" cannot provide an account of social identity that is useful for feminist theorizing, then it is unlikely to help us understand group formation. For "Lacanianism," affiliation falls under the rubric of the imaginary. To affiliate with others, then, to align oneself with others in a social movement, would be to fall prey to the illusions of the imaginary ego. It would be to deny loss and lack, to seek an impossible unification and fulfillment. Thus, from the perspective of "Lacanianism," collective movements would by definition be vehicles of delusion; they could not even in principle be emancipatory.[26]

Moreover, insofar as group formation depends on linguistic innovation, it is untheorizable from the perspective of "Lacanianism." Since "Lacanianism" posits a fixed, monolithic symbolic system and a speaker who is wholly subjected to it, it is inconceivable how there could ever be any linguistic innovation. Speaking subjects could only ever reproduce the existing symbolic order; they could not possibly alter it.

From this perspective, the question of cultural hegemony cannot be posed. There can be no question about how the cultural authority of dominant groups in society is established and contested, no question of unequal negotiations between different social groups occupying different discursive positions. For "Lacanianism," on the contrary, there is simply "*the* symbolic order," a single universe of discourse that is so systematic, so all-pervasive, so monolithic that one cannot even conceive of such things as alternative perspectives, multiple discursive sites, struggles over social meanings, contests between hegemonic and counterhegemonic definitions of social situations, conflicts of interpretation of social needs. One cannot even conceive, really, of a plurality of different speakers.

With the way blocked to a political understanding of identities, groups, and cultural hegemony, the way is also blocked to an understanding of political practice. For one thing, there is no conceivable agent of such practice. "Lacanianism" posits a view of the person as a nonsutured congeries of three moments, none of which can qualify as a political agent. The speaking subject is simply the grammatical "I," a shifter wholly subjected to the symbolic order; it can only and forever reproduce that order. The ego is an imaginary projection, deluded about its own stability and self-possession, hooked on an impossible narcissistic desire for unity and self-completion; it therefore can only and forever tilt at windmills. Finally, there is the ambiguous unconscious, sometimes an ensemble of repressed libidinal drives, sometimes the face of language as Other, but never anything that could count as a social agent.

This discussion shows, I think, that "Lacanianism" suffers from many conceptual shortcomings.[27] I have stressed those deficiencies that have their roots in the presupposition of the structuralist conception of language.

"Lacanianism" seemed to promise a way to get beyond structuralism by introducing the concept of the speaking subject. This in turn seemed to hold out the promise of a way of theorizing discursive practice. However, as I hope I have shown, these promises remain unfulfilled. The speaking subject introduced by "Lacanianism" is not the agent of discursive practice. It is simply an effect of the symbolic order conjoined to some repressed libidinal drives. Thus, the introduction of the speaking subject has not succeeded in dereifying linguistic structure. On the contrary, a reified conception of language as system has colonized the speaking subject.

Julia Kristeva between Structuralism and Pragmatics

So far, I have been arguing that the structuralist model of language is of limited usefulness for feminist theorizing. Now I want to suggest that the pragmatics model is more promising. Indeed, there are good prima facie reasons for feminists to prefer a pragmatics approach to the study of language. Unlike the structuralist approach, the pragmatics view studies language as social practice in social context. This model takes discourses, not structures, as its object. Discourses are historically specific, socially situated, signifying practices. They are the communicative frames in which speakers interact by exchanging speech acts. Yet discourses are themselves set within social institutions and action contexts. Thus, the concept of a discourse links the study of language to the study of society.

The pragmatics model offers several potential advantages for feminist theorizing. First, it treats discourses as contingent, positing that they arise, alter, and disappear over time. Thus, the model lends itself to historical contextualization, and it allows us to thematize change. Second, the pragmatics approach understands signification as action rather than as representation. It is concerned with how people "do things with words." Thus, the model allows us to see speaking subjects not simply as effects of structures and systems but, rather, as socially situated agents. Third, the pragmatics model treats discourses in the plural. It starts from the assumption that there is a plurality of different discourses in society, therefore a plurality of communicative sites from which to speak. Because it posits that individuals assume different discursive positions as they move from one discursive frame to another, this model lends itself to a theorization of social identities as non-monolithic. Next, the pragmatics approach rejects the assumption that the totality of social meanings in circulation constitutes a single, coherent, self-reproducing "symbolic system." Instead, it allows for conflicts among social schemas of interpretation and among the agents who deploy them. Finally, because it links the study of discourses to the study of society, the pragmatics approach allows us to focus on power and inequality. In short, the pragmatics approach has many of the features one needs in order to understand the complexity of social identities, the formation of social groups, the securing and contesting of cultural hegemony, and the possibility and actuality of political practice.

Let me illustrate the uses of the pragmatics model for feminist theorizing by considering the ambiguous case of Julia Kristeva. Kristeva's case is instructive in that she began her career as a critic of structuralism and a proponent of a pragmatics alternative. Having fallen under the sway of "Lacanianism," however, she has not managed to maintain a consistent orientation to pragmatics. Instead, she has ended up producing a strange, hybrid theory, one that oscillates between structuralism and pragmatics. In what follows, I shall argue that the aspects of Kristeva's thought that are fruitful for political theory are linked to its pragmatics dimensions, while the impasses she arrives at derive from structuralist lapses.

Kristeva's intention to break with structuralism is most clearly and succinctly announced in a brilliant 1973 essay called "The System and the Speaking Subject."[28] Here she argues that, because it conceives language as a symbolic system, structuralist semiotics is necessarily incapable of understanding oppositional practice and change. To remedy these lacunae, she proposes a new approach oriented to "signifying practices." These she defines as norm-governed, but not necessarily all-powerfully constraining, and as situated in "historically determined relations of production." As a complement to this concept of signifying practices, Kristeva also proposes a new concept of the "speaking subject." This subject is socially and historically situated, to be sure, but it is not wholly subjected to the reigning social and discursive conventions. It is a subject, rather, who is capable of innovative practice.

In a few bold strokes, then, Kristeva rejects the exclusion of context, practice, agency, and innovation, and she proposes a new model of discursive pragmatics. Her general idea is that speakers act in socially situated, norm-governed signifying practices. In so doing, they sometimes transgress the established norms in force. Transgressive practice gives rise to discursive innovations and these in turn may lead to change. Innovative practice may subsequently be normalized in the form of new or modified discursive norms, thereby "renovating" signifying practices.[29]

The uses of this sort of approach for feminist theorizing should by now be apparent. Yet there are also some warning signs of possible problems. First,

there is Kristeva's antinomian bent, her tendency, at least in this early quasi-Maoist phase of her career, to valorize transgression and innovation per se irrespective of its content and direction.[30] The flip side of this attitude is a penchant for inflecting norm-conforming practice as negative *tout court,* irrespective of the content of the norms. This attitude is highly problematic for feminist theorizing given that feminist politics requires ethical distinctions between oppressive and emancipatory social norms.

A second potential problem here is Kristeva's aestheticizing bent, her association of valorized transgression with "poetic practice." Kristeva tends to treat avant-garde aesthetic production as the privileged site of innovation. By contrast, communicative practice in everyday life appears as conformism *simpliciter.* This tendency to enclave or regionalize innovative practice is also problematic for feminist theorizing. We need to recognize and assess the emancipatory potential of oppositional practice *wherever* it appears—in bedrooms, on shop floors, in the caucuses of the American Philosophical Association.

The third and most serious problem that I want to discuss is Kristeva's additive approach to theorizing. By this I mean her penchant for remedying theoretical problems by simply *adding* to deficient theories instead of by scrapping or overhauling them. This, I submit, is how she ends up handling certain features of structuralism; rather than eliminating certain structuralist notions altogether, she simply adds other, antistructuralist notions alongside them.

Kristeva's additive, dualistic style of theorizing is apparent in the way she analyzes and classifies signifying practices. She takes such practices to consist in varying proportions of two basic ingredients. One of these is "the symbolic," a linguistic register keyed to the transmission of propositional content by means of the observance of grammatical and syntactical rules. The other is "the semiotic," a register keyed to the expression of libidinal drives by means of intonation and rhythm and not bound by linguistic rules. The symbolic, then, is the axis of discursive practice that helps reproduce the social order by imposing linguistic conventions on anarchic desires. The semiotic, in contrast, expresses a material, bodily source of revolutionary negativity, the power to break through convention and initiate change. According to Kristeva, all signifying practices contain some measure of each of these two registers of language, but with the signal exception of poetic practice, the symbolic register is always the dominant one.

In her later work, Kristeva provides a psychoanalytically grounded gender subtext to her distinction between the symbolic and the semiotic. Following "Lacanianism," she associates the symbolic with the paternal, and she describes it as a monolithically phallocentric, rule-bound order to which subjects submit as the price of sociality when they resolve the Oedipal complex by accepting the Father's Law. But then Kristeva breaks with "Lacanianism" in insisting on the underlying persistence of a feminine, maternal element in all signifying practice. She associates the semiotic with the pre-Oedipal and the maternal, and she valorizes it as a point of resistance to paternally coded cultural authority, a sort of oppositional feminine beachhead within discursive practice.

This way of analyzing and classifying signifying practices may seem at first sight to have promise for feminist theorizing. It seems to contest the presumption of "Lacanianism" that language is monolithically phallocentric and to identify a locus of feminist opposition to the dominance of masculine power. However, on closer inspection, this promise turns out to be largely illusory. In fact, Kristeva's analysis of signifying practices betrays her best pragmatics intentions. The decomposition of such practices into symbolic and semiotic constituents does not lead beyond structuralism. The "symbolic," after all, is a repetition of the reified, phallocentric symbolic order of "Lacanianism." And while the "semiotic" is a force that momentarily disrupts that symbolic order, it does not constitute an alternative to it. On the contrary, as Judith Butler has shown, the contest between the two modes of signification is stacked in favor of the symbolic: the semiotic is by definition transitory and subordinate, always doomed in advance to reabsorption by the symbolic order.[31] Moreover, and more fundamentally problematic, I think, is the fact that the semiotic is defined parasitically over against the symbolic as the latter's mirror image and abstract negation. Simply adding the two together, then, cannot lead beyond structuralism to pragmatics. Rather, it yields an amalgam of structure and antistructure. Moreover, this amalgam is, in Hegel's phrase, a "bad infinity" that leaves us oscillating ceaselessly between a structuralist moment and an antistructuralist moment without ever getting to anything else.

Thus, by resorting to an additive mode of theorizing, Kristeva surrenders her promising pragmatics conception of signifying practice to a quasi-"Lacanianist" neostructuralism. In the process, she ends up reproducing some of "Lacanianism's" most unfortunate conceptual shortcomings. She, too, lapses into symbolicism, treating the symbolic order as an all-powerful causal mechanism and conflating linguistic structure, kinship structure, and social structure in general.[32] On the other hand, Kristeva sometimes does better than "Lacanianism" in appreciating the historical specificity and complexity of particular cultural traditions, especially in those portions of her work that analyze cultural representations of gender in such traditions. Even there, however, she often lapses into psychologism; for example, she mars her potentially very interesting studies of cultural representations of femininity and maternity in Christian theology and in Italian Renaissance painting by falling back on reductive schemes of interpretation that treat the historical material as reflexes of autonomous, ahistorical, psychological imperatives like "castration anxiety" and "feminine paranoia."[33]

All told, then, Kristeva's conception of discourse surrenders many of the potential advantages of pragmatics for feminist theorizing. In the end, she loses the pragmatics stress on the contingency and historicity of discursive practices, their openness to possible change. Instead, she lapses into a quasi-structuralist emphasis on the recuperating power of a reified symbolic order and thereby surrenders the possibility of explaining change. Likewise, her theory loses the pragmatics stress on the plurality of discursive practices. Instead, it lapses into a quasi-structuralist homogenizing and binarizing orientation, one that distinguishes practices along the sole axis of proportion of semiotic to symbolic, feminine to masculine, and thereby surrenders the potential to understand complex identities. In addition, Kristeva loses the pragmatics stress on social context. Instead, she lapses into a quasi-structuralist conflation of "symbolic order" with social context and thereby surrenders the capacity to link discursive dominance to societal inequality. Finally, her theory loses the pragmatics stress on interaction and social conflict. Instead, as Andrea Nye has shown, it focuses almost exclusively on *intra*subjective tensions and thereby surrenders its ability to understand *inter*subjective phenomena, including affiliation, on the one hand, and struggle, on the other.[34]

This last point can be brought home by considering Kristeva's account of the speaking subject. Far from being useful for feminist theorizing, her view replicates many of the disabling features of "Lacanianism." Her subject, like its, is split into two halves, neither of which is a potential political agent. The subject of the symbolic is an oversocialized conformist, thoroughly subjected to symbolic conventions and norms. To be sure, its conformism is put "on trial" by the rebellious, desiring ensemble of bodily based drives associated with the semiotic. But, as before, the mere addition of an antistructuralist force doesn't lead beyond structuralism. The semiotic "subject" cannot itself be an agent of feminist practice for several reasons. First, it is located beneath, rather than within, culture and society; so it is unclear how its practice could be *political* practice.[35] Second, it is defined exclusively in terms of the transgression of social norms; thus, it cannot engage in the reconstructive moment of feminist politics, a moment essential to social transformation. Finally, it is defined in terms of the shattering of social identity, and so it cannot figure in the reconstruction of the new, politically constituted, *collective* identities and solidarities that are essential to feminist politics.

By definition, then, neither half of Kristeva's split subject can be a feminist political agent. Nor, I submit, can the two halves be joined together. They tend rather simply to cancel each other out, the first forever shattering the identitarian pretensions of the second, the second forever recuperating the first and reconstituting itself as before. The upshot is a paralyzing oscillation between identity and nonidentity without any determinate practical issue. Here, then, is another instance of a "bad infinity," an amalgam of structuralism and its abstract negation.

If there are no individual agents of emancipatory practice in Kristeva's universe, then there are no such collective agents either. This can be seen by examining one last instance of her additive pattern of thinking, namely, her treatment of the feminist movement itself. This topic is most directly addressed in an essay called "Women's Time" for which Kristeva is best known in feminist circles.[36] Here, she identifies three "generations" of feminist movements: first, an egalitarian, reform-oriented, humanist feminism, aiming to secure women's full participation in the public sphere, a feminism best personified in France perhaps by Simone de Beauvoir; second, a culturally oriented gynocentric feminism, aiming to foster the expression of a non-male-defined feminine sexual and symbolic specificity, a feminism represented by the proponents of *écriture féminine* and *parler femme;* and finally, Kristeva's own, self-proclaimed brand of feminism—in my view, actually postfeminism—a radically nominalist, antiessentialist approach that stresses that "women" don't exist and that collective identities are dangerous fictions.[37]

Despite the explicitly tripartite character of this categorization, the deep logic of Kristeva's thinking about feminism conforms to her additive, dualistic pattern. For one thing, the first, egalitarian humanist moment of feminism drops out of the picture in that Kristeva falsely—and astoundingly—assumes its program has already been achieved. Thus, there are really only two "generations" of feminism she is concerned with. Next, despite her explicit criticisms of gynocentrism, there is a strand of her thought that implicitly partakes of it—I mean Kristeva's quasi-biologistic, essentializing identification of women's femininity with maternity. Maternity, for her, is the way that women, as opposed to men, touch base with the pre-Oedipal, semiotic residue. (Men do it by writing avant-garde poetry; women do it by having babies.) Here, Kristeva dehistoricizes and psychologizes motherhood, conflating conception, pregnancy, birthing, nursing, and child-rearing, abstracting all of them from sociopolitical context, and erecting her own essentialist stereotype of femininity. But then she reverses herself and recoils from her construct, insisting that "women" don't exist, that feminine identity is fictitious, and that feminist movements therefore tend toward the religious and the protot otalitarian. The overall pattern of Kristeva's thinking about feminism, then, is additive and dualistic: she ends up alternating essentialist gynocentric moments with antiessentialist nominalistic moments, moments that consolidate an ahistorical, undifferentiated, maternal feminine gender identity with moments that repudiate women's identities altogether.

With respect to feminism, then, Kristeva leaves us oscillating between a regressive version of gynocentric-maternalist essentialism, on the one hand, and a postfeminist antiessentialism, on the other. Neither of these is useful for feminist theorizing. In Denise Riley's terms, the first *overfeminizes* women by defining us maternally. The second, by contrast, *underfeminizes* us by insisting that "women" don't exist and by dismissing the feminist movement as a prototot alitarian fiction.[38] Simply putting the two together, moreover, does not overcome the limits of either. On the contrary, it constitutes another "bad infinity" and so, another proof of the limited usefulness for feminist theorizing of an approach that merely conjoins an abstract negation of structuralism to a structuralist model left otherwise intact.

Conclusion

I hope the foregoing has provided a reasonably vivid and persuasive illustration of my most general point, namely, the superiority for feminist theorizing of pragmatics over structuralist approaches to the study of language. Instead of reiterating the advantages of pragmatics models, I shall close with one specific example of their uses for feminist theorizing.

As I argued, pragmatics models insist on the social context and social practice of communication, and they study a plurality of historically changing discursive sites and practices. As a result, these approaches offer us the possibility of thinking of social identities as complex, changing, and discursively constructed. This in turn seems to me our best hope for avoiding some of Kristeva's difficulties. Complex, shifting, discursively constructed social identities provide an alternative to reified, essentialist conceptions of gender identity, on the one hand, and to simple negations and dispersals of identity, on the other. They thus permit us to navigate safely between the twin shoals of essentialism and nominalism, between reifying women's social identities under stereotypes of femininity, on the one hand, and dissolving them into sheer nullity and oblivion, on the other.[39] I am claiming, therefore, that with the help of a pragmatics conception of discourse we can accept the critique of essentialism without becoming postfeminists. This seems to me to be an invaluable help, for it will not be time to speak of post-feminism until we can legitimately speak of postpatriarchy.[40]

Notes

1. I am grateful for helpful comments and suggestions from Jonathan Arac, David Levin, Paul Mattick, Jr., John McCumber, Diana T. Meyers, and Eli Zaretsky.

2. See, for example, Fraser, "Struggle over Needs," in *Unruly Practices: Power, Discourse and Gender in Contemporary Social Theory* (Minneapolis: University of Minnesota Press, 1989).

3. I group these writers together not because all are Lacanians—clearly only Kristeva and Lacan himself are—but rather because, disclaimers notwithstanding, all continue the structuralist reduction of discourse to symbolic system. I shall develop this point later in this chapter.

4. Thus, the fund of interpretive possibilities available to me, a late-twentieth-century American, overlaps very little with that available to the thirteenth-century Chinese woman I may want to imagine as my sister. And yet in both cases, hers and mine, the interpretive possibilities are established in the medium of social discourse. It is in the medium of discourse that each of us encounters an interpretation of what it is to be a person, as well as a menu of possible descriptions specifying the particular sort of person each is to be.

5. See Elizabeth V. Spelman, *Inessential Woman* (Boston: Beacon Press, 1988).

6. See Denise Riley, *"Am I That Name?" Feminism and the Category of "Women" in History* (Minneapolis: University of Minnesota Press, 1988).

7. See Jane Jenson, "Paradigms and Political Discourse: Labour and Social Policy in the U.S.A. and France before 1914," Working Paper Series, Center for European Studies, Harvard University, winter 1989.

8. See Fraser, "Struggle over Needs," and Riley, *"Am I That Name?"*

9. Antonio Gramsci, *Selections from the Prison Notebooks of Antonio Gramsci*, ed. and trans. Quinton Hoare and Geoffrey Nowell Smith (New York: International Publishers, 1972).

10. For a critique of "cultural feminism" as a retreat from political struggle, see Alice Echols, "The New Feminism of Yin and Yang," in *Powers of Desire: The Politics of Sexuality*, ed. Ann Snitow, Christine Stansell, and Sharon Thompson (New York: Monthly Review Press, 1983).

11. Fernand de Saussure, *Course in General Linguistics*, ed. Charles Baily and Albert Sechehaye with the collaboration of Albert Riedlinger, trans. Roy Harris (LaSalle: Open Court, 1986). For a brilliant critique of this move, see Pierre Bourdieu, *Outline of a Theory of Practice* (Cambridge: Cambridge University Press, 1977). Similar objections are found in Julia Kristeva's "The System and the Speaking Subject," in *The Kristeva Reader*, ed. Toril Moi (New York: Columbia University Press, 1986), to be discussed below, and in the Soviet Marxist critique of Russian formalism from which Kristeva's views derive.

12. I leave it to linguists to decide whether it is useful for other purposes.

13. These criticisms pertain to what may be called "global" structuralisms, that is, approaches that treat the whole of language as a single symbolic system. They are not intended to rule out the potential utility of approaches that analyze structural relations in limited, socially situated, culturally and historically specific sublanguages or discourses. On the contrary, it is possible that approaches of this latter sort can be usefully articulated with the pragmatics model discussed below.

14. In earlier versions of this chapter, I was not as careful as I should have been in distinguishing "Lacanianism" from Lacan. In taking greater pains to make this distinction here, however, I do not mean to imply that I believe Lacan to be free of difficulties. On the contrary, I suspect that many of the basic critical points made here against "Lacanianism" tell against Lacan as well. But a much longer, more complex textual argument would be required to demonstrate this.

15. For the tensions between the Hegelian and Saussurean dimensions in Lacan's thought, see Peter Dews, *Logics of Disintegration: Post-Structuralist Thought and the Claims of Critical Theory* (New York: Verso, 1987).

16. For the notion of "neostructuralism," see Manfred Frank, *What is Neo-Structuralism?* trans. Sabine Wilke and Richard Gray (Minneapolis: University of Minnesota Press, 1989).

17. Dorothy Leland, "Lacanian Psychoanalysis and French Feminism," in *Revaluing French Feminism: Critical Essays on Difference, Agency, and Culture,* ed. Nancy Fraser and Sandra Bartky (Bloomington: Indiana University Press, 1991).

18. Here I believe one can properly speak of Lacan. Lacan's claim to have overcome biologism rests on his insistence that the phallus is not the penis. However, many feminist critics have shown that he fails to prevent the collapse of the symbolic signifier into the organ. The clearest indication of this failure is his assertion, in "The Meaning of the Phallus," that the phallus becomes the master signifier because of its "turgidity," which suggests "the transmission of vital flow" in copulation. See Jacques Lacan, "The Meaning of the Phallus," in *Feminine Sexuality: Jacques Lacan and the école freudienne,* ed. Juliet Mitchell and Jacqueline Rose (New York: Norton, 1982).

19. A similar argument is made by Leland in "Lacanian Psychoanalysis and French Feminism."

20. Deborah Cameron, *Feminism and Linguistic Theory* (New York: St. Martin's Press, 1985).

21. For an account of the declining significance of kinship as a social structural component of modern capitalist societies, see Linda J. Nicholson, *Gender and History: The Limits of Social Theory in the Age of the Family* (New York: Columbia University Press, 1986).

22. In fact, the main function of this broad usage seems to be ideological, for it is only by collapsing into a single category what is supposedly ahistorical and necessary and what is historical and contingent that "Lacanianism" could endow its claim about the inevitability of phallocentrism with a deceptive appearance of plausibility.

23. See "The Blind Spot in an Old Dream of Symmetry" in Luce Irigaray, *Speculum of the Other Woman,* trans. Gillian C. Gill (Ithaca: Cornell University Press, 1985). Here she shows how the use of a phallic standard to conceptualize sexual difference casts woman negatively as "lack."

24. For a brilliant critical discussion of this issue as it emerges in relation to the very different—feminist object-relations—version of psychoanalysis developed in the United States by Nancy Chodorow, see Spelman, *Inessential Woman.*

25. Jacqueline Rose, "Introduction—II," in *Feminine Sexuality: Jacques Lacan and the école freudienne.*

26. Even Lacanian feminists have been known on occasion to engage in this sort of movement-baiting. It seems to me that, in Jane Gallop's introductory chapter to *The Daughter's Seduction: Feminism and Psychoanalysis* (Ithaca: Cornell University Press, 1982), she comes perilously close to dismissing the politics of a feminist movement informed by ethical commitments as "imaginary."

27. I have focused here on conceptual as opposed to empirical issues, and I have not directly addressed the question, is "Lacanianism" true? Yet recent research on the development of subjectivity in infants and young children seems not to support its views. It now appears that even at the earliest stages children are not passive, blank slates on which symbolic structures are inscribed but, rather, active participants in the interactions that construct their experience. See, for example, Beatrice Beebe and Frank Lachman, "Mother-Infant Mutual Influence and Precursors of Psychic Structure," in *Frontiers in Self Psychology, Progress in Self Psychology*, ed. Arnold Goldberg (Hillsdale N.J.: Analytic Press, 1988), 3–25. I am grateful to Paul Mattick, Jr., for alerting me to this work.

28. Kristeva, "The System and the Speaking Subject."

29. "Renovation" and "renewal" are standard English translations of Kristeva's term, "renouvellement." Yet they lack some of the force of the French. Perhaps this explains why readers have not always noticed the change-making aspect of her account of transgression, why they have instead tended to treat it as pure negation with no positive consequences. For an example of this interpretation, see Judith Butler, "The Body Politics of Julia Kristeva," in *Revaluing French Feminism*, ed. Nancy Fraser and Sandra Bartky (Bloomington: Indiana University Press, 1991).

30. This tendency fades in her later writings, where it is replaced by an equally one-sided, undiscriminating, neoconservative emphasis on the "totalitarian" dangers lurking in every attempt at uncontrolled innovation.

31. Butler, "The Body Politics of Julia Kristeva."

32. For an example, see Julia Kristeva, *Powers of Horror: An Essay on Abjection,* trans. Leon S. Roudiez (New York: Columbia University Press, 1982).

33. See Julia Kristeva, "Stabat Mater," in *The Kristeva Reader,* ed. Toril Moi (New York: Columbia University Press, 1986); and "Motherhood According to Giovanni Bellini" in Julia Kristeva, *Desire in Language: A Semiotic Approach to Art and Literature,* ed. Leon S. Roudiez, trans. Thomas Gora, Alice Jardine, and Leon S. Roudiez (New York: Columbia University Press, 1980).

34. For a brilliant critical discussion of Kristeva's philosophy of language, one to which the present account is much indebted, see Andrea Nye, "Woman Clothed with the Sun," *Signs* 12, no. 4 (1987): 664–86.

35. Butler makes this point in "The Body Politics of Julia Kristeva."

36. Reprinted in *The Kristeva Reader,* ed. Toril Moi (New York: Columbia University Press, 1986).

37. I take the terms "humanist feminism" and "gynocentric feminism" from Iris Young, "Humanism, Gynocentrism and Feminist Politics," in Young, *Throwing Like a Girl and Other Essays in Feminist Philosophy and Social Theory* (Bloomington: Indiana University Press, 1990). I take the term "nominalist feminism" from Linda Alcoff, "Cultural Feminism versus Poststructuralism: The Identity Crisis in Feminist Theory," *Signs* 13, no. 3 (spring 1988): 405–36.

38. For the terms "underfeminization" and "overfeminization," see Riley, *"Am I That Name?"* For a useful discussion of Kristeva's neoliberal equation of collective liberation

movements with "totalitarianism," see Ann Rosalind Jones, "Julia Kristeva on Femininity: The Limits of a Semiotic Politics," *Feminist Review* 18 (1984): 56–73.

39. This point builds on work that Linda Nicholson and I did jointly and that she is continuing. See our "Social Criticism without Philosophy: An Encounter between Feminism and Postmodernism," in *Feminism/Postmodernism,* ed. Nicholson (New York: Routledge, 1993).

40. I borrow this line from Toril Moi, who uttered it in another context in her talk at the conference "Convergence in Crisis: Narratives of the History of Theory," Duke University, 24–27 September 1987.

PART III

FEMINIST INTERVENTIONS

7

Multiculturalism, Antiessentialism, and Radical Democracy

A Genealogy of the Current Impasse in Feminist Theory

"Democracy" is today an intensely contested word that means different things to different people, even as everyone claims to be for it. Should we take it to mean free-market capitalism plus multiparty elections, as many former Cold Warriors now insist? Or should we understand democracy in the stronger sense of self-rule? And if so, does that mean that every distinct nationality should have its own sovereign state in an "ethnically cleansed" territory? Or does it rather mean a process of communication across differences, where citizens participate together in discussion and decision making to determine collectively the conditions of their lives? And in that case, finally, what is required to ensure that *all* can participate *as peers*? Does democracy require social equality? The recognition of difference? The absence of systemic dominance and subordination?[1]

"Radical democracy" must be distinguished from rival conceptions of democracy by a distinctive set of answers to these questions. What, then, might its distinctive answers be? I assume that to be a radical democrat today is to appreciate—and to seek to eliminate—two different kinds of impediments to democratic participation. One such impediment is social inequality; the other is the misrecognition of difference. Radical democracy, on this interpretation, is the view that democracy today requires both economic redistribution and multicultural recognition.

This, however, is only the outline of an answer. To try to flesh it out is to become immediately embroiled in difficult questions about the relation between equality and difference. These questions are variously debated today with respect to gender, sexuality, nationality, ethnicity, and "race." What are the differences that make a difference for democracy? Which differences merit public recognition and/or political representation? Which differences, in contrast, should be considered irrelevant to political life and treated instead as private matters? Which kinds of differences, finally, should a democratic society seek to promote? And which, on the contrary, should it aim to abolish?

Radical democrats, like everyone else, cannot avoid confronting these questions. But to answer them is no simple matter. Current U.S. discussions are at an impasse, I think, impeded by some unfortunate tendencies. One is the tendency to focus one-sidedly on cultural politics to the neglect of political economy. This is the thrust of current arguments over identity politics, which rage across the whole spectrum of "new social movements." These arguments pit antiessentialists, committed to deconstructing group identities, against multiculturalists, eager to recognize and revalue group differences. The issue at bottom is the politics of recognition: *Which* politics of recognition best serves the victims of misrecognition? Revaluation of difference or deconstruction of identity?

The argument in this form is unresolvable. It remains on the terrain of identity politics, where the misrecognition of difference is constructed as a "cultural" problem and dissociated from political economy. In fact, injustices of recognition are thoroughly imbricated with injustices of distribution. They cannot be adequately addressed in isolation from the latter. Radical democrats will never succeed in untying the gordian knots of identity and difference until we leave the terrain of identity politics. This means resituating cultural politics in relation to social politics and linking demands for recognition with demands for redistribution.

This, at any rate, is the thesis I shall argue in this chapter. I shall approach it somewhat indirectly, however. I shall reconstruct the history of recent U.S. feminist debates about difference in order to show how and where our present difficulties arise. Where possible, I shall also suggest ways of getting around them.

This approach requires a clarification. Despite the explicit focus on feminist debates, my interest here is not confined to feminism per se. Rather, I aim to use a reconstruction of feminist debates to illustrate a more general trajectory. Analogous lines of argument could be developed from other starting points, such as the debates concerning "race." They, too, I believe, would reveal a progressive tendency to divorce the cultural politics of recognition from the social politics of redistribution—to the detriment of efforts to develop a credible vision of radical democracy.

"Gender Difference": Equality or Difference?

Academic feminist theory in the United States is at an impasse today, perfectly mirroring the larger radical-democratic impasse. We are currently spinning our wheels arguing over identity politics, having succumbed to two unfortunate temptations. One is the tendency to adopt an undiscriminating form of antiessentialism, which treats all identities and differences as repressive fictions. The other is the mirror-opposite tendency to adopt an undiscriminating version of multiculturalism, which celebrates all identities and differences as worthy of recognition. In fact, both of these tendencies share a common root: they fail to connect the cultural politics of identity and difference to the social politics of justice and equality. Dissociating the politics of recognition from the politics of redistribution, both tendencies impede feminist efforts to develop a credible vision of radical democracy.

To see this, we need only reconstruct the history of debates about difference in second-wave U.S. feminism. These debates divide roughly into three phases. In the first phase, which lasted from the late 1960s through about the mid-1980s, the main focus was "gender difference." In the second phase, which ran roughly from the mid-1980s to the early 1990s, the main focus shifted to "differences among women." A third phase, which is currently under way, is focused on "multiple intersecting differences." Of course, to plot the trajectory of debate in this way is necessarily to simplify and abstract. But it also makes possible the sort of bird's-eye view that can reveal an otherwise hidden inner logic.

In the first phase, the principal antagonists were "equality feminists" and "difference feminists." And the main questions that divided them were, first, the nature and causes of gender injustice, and second, its appropriate remedy, hence, the meaning of gender equity. Let me describe the two sides schematically, ignoring many nuances and subtleties.

Equality feminists saw gender difference as an instrument and artifact of male dominance. What passes for such difference in a sexist society, they claimed, are either misogynist lies told to rationalize women's subordination (for example, we are said to be irrational and sentimental, *therefore* unfit for intellectual work but well suited to domesticity) or the socially constructed results of inequality (we have actually *become* anxious about math or fearful of success *because* we have been differently treated). In either case, to stress gender difference is to harm women. It is to reinforce our confinement to an inferior domestic role, hence to marginalize or exclude us from all those activities that promote true human self-realization, such as politics, employment, art, the life of the mind, and the exercise of legitimate authority. It is also to deprive us of our fair share of essential social goods, such as income, jobs, property, health, education, autonomy, respect, sexual pleasure, bodily integrity, and physical safety.

From the equality perspective, then, gender difference appeared to be inextricable from sexism. The political task was thus clear: the goal of feminism was to throw off the shackles of "difference" and establish equality, bringing women and men under a common measure. To be sure, liberal feminists, radical feminists, and socialist feminists might dispute how best to achieve this goal, but they nevertheless shared a common vision of gender equity, which involved minimizing gender difference.

This equality perspective dominated the U.S. women's movement for nearly a decade from the late 1960s. In the late 1970s, however, it was sharply challenged by the rise of a new, "difference" feminism, which has also been called "cultural feminism." Difference feminists rejected the equality view as androcentric and assimilationist. From their perspective, getting women included in traditionally male pursuits was an insufficiently radical goal because it uncritically adopted the biased masculinist view that only men's activities were truly human, thereby depreciating women's. Far from challenging sexism, then, equality feminism actually reproduced it—by devaluing femininity. What was needed instead was another sort of feminism, one that opposed the undervaluation of women's worth by recognizing gender difference and revaluing femininity.

Difference feminists accordingly proposed a new, positive, interpretation of gender difference. Women really did differ from men, they claimed, but such difference did not mean inferiority. Some insisted, on the contrary, that nurturing, peace-loving women were morally superior to competitive, militaristic men. Others preferred to drop all talk of inferiority and superiority, to recognize two different "voices" of equivalent value, and to demand a respectful hearing for woman's voice. In either case, they agreed that gender difference was real and deep, the most fundamental human difference. All women shared a common "gender identity" *as women*. All suffered a common harm when that identity was depreciated. All, therefore, were sisters under the skin. Feminists need only articulate the positive content of femininity in order to mobilize this latent solidarity. The way to do justice to women, in sum, was to *recognize,* not minimize, gender difference.

Here, then, were the stakes in the first difference debate within second-wave U.S. feminism. The movement stood poised between two conflicting views of gender difference, two alternative accounts of gender injustice, and two opposing visions of gender equity. The proponents of equality saw gender difference as the handmaiden of male domination. For them, the central injustices of sexism were women's marginalization and the maldistribution of social goods. And the key meaning of gender equity was equal participation and redistribution. Difference feminists, in contrast, saw gender difference as the cornerstone of women's identity. For them, accordingly, androcentrism was sexism's chief harm. And the centerpiece of gender equity was the recognition and revaluation of femininity.

This debate raged for several years on both the cultural and the political planes, but it was never definitively settled. Part of the difficulty was that each side had convincing criticisms of the other. The proponents of difference successfully showed that the egalitarians presupposed "the male as norm," a standard that disadvantaged women. The egalitarians argued just as cogently, however, that the difference side relied on stereotypical notions of femininity, which reinforced existing gender hierarchies. Neither side, therefore, had a fully defensible position. Yet each had an important insight. The egalitarian insight was that no adequate account of sexism could overlook women's social marginalization and unequal share of resources; hence, no persuasive vision of gender equity could omit the goals of equal participation and fair distribution. The difference insight was that no adequate account of sexism could overlook the problem of androcentrism in the construction of cultural standards of value; hence, no persuasive vision of gender equity could omit the need to overcome such androcentrism.

What, then, was the moral to be drawn? Henceforth, feminists would have to find a way to accommodate both of these insights. We would need to develop a perspective that opposed social inequality and cultural androcentrism simultaneously. Such a perspective would effectively combine a politics of redistribution with a politics of recognition, but not as two separate matters. Rather, it would have to integrate social demands with cultural demands, seeking to change culture and political economy in tandem.

"Differences among Women"

As it turned out, U.S. feminists did not resolve the equality/difference impasse by developing such a new perspective. Rather, by the mid-1980s, the entire framework of the debate had been altered so radically that the problem could no longer be posed in those terms. In the interim, leading feminist currents had come to reject the view that gender difference could be fruitfully discussed in isolation from other axes of difference, especially "race," ethnicity, sexuality, and class. And so the equality/difference debate was displaced. The focus on "gender difference" gave way to a focus on "differences among women," inaugurating a new phase of feminist debate.

This shift in focus was largely the work of lesbians and feminists of color. For many years they had protested forms of feminism that failed to illuminate their lives and address their problems. African-American women, for example, had invoked their history of slavery and resistance, waged work, and community activism to contest assumptions of universal female dependence on men and confinement to domesticity. Meanwhile, Latina, Jewish, Native-American, and Asian-American feminists had protested the implicit reference to white Anglo women in many mainstream feminist texts. Lesbians, finally, had unmasked assumptions of normative heterosexuality in the classic feminist accounts of mothering, sexuality, gender identity, and reproduction.

Mainstream U.S. feminism, all these voices insisted, was *not* a feminism for all women. It privileged the standpoint of the white Anglo heterosexual middle-class women who had so far dominated the movement. It falsely extrapolated from their experiences and conditions of life in ways that were inappropriate, even harmful, to other women. Thus, the very movement that claimed to liberate women ended up reproducing within its own ranks the racism and the heterosexism, the class hierarchies and the ethnic biases, that were endemic in U.S. society.

For many years, such voices had been largely confined to the margins of U.S. feminism. By the mid to late 1980s, however, they had moved, in the prophetic words of bell hooks, "from [the] margins to [the] center" of discussion.[2] Many erstwhile doubters were now willing to concede the point: the movement had been so exclusively preoccupied with gender difference that it had neglected the differences among women.

"Difference feminism" was the most obvious culprit. Its purportedly universal accounts of feminine gender identity and women's different voice could now be seen for what they actually were: culturally specific stereotypical idealizations of middle-class, heterosexual, white-European femininity, idealizations that had as much to do with hierarchies of class, "race," ethnicity, and sexuality as with hierarchies of gender. And yet, equality feminism was culpable, too. Assuming that all women were subordinated to all men in the same way and to the same degree, it had falsely universalized the specific situation of white, middle-class heterosexual women and concealed their implication in hierarchies of class, "race," ethnicity, and sexuality. Thus, neither side of the old equality/difference debate could withstand the critique. Although one side had stressed male/female similarity and the other side male/female difference, the end result was effectively the same: both had obscured important differences among women. In both cases, consequently, the attempt to build sisterhood backfired. False universalizations of *some* women's situation and *some* women's identity ideals had not promoted feminist solidarity. They led, on the contrary, to anger and schism, to hurt and mistrust.

But the difficulty went deeper still. In repressing differences among women, the mainstream movement had also repressed axes of subordination other than gender—once again, class, "race," ethnicity, nationality, and sexuality.[3] It therefore repressed what Deborah King has called "multiple jeopardy," the multiple forms of subordination faced by lesbians, women of color, and/or poor and working-class women.[4] Consequently, the mainstream movement failed to grasp the multiple affiliations of such women, their loyalty to more than one social movement. For example, many women of color and/or lesbians remain committed to fighting *alongside* men of color and/or gays in antiracist and/or gay-liberation movements, while simultaneously fighting *against* the sexism of their male comrades. But a feminism focused only on gender difference failed fully to grasp this situation. By suppressing axes of subordination other than gender, it also suppressed differences *among men.* And that created a double bind for women who are subject to multiple jeopardy: it effectively pressured them to choose between loyalty to their gender and loyalty to their "race," class, and/or sexuality. The either/or imperative denied their reality of multiple jeopardy, multiple affiliation, and multiple identity.

The exclusive focus on "gender difference" proved increasingly counterproductive as "identity politics" proliferated in the 1980s. Now the political scene was crowded with "new social movements," each politicizing a different "difference." Gays and lesbians were mobilized around sexual difference in order to fight against heterosexism; movements of African Americans, Native Americans, and other peoples of color had politicized "racial" difference in order to contest racial subordination; and a wide range of ethnically and religiously identified groups were struggling for recognition of cultural differences within an increasingly multiethnic nation.[5] Thus, feminists found themselves sharing political space with all these movements, but not in the sense of a parallel, side-by-side coexistence. Rather, all the various movements cut across one another. And each was going through an analogous process of discovering the other differences within itself.

In this context, the need for a reorientation was clear. Only if feminists were willing to abandon an exclusive focus on gender difference could we cease interpreting other difference claims as threats to the unity of women. Only if we were willing to grapple with axes of subordination other than gender could we theorize our relation to the other political struggles surrounding us. Only by abandoning the view of ourselves as a self-contained social movement, finally, could we fully grasp the true situation: that gender struggles were occurring on the broader terrain of civil society, where multiple axes of difference were being contested simultaneously and where multiple social movements were intersecting.

"Multiple Intersecting Differences": Antiessentialism or Multiculturalism?

By around 1990, therefore, the decisive U.S. feminist debate was poised to shift from "differences among women" to "multiple intersecting differences." The result should have been an enormous gain. What had appeared at first to be a turning inward (instead of focusing on our relation to men, we would focus on the relations among ourselves) seemed instead to invite a turning outward (instead of focusing on gender alone, we would focus on its relation to other crosscutting axes of difference and subordination). In this way, the whole range of politicized differences would become grist for the feminist mill. Not only gender but also "race," ethnicity, nationality, sexuality, and class would now require feminist theorization.[6] And all struggles against subordination would now need somehow to be linked up with feminism.

To make such a shift should not in principle have required scuttling the project of combining a politics of redistribution with a politics of recognition. Indeed, the discussions of "differences among women" never explicitly challenged that project. Nor did anything in the logic of attending to such differences entail the need to abandon efforts to integrate a cultural politics of identity and difference with a social politics of justice and equality. But to make such a shift did complicate that project. Henceforth, it would be necessary to resituate the task of integrating redistribution and recognition in a new, more complex political field. Cultural demands would have to interimbricate with social demands across the entire spectrum of crosscutting axes of domination.

Once again, however, U.S. feminists have not (yet) developed such an approach. On the contrary, as we enter the third and current phase of debate about difference, the politics of recognition is becoming increasingly dissociated from the politics of redistribution, and the former is increasingly eclipsing the latter. The result is a truncated problematic, which is impeding efforts to develop a credible vision of radical democracy.

In the current phase, the feminist discussion joins the more general discussion of radical democracy. Today, "radical democracy" is being proposed as a rubric for mediating various struggles over "multiple intersecting differences," hence for linking various social movements.[7] As such, it appeals on at least two planes. On the one hand, it seems to correct the balkanizing tendencies of identity politics and to promote broader political alliances. On the other hand, and at the same time, it seems to offer a "postsocialist" vision of the good society and to contest hegemonic conservative understandings of democracy. It is no wonder, then, that feminists seeking to develop a viable theoretical and political outlook oriented to "multiple intersecting differences" are increasingly turning to radical democracy.[8]

Yet the meaning of "radical democracy" remains underdeveloped. Functioning chiefly as a counterweight to identity politics, it remains largely confined to the cultural-political plane. Thus, current discussion tends to bracket political economy. It is so far unclear, therefore, how precisely the project of a radical democracy can connect a cultural politics of recognition to a social politics of redistribution. Unless it manages to connect them, however, "radical democracy" will not be genuinely democratic. It will not succeed in forging democratic mediations among "multiple intersecting differences."

The difficulties become clear when we examine the current debates that form the context for discussions of radical democracy. These debates focus chiefly on group identity and cultural difference, and they divide into two related streams. One of the streams can be designated "antiessentialism"; it cultivates a skeptical attitude toward identity and difference, which it reconceptualizes as discursive constructions. A second stream can be designated "multiculturalism"; it cultivates a positive view of group differences and group identities, which it seeks to revalue and promote. Although both streams of discussion are in some respects insightful, neither is entirely satisfactory. Meanwhile, the conjoining of the two in current debates about radical democracy results in a one-sided, truncated, "culturalist" problematic.

One problem is that both discussions rely on one-sided views of identity and difference. The antiessentialist view is skeptical and negative; it sees all identities as inherently repressive and all differences as inherently exclusionary. The multiculturalist view, in contrast, is celebratory and positive; it sees all identities as deserving of recognition and all differences as meriting affirmation. Thus, neither approach is sufficiently differentiated. Neither provides a basis for distinguishing democratic from antidemocratic identity claims, just from unjust differences. Neither, as a result, can sustain a viable politics or a credible vision of radical democracy.

A second problem, which undergirds the first, is that both current approaches have lost the dual focus on redistribution and recognition. Both antiessentialism and multiculturalism are concerned virtually exclusively with injustices of cultural misrecognition. Both neglect injustices of political-economic maldistribution. Neither, therefore, provides an adequate political framework.

Let me briefly sketch the main contours of each approach, focusing on its understanding of difference. I shall try to show that the weaknesses in both cases can be traced to a common source, namely, a failure to appreciate that cultural differences can be freely elaborated and democratically mediated only on the basis of social equality.

I begin with antiessentialism—as it is debated within feminist circles. Proponents of antiessentialism propose to avoid the errors of difference feminism by radically reconceiving identity and difference. They begin from the assumption that the differences among women go "all the way down"; hence, there is no way of being a woman that is not already "raced," sexed, and classed; therefore, gender has no invariant essence or core. Yet they also reject approaches that would divide women (and men) into ever smaller subgroups, each with its own distinct identity and its own claim for recognition.[9] In contrast to such approaches, antiessentialists appreciate that neither differences nor identities are simply given as a matter of fact in virtue of a group's "objective" character or social position. Rather, they are discursively constructed. Differences and identities are performatively created through cultural processes of being claimed and elaborated; they do not preexist such processes. They could always in principle be otherwise. Thus, existing differences and identities can be performatively undone or altered by being dis-claimed or differently elaborated.[10]

What follows politically from this view? Clearly, antiessentialism rejects any politics—feminist or otherwise—that essentializes identity and difference. But some of its exponents go further still. Stressing that all collective identities are "fictional" because constructed, they regard all with a skeptical eye. From this perspective, politicized identity terms such as *women* must always necessarily be exclusionary; they can be constructed only through the repression of difference. Any collective identification, therefore, will be subject to critique from the standpoint of what it excludes. Feminist identity is no exception. Thus, the black-feminist critique of white bias in feminism is not only a protest against racism; it also protests a logical necessity. Any attempt to claim a black feminist identity, therefore, could only repeat the exclusionary gesture.

I shall henceforth call this "the deconstructive version of antiessentialism." In this version, the only "innocent" political practice is negative and deconstructive. It involves unmasking the repressive and exclusionary operation that enables every construction of identity. Thus, it is not the job of feminism, in this view, to construct a feminine identity or a collective feminist subject; it is, rather, our task to deconstruct every construction of "women." Rather than take for granted the existence of gender difference and hence of "women," we should expose the processes by which gender binarism and, therefore, "women" are constructed. The political aim of feminism, then, is to destabilize gender difference and the gender identities that accompany it. A privileged strategy is dissidence and parody.[11] But beyond this, we should ally with other social movements with analogous deconstructive aims, for example, with critical "race" theorists committed to deconstructing black/white difference and with queer theorists working to deconstruct the homo/hetero difference but not, in contrast, with Afrocentrists seeking to consolidate black identity, nor with proponents of gay and lesbian identity.

What should we make of this discussion? In my view the outcome is mixed. On the one hand, antiessentialism makes a major advance by conceptualizing identities and differences as discursively constructed instead of as objectively given. But the politics of the deconstructive version are simplistic. By this, I do not mean only the obvious difficulty that sexism cannot be dismantled by an exclusively negative, deconstructive practice. I mean also the further difficulties that arise when deconstructive antiessentialists try the theoretical equivalent of pulling a rabbit out of a hat, when they try, that is, to deduce a normative politics of culture from an ontological conception of identity and difference. And I mean, finally, limitations linked to the failure to pursue the question of how to integrate an antiessentialist politics of recognition with an egalitarian politics of redistribution.

The difficulty can be put like this: Deconstructive antiessentialists appraise identity claims on ontological grounds alone. They do not ask, in contrast, how a given identity or difference is related to social structures of domination and to social relations of inequality. Nor do they ask what sort of political economy would be required to sustain nonexclusionary identities and antiessentialist understandings of difference. They risk succumbing, as a result, to a night in which all cows are gray: all identities threaten to become equally fictional, equally repressive, and equally exclusionary. But this is tantamount to surrendering any possibility of distinguishing emancipatory and oppressive identity claims, benign and pernicious differences. Thus, deconstructive antiessentialists evade the crucial political questions of the day: Which identity claims are rooted in the defense of social relations of inequality and domination? And which are rooted in a challenge to such relations? Which identity claims carry the potential to expand actually existing democracy? And which, in contrast, work against democratization? Which differences, finally, should a democratic society seek to foster, and which, on the contrary, should it aim to abolish?

Yet antiessentialism has no monopoly on these problems. They are shared, I contend, by the other major stream of U.S. discussion, the stream focused on "multiculturalism." Multiculturalism has become the rallying cry for a potential alliance of new social movements, all of whom seem to be struggling for the recognition of difference. This alliance potentially unites feminists, gays and lesbians, members of racialized groups and of disadvantaged ethnic groups in opposition to a common enemy: namely, a culturally imperialist form of public life that treats the straight, white-Anglo, middle-class male as the human norm, in relation to which everyone else appears deviant. The goal of the struggle is to create multicultural public forms, which recognize a plurality of different, equally valuable ways of being human. In such a society, today's dominant understanding of difference as deviance would give way to a positive appreciation of human diversity. All citizens would enjoy the same formal legal rights in virtue of their common humanity. But they would also be recognized for what differentiates them from one another, their cultural particularity.

This, at least, is the most common U.S. understanding of multiculturalism. It has dominated intense debates over education in the mainstream public sphere. Conservatives have attacked proponents of Women's Studies, African-American Studies, Gay-and-Lesbian Studies, and Ethnic Studies, charging that we have inappropriately politicized the curriculum by replacing Great Works selected for their enduring universal value with inferior texts chosen on ideological, affirmative-action grounds. Thus, the argument turns on the interpretation of "difference." Whereas defenders of traditional education persist in viewing difference negatively, as deviance from a single universal norm, multiculturalists view difference positively, as cultural variation and diversity, and demand its representation in educational curricula, as well as elsewhere in public life.

Feminists and radical democrats are understandably committed to defending some version of multiculturalism against the conservative attacks. But we should nevertheless reject the version I have just sketched, which I will

henceforth call "the pluralist version."[12] The pluralist version of multiculturalism is premised on a one-sided understanding of difference: difference is
viewed as intrinsically positive and inherently cultural. This perspective
accordingly celebrates difference uncritically while failing to interrogate its
relation to inequality. Like the American pluralist tradition from which it
descends, it proceeds—contrary to fact—as if U.S. society contained no
class divisions or other deep-seated structural injustices, as if its political
economy were basically just, as if its various constituent groups were socially
equal. Thus, it treats difference as pertaining exclusively to culture.[13] The
result is to divorce questions of difference from material inequality, power
differentials among groups, and systemic relations of dominance and subordination.

All this should ring warning bells for feminists who would be radical
democrats. We should recognize this view as a cousin of the old "difference
feminism." The latter's core elements are recycled here in a more general
form and extended to differences other than gender. Where difference feminism made cultural androcentrism the central injustice and revaluation of
femininity the chief remedy, pluralist multiculturalism substitutes the more
general injustice of cultural imperialism and the more general remedy of
revaluing all disrespected identities. But the structure of the thinking is the
same. And so are the structural weaknesses.

Like difference feminism, pluralist multiculturalism tends to substantialize
identities, treating them as given positivities instead of as constructed relations. It tends, consequently, to balkanize culture, setting groups apart from
one another, ignoring the ways they cut across one another, and inhibiting
cross-group interaction and identification. Losing sight of the fact that differences intersect, it regresses to a simple additive model of difference.

Like difference feminism, moreover, pluralist multiculturalism valorizes
existing group identities. It assumes that such identities are fine as they are,
only some need additional respect. But some existing group identities may
be importantly tied to existing social relations of domination, and they
might not survive the transformation of those relations. Moreover, some
group identities—or strands thereof—are incompatible with others. For
example, one cannot consistently affirm a white-supremacist identity and an
antiracist identity simultaneously; affirming some identities—or some
strands of some identities—requires transforming others. Thus, there is no
avoiding political judgments about better and worse identities and differences. These, however, pluralist multiculturalism cannot make.

Pluralist multiculturalism, finally, is the mirror image of deconstructive
antiessentialism. Whereas that approach threatened to delegitimate all iden-

tities and differences, this one seems to celebrate them all indiscriminately. Thus, its politics are equally one-sided. It, too, maintains an exclusive and one-sided focus on the cultural politics of recognition, while neglecting the social politics of redistribution. Consequently, it too evades the crucial political questions of the day: Which identity claims are rooted in the defense of social relations of inequality and domination? And which are rooted in a challenge to such relations? Which identity claims carry the potential to expand actually existing democracy? And which, in contrast, work against democratization? Which differences, finally, should a democratic society seek to foster, and which, on the contrary, should it aim to abolish?

Concluding Theses: Toward a Credible Vision of Radical Democracy

It is no accident that both deconstructive antiessentialism and pluralist multiculturalism fail in the same way, for the weaknesses of both share a common root: both fail to connect a cultural politics of identity and difference to a social politics of justice and equality. Both fail, that is, to link struggles for recognition to struggles for redistribution. Neither appreciates the crux of the connection: *cultural differences can be freely elaborated and democratically mediated only on the basis of social equality.*

In this sense, both approaches are victims of an unmastered history. With the wisdom of hindsight, we can now see that both are haunted by echoes of the old equality/difference debate. The failure to resolve that debate left both current discussions with a truncated problematic. Both antiessentialism and multiculturalism have sought to correct the deficiencies of difference feminism, but they remain on the latter's own terms. Both approaches restrict themselves to the plane of culture, which they treat in abstraction from social relations and social structures, including political economy. And so both try to elaborate a cultural politics of difference in abstraction from a social politics of equality. Put differently, both approaches repress the insights of equality feminism concerning the need for equal participation and fair distribution. As a result, both are left without the resources needed to make crucial political distinctions. Thus, neither can sustain a viable politics in a period of multiple, intersecting difference claims. And neither can model a credible vision of radical democracy.

What, finally, can we learn from this story? How can we use its lessons to develop a credible vision of radical democracy? And where should we go from here?

Let me conclude by proposing three theses.

First, there is no going back to the old equality/difference debate in the sense of an exclusive focus on any single axis of difference. The shift from "gender difference" to "differences among women" to "multiple intersecting differences" remains an unsurpassable gain, but this does not mean that we should simply forget the old debate. Rather, we now need to construct a new equality/difference debate, one oriented to multiple intersecting differences. We need, in other words, to reconnect the problematic of cultural difference with the problematic of social equality.

Second, there is no going back to essentialized understandings of identity and difference. The antiessentialist view of identities and differences as relationally constructed represents an unsurpassable gain, but this does not mean that we should pursue an exclusively deconstructive politics. Rather, we should develop an alternative version of antiessentialism, one that permits us to link an antiessentialist cultural politics of recognition with an egalitarian social politics of redistribution.

Third, there is no going back to the monocultural view that there is only one valuable way of being human. The multicultural view of a multiplicity of cultural forms represents an unsurpassable gain, but this does not mean that we should subscribe to the pluralist version of multiculturalism. Rather, we should develop an alternative version that permits us to make normative judgments about the value of different differences by interrogating their relation to inequality.

In sum, we must find a way to combine the struggle for an antiessentialist multiculturalism with the struggle for social equality. Only then will we be able to develop a credible model of radical democracy and a politics that is adequate to our time. A promising rallying cry for this project is "No recognition without redistribution."[14]

Notes

1. Research for this essay was supported by the Institut für die Wissenschaften vom Menschen, Vienna, and the Dean of the Graduate Faculty of the New School for Social Research. I am grateful for helpful comments from Cornelia Klinger and Eli Zaretsky.

2. bell hooks, *Feminist Theory: From Margin to Center* (Boston: South End Press, 1984).

3. An important exception was the socialist-feminist current of the late 1960s and the 1970s. Socialist-feminists had always insisted on relating gender divisions to class divisions and, to a lesser degree, to racial divisions, but with the decline of the New Left, their influence waned.

4. Deborah King, "Multiple Jeopardy, Multiple Consciousness," *Signs* 14, no. 1 (autumn 1988): 42–72.

5. The relative absence of nationalist struggles—the exceptions being some Native-American and Puerto-Rican currents—distinguishes U.S. identity politics from that in many other areas of the world.

6. The reverse is also true: gender must now be theorized from the perspective of these other differences.

7. See, for example, Ernesto Laclau and Chantal Mouffe, *Hegemony and Socialist Strategy* (London: Verso, 1985), and David Trend, ed., *Radical Democracy* (New York: Routledge, 1995).

8. See, for example, Judith Butler, *Bodies That Matter* (New York: Routledge, 1993), and the various contributors to Trend, *Radical Democracy.*

9. This seems to be the logic of many multicultural approaches to difference. It mars the otherwise very thoughtful discussion in Elizabeth V. Spelman, *Inessential Woman: Problems of Exclusion in Feminist Thought* (Boston: Beacon Press, 1988).

10. For an argument to this effect, see Judith Butler, *Gender Trouble: Feminism and the Subversion of Identity* (New York: Routledge, Chapman & Hall, 1990), which elaborates a performative theory of gender.

11. Ibid.

12. Not all versions of multiculturalism are "pluralist" in the sense I describe here. The pluralist version is an ideal-typical reconstruction of what I take to be the majority understanding of multiculturalism. It is also mainstream in the sense of being the version that is usually debated in mainstream public spheres. Other versions are discussed in Linda Nicholson, "To Be or Not to Be: Charles Taylor on The Politics of Recognition," *Constellations* 3, no. 1 (1996): 1–16, and in Michael Warner et al., "Critical Multiculturalism," *Critical Inquiry* 18, no. 3 (spring 1992): 530–56.

13. In so doing, pluralist multiculturalism construes difference on the standard U.S. model of ethnicity, in which an immigrant group preserves some identification with its "old country" cultural heritage, while integrating into U.S. society; since the ethnic group is thought not to occupy any distinctive structural position in the political economy, its difference is wholly cultural. Pluralist multiculturalism generalizes this ethnicity model to gender, sexuality, and "race," which the model does not in fact fit. For a critique of the ethnicity model, see Nicholson, "To Be or Not to Be."

14. For a first attempt to work out some of the implications of this project, see Fraser, "From Redistribution to Recognition?" chapter 1 in this volume.

8

Culture, Political Economy, and Difference

On Iris Young's Justice and the Politics of Difference

T he practical decoupling of the politics of recognition from the politics of redistribution in social life has a theoretical counterpart in intellectual life. In the life of the mind today, theorists of cultural politics pay little heed to the work of theorists of social politics, and the latter seem pleased to return the favor. Within the discipline of political philosophy, for example, theorists of distributive justice tend simply to ignore identity politics, apparently assuming that it represents false consciousness. And theorists of recognition tend likewise to ignore distribution, as if the problematic of cultural difference had nothing to do with that of social equality. Both camps, in sum, tend to evade the crucial questions of the day: What is the relationship between redistribution and recognition? Do they constitute two distinct conceptions of justice, belonging to two distinct theoretical paradigms? Or can both be accommodated within a single comprehensive theory? On the practical-political plane, moreover, do claims for recognition work against claims for redistribution? Or can both be pursued simultaneously without mutual interference?[1]

Iris Marion Young's 1990 book, *Justice and the Politics of Difference*, is virtually unique in inviting such questions.[2] Not that she herself poses them

189

in precisely these terms, to be sure. But Young's book is unusual—and significant—in that it aspires to be "bifocal." It seeks to explicate a theory of justice that encompasses claims of both redistribution and recognition, of both equality and difference, of both culture and political economy. On this ground alone it represents an important step forward in political theory.

Integrating recognition and redistribution in a single theory is no easy task, however. And Young's effort is not free of difficulties. In what follows, I shall examine the unresolved tensions between the cultural and political-economic dimensions of her framework. By identifying some ambiguities in several of her core conceptions, I shall argue that she unself-consciously mixes elements of the two paradigms, without however successfully integrating them. Because she has not thought through the relations between them, moreover, the two paradigms interfere with each other. The difficulties become especially serious, I contend, when Young seeks to defend a wholesale, undifferentiated and uncritical version of the politics of difference, for this version is at odds with her own professed commitment to the politics of redistribution.

My discussion proceeds in six parts. In the first section, I present the general contours of Young's "bifocal" concern with culture and political economy. Then, in the second, third, and fourth sections, I examine her conceptions of oppression, social group, and the "five faces of oppression," respectively. In the fifth section, I consider some real-world applications. I conclude in the sixth section by rejecting Young's wholesale endorsement of the politics of difference and by proposing a more differentiated alternative.

The Predominance of Recognition in a Bifocal Schema

Young herself does not use the terms 'recognition' and 'redistribution'. In fact, she claims to reject the sort of categorial dualism that would divide issues of justice in this way; she prefers an alternative fivefold classification of oppressions that purports to bypass the distinction between culture and political economy. Moreover, she explicitly criticizes what she calls the "distributive paradigm" of justice, and she supposes that her framework supersedes it.

Nevertheless, a bifocal interest in recognition and redistribution runs throughout *Justice and the Politics of Difference*. Young's account of oppression encompasses both injustices rooted in political economy, such as exploitation, and also injustices rooted in culture, such as "cultural imperialism." She thus follows contemporary "postsocialist" social-movement thought in giving considerable attention to culture. Yet she refuses to follow those extreme culturalists who would jettison altogether a focus on political economy. She insists, rather, on maintaining a "quasi-socialist" interest in that problematic as well. Indeed, it is this dual focus, this interest in both recognition and redistribution, that marks the innovation, and the promise, of her book.

Thus, Young's critique of "the distributive paradigm" should not be taken entirely at face value. It is, in my view, ambiguous and confused. In one aspect, it recapitulates the Marxian objection to approaches that focus exclusively on end-state patterns of allocation among individuals of tangible goods and positions, such as income and jobs or offices, while neglecting the underlying structural processes that produce them. Here the target of the critique is "the standpoint of distribution," as opposed to "the standpoint of production." In another aspect, however, Young recapitulates Amartya Sen's objection to approaches that focus on the distribution of commodities, as opposed to capabilities, thereby casting people as passive consumers instead of as agents.[3] Here the critique is aimed, not at distribution per se but at distribution of the wrong goods. In a third aspect, finally, Young's critique is aimed precisely at approaches, like Sen's, that treat nontangibles such as capabilities as foci and objects of distribution. Here the target is "reification."

No matter how we resolve these ambiguities, the important point is this: none of Young's objections to "the distributive paradigm" constitutes a persuasive argument against approaches that assess the justice of social arrangements in terms of how they distribute economic advantages and disadvantages. Although made from the "standpoint of distribution," such judgments need not entail that remedies for injustice be limited to such measures as equalizing income through redistributive taxation, which alter end-state patterns of allocation without disturbing the deep structural mechanisms that generate them.[4] Instead, they can provide good reasons for condemning the underlying "basic structure" of a society and for seeking its wholesale transformation. Young herself makes such judgments throughout her book. In so doing, she generally follows Sen in defining economic advantage and disadvantage in terms of capabilities. This, however, puts her squarely inside the distributive paradigm, broadly conceived, her qualms about reification notwithstanding. Nor could she escape that paradigm with respect to socioeconomic justice, finally, by opposing its extension to issues of cultural justice as well. Rather, as I shall show, she effectively adds a second, recognition problematic alongside it. Despite Young's explicit caveats, then, redistribution remains relevant to *Justice and the Politics of Difference*.

If redistribution represents an implicit presence in Young's book, then recognition constitutes its gravitational center. The recognition paradigm undeniably dominates the book, reflecting Young's identification with contemporary "new" social movements. Her stated aim is, in fact, to explicate, and defend, the theory of justice that is implicit in the political practice of movements such as feminism, gay and lesbian liberation, and antiracism. What is distinctive about these movements, as she presents them, is their view of the dominant culture as a locus of oppression, their rejection of the "ideal of assimilation," and their demand for the recognition of difference. Theorizing cultural recognition is therefore central to the project of Young's book.

Accordingly, Young mounts a challenge to theories that would exclude the domain of culture from the scope of justice. She makes a compelling case for the view that the dominant images, symbolic associations, and interpretations of a culture may unjustly depreciate and degrade some social groups; such cultural deprecation may even find expression in unconscious and preconscious reactions of bodily aversion in everyday life in ways that constitute serious harm. Culture, therefore, may be oppressive and unjust. No theory of justice can with justice ignore it.

Young also follows contemporary social movements in defending the "politics of difference." By this she means a "cultural revolution" in which social-group differences cease to be viewed as deviations from a single norm and are seen, rather, as cultural variations. Far from seeking to abolish such differences, then, Young aims to preserve and affirm them. This politics of difference is so central to her vision that it appears in the title of her book. It is her own distinctive and preferred version of the politics of recognition.

Despite her continuing interest in the politics of redistribution, then, Young's primary focus is the politics of recognition. She returns to the latter again and again, in virtually every chapter of the book. Her treatment of political economy, by contrast, is somewhat cursory. To be sure, at least three of the five forms of oppression that Young identifies are based in political economy, as we shall see; but that domain receives only one chapter-length elaboration—namely, in the chapter that criticizes "the myth of merit" and the division between task-defining and task-executing labor. Virtually every other chapter, in contrast, focuses primarily on cultural oppression and its remedy, the "politics of difference."

The dominance of the cultural paradigm over the political-economy paradigm is not merely a matter of length of treatment, however. It can also be read in some of Young's central categorial conceptions, as indeed can some unresolved tensions between the cultural and the political-economic dimensions of her framework.

Defining Oppression

Consider, first, Young's general definition of oppression as "the institutional constraint on self-development" (37). To be oppressed, in her view, is to be inhibited from "developing and exercising one's capacities and expressing one's experience" (37). More elaborately: "Oppression consists in systematic institutional processes which prevent some people from learning and using satisfying and expansive skills in socially recognized settings, or institutional processes which inhibit people's ability to play and communicate with others or to express their feelings and perspectives on social life in contexts where others can listen" (38).

There are many interesting and attractive features of this definition. The focus on capacities, for example, provides a welcome corrective to approaches that focus on resource distribution and implicitly posit people as inactive consumers. As I noted, this point recalls Amartya Sen's argument in *Commodities and Capabilities.*

For present purposes, however, I want to focus on something else: the two-pronged or bipartite character of the definition, the way in which it turns one of its two faces toward problems of culture and the other toward problems of political economy. The cultural face of the definition is captured in the clauses that concern constraints on "expressing one's experience," and processes that "inhibit people's ability to play and communicate with others or to express their feelings and perspectives on social life in contexts where others can listen." These clauses define oppression as inhibited expression and communication, rooted in a lack of cultural recognition. The political-economic face, in contrast, appears in the clauses about constraints on "developing and exercising one's capacities," and "systematic institutional processes which prevent some people from learning and using satisfying and expansive skills in socially recognized settings." These clauses define oppression as inhibited development of expansive skills, rooted in inequities in the division of labor.

Here, then, we see Young's dual focus on redistribution and recognition. She has sought to yoke culture and political economy together under a single, albeit bipartite definition of oppression. But the two sides are not adequately integrated with each other. And the definition contains an unresolved tension. The cultural dimension of the definition suggests that the capacities and abilities of oppressed people are essentially undamaged and intact; they suffer chiefly from misrecognition and undervaluation of their group-specific modes of cultural expression. The political-economy face, in contrast, suggests that certain skill-developing capacities and abilities of the oppressed are stunted or unrealized; the oppressed suffer from lack of opportunity to grow, learn, and enhance their skills in socially valued work. The cultural face of the definition, then, is a problem of undervaluation; the political-economic face, in contrast, is a problem of underdevelopment.

These two understandings of oppression are clearly in tension with each other. And the tension has significant political consequences. Arrangements that positively affirm the culture of oppressed groups constitute a plausible remedy for the cultural face of oppression. But they are far less plausible as a remedy for the political-economic face. To remedy that face of oppression, opportunities for self-development are required. Recognition of cultural difference, in sum, is no substitute for redistribution. In some cases, as we shall see, it could interfere with the latter.

Young appears not to notice this problem, but it surfaces repeatedly throughout her book. Not just oppression but also other key conceptions evince a bipartite structure. In them, too, as we shall see, cultural and political-economic elements are unself-consciously mixed but not successfully integrated with one another. Consequently, those conceptions, too, manifest theoretical tensions, which ultimately call into question Young's politics of difference.

Defining a Social Group

Consider, as another example, Young's conception of a social group. Groups, according to her, are the entities that suffer oppression. Individuals are oppressed by virtue of belonging to oppressed groups. Groups, moreover, are prior to individuals in that they are constitutive of individual identities. Groups in Young's sense, then, are neither aggregates, which are classified externally by an observer on the basis of objective similarities, nor voluntary associations, which individuals might join or not join, without any shifts in their identities. Rather, in Young's words: "a social group is a collective of persons differentiated from at least one other group by *cultural forms, practices, or way of life.* Members of a group have a specific affinity with one another *because of their similar experience or way of life,* which prompts them to associate with one another more than with those not identified with the group, or in a different way" (43, my emphasis). Elsewhere: "a social group is a collective of people who have affinity with one another *because of a set of practices or way of life.* They differentiate themselves from or are differentiated by at least one other group *according to these cultural forms*" (186, my emphasis).[5]

This conception, too, has many attractive features. For example, it neatly bypasses all the dilemmas associated with the standard Marxian distinction between the class-in-itself, defined by its objective structural position, and the class-for-itself, defined as the group's accurate subjective awareness of its objective position. Young's idea of an affinity group is reducible neither to an objective position nor to its reflection in consciousness. Rather, it is a lived sense of connection and differentiation.

How, then, does group differentiation arise? On what precisely is lived affinity based? In the passages quoted above, Young refers alternatively to "cultural forms," "ways of life," "similar experiences," and "set[s] of practices." These expressions, although somewhat vague, suggest that groups may be formed in a variety of different ways and on a multiplicity of different bases. Elsewhere in her book, in fact, Young elaborates several different scenarios. She notes that in some cases the affinities that constitute a social group arise simply as a result of shared cultural forms; an example is an ethnic group. In other cases, however, Young declares that group affinities can arise as a result of people's shared position in the division of labor; here, interestingly, she mentions gender as an example. In still other cases, finally, she suggests that group affinities may arise even in the absence of a shared culture or a shared position in the division of labor, as the result of a shared experience of hostility from the outside. This sort of group affinity is constituted when members of another group brand people as "Other" from without and proceed to oppress them; here Young cites the example of assimilated German Jews under Nazism.

Once again, we find that Young invokes a single conception—the social group—to cover both cultural and political-economic phenomena. Thus, this conception of a social group, too, is bipartite. It encompasses both those modes of collectivity, such as ethnicity, that are rooted in culture alone, and also those modes of collectivity, such as class, that are rooted in political economy. Young apparently sees no need to maintain such distinctions. For our purposes, however, it will be useful to avoid collapsing them, at least until we have had a chance to interrogate them.

Let me therefore introduce the following terminology: insofar as group affinity rests on shared cultural forms, I shall call the result "a culture-based group." Insofar as affinity rests on shared position in the division of labor, in contrast, I shall call the result "a political-economy-based group."[6] To repeat: the best familiar model for the culture-based group is the ethnic group. The best model for the political-economy-based group, in contrast, is class, especially the lived experience of social class theorized by Pierre Bourdieu as "class habitus," which is not limited to the classes recognized by Marxism.[7] In Young's framework, as we saw, this distinction disappears. Nevertheless, insofar as it encompasses both culture-based groups and political-economy-based groups, her conception of a social group is bipartite.

The bipartite character of Young's conception is simultaneously appealing and troubling. The appeal is the attraction of parsimony—the possibility that a single conception might encompass several disparate modes of collectivity. The difficulty is the possibility that it might not do justice to them all. It could be the case, for example, that important conceptual distinctions will be lost if we assimilate genders, "races," ethnic groups, sexualities, nationalities, and social classes to the single model of the affinity group. It could also be the case that one of these modes of collectivity will implicitly predominate, that its distinctive characteristics will be projected as characteristics of all social groups, and that other modes of collectivity will be distorted.

This does in fact happen in the course of Young's argument. She implicitly privileges the culture-based social group. As a result, the ethnic group surreptitiously becomes the paradigm not only for such collectivities as Jews, Irish Americans, and Italian Americans, where it is clearly apt, but also for such collectivities as gays and lesbians, women, African Americans, old people, people with disabilities, Native Americans, and working-class people, where it distorts.

This, too, has unfortunate political consequences. The politics of difference embraced by Young is a vision of emancipation especially suited to the situation of ethnic groups. Where the differences in question are those of ethnic cultures, it is prima facie plausible to consider that justice would be served by affirming them and thereby fostering cultural diversity. Where, in contrast, cultural differences are linked to differentially desirable locations in the political economy, a politics of difference may be misplaced. There justice may require precisely undermining group differentiation by, for example, restructuring the division of labor. In that case, redistribution could obviate the need for recognition.

It is true, of course, that modeling the character of oppressed groups on ethnicity fits the self-understanding of many of the new social movements Young supports. Thus, in settling on such a conception, she has succeeded in her professed aim of articulating the implicit theories of such groups. At the same time, however, to the extent that these movements may misunderstand themselves, she risks reproducing their self-misunderstandings. In noting this, I mean to signal a broader unease with a theoretical stance that could be too closely identified with its subjects to be critical of their self-understandings.

Equally troubling, there is something specifically, and even quintessentially, American about this way of understanding collectivities. Where else but in the United States does ethnicity so regularly eclipse class, nation, and party? This, of course, is not an indefeasible criticism of Young's concept of a social group, but it should give one pause about its applicability.

Five Faces of Oppression

I have already noted that Young disclaims the sort of categorial dualism I have been at pains to uncover in her book. Instead, she proposes a five-part classification of oppressions, which purports to scramble the distinction between culture and political economy. In this section, I examine her classificatory schema in order to show that it, too, is implicitly bipartite.

Young's classification of oppressions is perhaps the most interesting part of her book. With this classification she aims to circumvent painful and unproductive squabbles among oppressed groups as to whose oppression is "primary" and whose merely "secondary," whose, therefore, should be prioritized in political struggle and whose should be put on the back burner. Her inspired move is to reconceptualize what it means to theorize oppression. Instead of classifying oppressions in terms of who suffers them, and thus distinguishing such varieties as sexism, racism, ableism, and homophobia, she classifies different types of capacity inhibition. Only then will she ask, which groups suffer which kind(s) of oppression? This approach generates five distinct "faces" or forms of oppression, which may attach to groups singly or in various combinations or permutations. Each of the five is a sufficient condition for calling a group oppressed; none is a necessary condition.

Very briefly, the five forms of oppression identified by Young are:

1. *Exploitation,* defined as a structural relation whereby some people exercise their capacities under the control of others, according to the purposes and for the benefit of others, thereby systematically augmenting the power of the others. Exploitation in Young's view is not restricted to Marxian class relations; it also occurs in gender-specific and "race"-specific forms, in unpaid activities as well as in paid work.[8] The remedy for exploitation, according to Young, is radical restructuring of both political economy and culture.

2. *Marginalization,* defined as the condition of expulsion or exile from the system of labor and from useful participation in social life. Those who suffer marginalization, according to Young, include the racially marked underclass, the old, youth, the disabled, and single mothers and their children. The harm of this oppression includes not only material deprivation but also curtailment of citizenship rights and loss of opportunities for develop-

ing and exercising capacities in socially recognized ways. The remedy is
political-economic restructuring.

3. *Powerlessness,* defined as the condition of having power exercised over
one by others without oneself exercising power in turn; hence, having to
take orders but never oneself giving them; occupying a position in the division of labor that affords little opportunity to develop and exercise skills; and
being subject as a result to disrespectful treatment because of low occupational status; being, viewed, moreover, as lacking "respectability." This
oppression is, according to Young, suffered by nonprofessional workers. Its
remedy is radical restructuring of the division of labor to eliminate the division between task-defining and task-executing work.

4. *Cultural imperialism,* defined as the universalization and establishment
as the norm of the dominant group's experience and culture, which has the
result of rendering invisible the oppressed group's perspective, while simultaneously stereotyping that group as Other. Cultural imperialism is suffered
by women, African Americans, Native Americans, gays and lesbians, and
many other social groups in contemporary U.S. society. The best remedy for
this form of oppression, according to Young, is "the politics of difference,"
or attention to and affirmation of social group differences.

5. *Violence,* defined as susceptibility to systematic, albeit random, irrational, unconsciously motivated, and socially tolerated attacks on group
members' persons and property. Included here are physical attacks, to be
sure, but also harassment, intimidation, and ridicule. Violence, according to
Young, is closely related to cultural imperialism. Many groups that suffer the
latter also suffer the former, for example, gays and lesbians, Jews, African
Americans, Latinos, and women. The remedy for it, too, is cultural revolution: changes in the images, stereotypes, and the mundane gestures of
everyday life wherein oppressed people meet aversive reactions to their bodily presence.

Each of these five definitions of the forms of oppression is extremely interesting and deserves some individual attention. Here, however, I shall
consider only the general configuration. Young presents the five as distinct
faces of oppression, and she declines to explore possible connections among
them. We may note, however, that they fall broadly into two groups.
Exploitation, marginalization, and powerlessness are rooted in political
economy; they involve inhibition of the sort of self-development that Young
believes comes from meaningful, skill-enhancing, and socially valued work.
Cultural imperialism and violence, in contrast, are said by Young to be rooted in culture; they involve inhibition with respect to expression and
communication.

Here, then, is another bipartite schema. Some oppressions—exploitation, marginalization, and powerlessness—are rooted in political economy; others—cultural imperialism and violence—are rooted in culture. Again, Young herself does not make this distinction, but for my purposes it will be useful to develop it. Let me therefore introduce the following terminology: those instances of oppression that are rooted in political economy I shall call "economically rooted oppressions"; those that are rooted in culture, in contrast, I shall call "culturally rooted oppressions."

Each of these two broad categories of oppressions has its own proper broad category of remedy. The remedy for the culturally rooted oppressions of cultural imperialism and violence, according to Young, is cultural revolution. This means breaking down the idea of a single universal set of cultural norms and affirming cultural pluralism and difference. The principal remedy for the economically rooted oppressions, on the other hand, is radical restructuring of the division of labor. This includes eliminating the division between, for example, task-defining and task-executing work and providing socially valued, skill-enhancing activities for all.

Each of these remedies seems well suited to redress its respective oppressions—assuming that we follow Young's characterizations. But there is a potentially disabling tension between them. Whereas the remedy for the culturally rooted oppressions promotes group differentiation, the remedy for the economically rooted oppressions may undermine it. In some cases, consequently, the effects of the two remedies will be contradictory.

The problem becomes evident when we take a closer look at the oppressions of cultural imperialism and violence. As we saw, Young's definitions suggested that both of them were culturally rooted, hence, best remedied by the politics of difference. This, however, begs the question.

Consider, first, that Young's account of cultural imperialism contains an important ambiguity. She defines this oppression as the universalization of the particular culture of the dominant group, but she does not specify the grounds of that group's dominance. One possibility, of course, is that its dominance consists precisely in the fact that its culture is universalized; in that case, cultural imperialist oppression would be culturally rooted. Another possibility, however, is that the group's dominance arises in some other way, such as through political-economic superordination, which then provides the basis for the universalization of its culture; in that case, cultural imperialist oppression would be economically rooted.[9] In the first case, moreover, affirmation of cultural difference is a plausible remedy for oppression. In the second case, however, political-economic restructuring is necessary. In that case, consequently, the politics of difference could be counterproductive because it tends to preserve those group differences that redistribution could very well undermine. Recognition, in sum, could work against redistribution.

Analogous problems arise with respect to the oppression of violence. As we saw, violence in Young's definition is closely linked to cultural imperialism, for it is said to be fostered by cultural othering. It, too, is thus open to ambiguity. In some instances, oppressive violence may be linked to autonomous processes of cultural othering; violence against gays is an example. In other cases, however, violence may be fostered by forms of cultural othering that are themselves in turn rooted in political economy; the lynching of blacks in the Jim Crow South is an example. In still other cases, finally, oppressive violence may flow directly out of political-economic oppression, with little or no intermediary cultural othering; violence against (ethnically majoritarian) unionizing and striking workers is an example. It follows that oppressive violence is not always best remedied by recognizing cultural difference. While clearly appropriate in the case of violence against gays, the politics of difference would be counterproductive in the case of violence against strikers, where the primary need is redistribution. The case of lynching is more complicated, I think, because both recognition and redistribution are needed. Yet it is still true that they stand in tension with each other, and that the first can interfere with the second.

Applications

The preceding discussion suggests that the politics of difference may be less globally applicable than Young thinks. To illustrate the multiplicity of possibilities here, let us consider some real-world applications that concern different cases of oppressed groups.

First, take the case of working-class nonprofessionals. In Young's account, they suffer primarily the oppression of powerlessness, although presumably also that of exploitation. As a consequence of powerlessness, moreover, they are said to develop a class habitus or affinity that marks them as lacking "respectability." Here, then, is an oppressed group whose existence and whose oppression are both rooted in political economy. Is the politics of difference apposite?

In my view the answer is no. This is because it is unlikely that an affinity group based on the shared experience of powerlessness and nonrespectability would survive as a group in the event that its economic oppression were remedied by redistribution. Suppose, for example, that the division of labor between task-defining work and task-executing work were abolished. In that case, all jobs would encompass both sorts of work, and the class division between professionals and nonprofessionals would be abolished. Cultural affinities that differentiate professionals from nonprofessionals would probably wither away as well, since they appear to have no other basis of existence. Thus, a politics of redistribution that successfully combated the political-economic oppression of powerlessness would effectively destroy the group as a group, much as Marx held that the task of the proletariat was to abolish itself as a class. The politics of difference, in contrast, would not foster the overcoming of oppression in this case. On the contrary, by entrenching the very specificities that redistribution would eliminate, it would work against the overcoming of oppression.

Consider, second, the case of women as an oppressed group. It is doubtful to me that women really do constitute a group in Young's sense of a felt connection of shared experience or affinity. Yet gender is unquestionably a structural principle of the division of labor, and as such it disadvantages women as an aggregate. Let us consider, therefore, the effects of a restructured division of labor on women as an oppressed group. Let us assume, further, that a long-term feminist goal is to subvert the existing gender division of labor and not merely to elevate the standing of women within it, hence to effect a radical redistribution. Let us ask, therefore, if the gender division of labor were effectively abolished, would gender-distinct cultural affinities survive? And if not, is the politics of difference an appropriate remedy for the oppression of women?

This case seems less clear-cut than the previous one. Gender affinities, if indeed they exist, could have additional bases beyond their basis in the division of labor, for example, in socialization, in culture, even in bodily experiences, such as menstruation. Thus, even a successful politics of redistribution might not abolish women as a group. They could still be culturally constructed as different from men and be depreciated and oppressed on that basis. Thus, a politics of difference could be in order here. This raises a further dilemma, however. The struggle to remedy women's cultural oppression by affirming women's "difference" on the model of ethnicity might militate against the struggle to abolish the gender division of labor, which entails decreasing the social salience of gender. The first, after all, calls attention to and exaggerates, if it does not performatively create, gender difference. The second, in contrast, would minimize such difference, if not abolish it altogether.

Consider, finally, the case of African Americans. This case seems different yet again. There is little reason to think that abolishing the racial division of labor would entail the disappearance of the affinity group, since that group has an independent cultural basis. A more likely result would be the transformation of a subordinate racialized caste into an ethnic group. And this would be historically new, since African Americans, like Native Americans, have never been allowed to be just another ethnic group.

What these examples show, I think, is that disadvantaged social collectivities differ from one another importantly—not only in the kinds of disadvantages they experience, as Young maintains, but also in the bases of their differentiation and in the roots of their oppression. In some cases, political-economic restructuring seems certain to entail group dedifferentiation, while in others it clearly does not. In still other cases, by contrast, the implications are harder to predict.

If this is right, then the politics of difference is not globally applicable. In some cases, such as that of nonprofessional workers, it is simply askew of the nature of the group and its oppression. In other cases, such as gays and lesbians, in contrast, the politics of difference is absolutely crucial for remedying oppression. The hardest cases, of course, are those, such as gender and "race," in which both redistribution and recognition are required to overcome a complex of oppression that is multiple and multiply rooted. The difficulty here stems from the real tensions and interferences that arise when one tries both to affirm and to abolish difference simultaneously. A glib and global endorsement of the politics of difference will not help us solve this problem. For that, we need to face the problem squarely and to develop a *critical* theory of recognition.

Toward a Differentiated Politics of Difference and a Critical Theory of Recognition

We have seen that the "politics of difference" is less globally applicable than Young thinks. In the case of some groups and some oppressions, such a politics is clearly apposite. In the case of others, however, such a politics may be counterproductive, since their oppressions may be better combated precisely by undermining the conditions of existence that differentiate the group as a group. Classes, subordinated sexualities, genders, subordinate racialized castes, and ethnic groups represent conceptually distinct kinds of collectivities. Not all of them are suitable vehicles for the "politics of difference." (Nor of course are what we might call "bad groups," such as neo-Nazi skinheads, who are certainly oppressed in Young's terms, since they suffer marginalization and cultural imperialism, but whose "differences" we do not wish to affirm.)

One might accept what I have said so far and still defend the broader applicability of the politics of difference, however. One might maintain that even where this politics is not a tenable long-term goal, it is indispensable as a transitional strategy. One might claim, for example, that this politics promotes group solidarity and thus is a necessary condition for the possibility of any sort of political struggle whatsoever.

It is certainly true that one cannot stand up for oneself when one is crippled by self-hatred. But it does not follow that affirming one's difference in Young's sense is the only or best way of overcoming internalized self-hatred. Here the history of second-wave feminism is instructive. The radical conscious-raising of the late 1960s and early 1970s helped heal wounds, forge solidarity, and galvanize struggle. But it was a far cry from the sort of difference feminism that Young's model would privilege, which celebrates the traditional feminine. It is far from clear, moreover, that such difference feminism really does foster solidarity of the sort that coheres with the long-term goal of debinarizing gender. It seems rather to have led to fractiousness and hurt by affirming traits specific to white middle-class heterosexual women and by promoting repressive forms of gender "correctness."

Young counterposes her ideal of the politics of difference to what she calls "the assimilationist ideal," which, she contends, perpetuates oppression. But are these really the only two possibilities? My argument suggests they are not. To convey a sense of additional possibilities, let me conclude by contrasting four possible attitudes toward "difference."

1. The first is the one Young calls humanism: it is the view that the differences that members of oppressed groups evince are precisely the damages of oppression or the lies that rationalize them. Difference, in other words, is an artifact of oppression, as in the stunting of skills and capacities. The proper political response is to abolish it. This is essentially the position of Catharine MacKinnon with respect to gender difference.[10]

2. A second position on difference is sometimes called cultural nationalism. Within feminism, it has been called (by Young) gynocentrism; within antiracist politics, it has been called Afrocentrism. It is the view that the differences that members of oppressed groups evince are marks of their cultural superiority over their oppressors. These differences, like feminine nurturance or Native-American connection to the land, merit revaluation. But this does not mean that they should be celebrated as differences. On the contrary, they should universalized and extended to those who currently manifest inferior traits such as competitiveness and instrumentalism.

3. A third position views difference as cultural variation. This is the view that the differences manifested by members of different groups are neither

superiorities nor inferiorities but simply variations. They should neither be eliminated nor universalized but rather affirmed as differences; they are valuable as expressions of human diversity. This is Young's position.

4. A fourth position, which is the one I wish to commend, is that there are different kinds of differences. Some differences are of type 1 and should be eliminated; others are of type 2 and should be universalized; still others are of type 3 and should be enjoyed. This position implies that we can make judgments about which differences fall into which categories. It also implies that we can make normative judgments about the relative value of alternative norms, practices, and interpretations, judgments that could lead to conclusions of inferiority, superiority, and equivalent value. It militates against any politics of difference that is wholesale and undifferentiated. It entails a more differentiated politics of difference.

Such a differentiated view of difference represents an important contribution to a critical theory of recognition. It can help us to identify, and defend, only those versions of the politics of difference that coherently synergize with the politics of redistribution. This is the sort of approach we need in order to meet the challenges of our time. The task is to integrate the egalitarian ideals of the redistribution paradigm with whatever is genuinely emancipatory in the paradigm of recognition.

Notes

1. This chapter is a revised version of a paper presented at an "Author Meets Author" session at the Eastern Division meetings of the American Philosophical Association, Washington, D.C., 29 December 1992. I am grateful to the Committee on the Status of Women for organizing the session. I am also grateful to the Center for Urban Affairs and Policy Research at Northwestern University and to the Institut für die Wissenschaften vom Menschen in Vienna for research support. Finally, I thank Jane Mansbridge, Linda Nicholson, Erik Olin Wright, Eli Zaretsky, and the editors of the *Journal of Political Philosophy* for helpful comments on previous drafts.

2. Iris Marion Young, *Justice and the Politics of Difference* (Princeton: Princeton University Press, 1990). Citations to this volume will appear in the text as page numbers in parentheses.

3. See, for example, Amartya Sen, *Commodities and Capabilities* (Amsterdam: North-Holland, 1985).

4. In "From Redistribution to Recognition?" chapter 1 of this volume, I distinguish this sort of "affirmative" redistribution from "transformative" redistribution, which alters end-state distributive patterns precisely by altering the underlying generative framework. The important point here is that in rejecting the first in favor of the second, one is not rejecting redistribution *tout court;* rather, one is opting for a different kind of redistribution.

5. Young also gives another definition: "What makes a group a group is a social process of interaction and differentiation in which some people come to have a particular affinity

with one another. My affinity group in a given social situation comprises those *people with whom I feel most comfortable, who are more familiar.* Affinity names the manner of *sharing assumptions, affective bonding, and networking* that recognizably differentiates groups from one another . . ." (172, my emphasis).

6. Another possibility is affinity rooted simultaneously in culture and political economy. I consider this possibility in "From Redistribution to Recognition?" under the designation "bivalent collectivity." See chapter 1 of this volume.

7. For class habitus, see, for example, Pierre Bourdieu, *Distinction: A Critique of Pure Taste,* trans. Richard Nice (Cambridge: Harvard University Press, 1984).

8. For an account that uses game-theoretical tools to construct a conception of exploitation that applies to gender as well as class, see Alan Carling, *Social Division* (London: Verso, 1991).

9. There are other possibilities as well. A group's dominance could be rooted in numerical superiority, military superiority, and/or political domination, any of which could then give rise to its cultural dominance. For the sake of simplicity, I leave aside these other possibilities here.

10. Catharine MacKinnon, "Difference and Dominance," in *Feminism Unmodified: Discourses on Life and Law* (Cambridge: Harvard University Press, 1987).

9

False Antitheses

A Response to Seyla Benhabib and Judith Butler

O stensibly, Seyla Benhabib and Judith Butler have debated the relation-ship of feminism to postmodernism.[1] In the course of their exchange, however, a dispute about "modernity" versus "postmodernity" was trans-muted into a debate over the relative merits of Critical Theory and poststructuralism. Benhabib has defended a feminism rooted in Critical Theory and premised on concepts of autonomy, critique, and utopia. Butler's feminism, in contrast, rests on conceptions of subjectivity, identity, and human agency that derive from poststructuralist thought. Benhabib claims that postmodernist and poststructuralist views of subjectivity are incompatible with feminist politics; Butler, that views like Benhabib's imply an authoritarian foundationalism antithetical to the feminist project. To complicate matters still further, the two feminist theorists disagree about how to characterize their disagreement. For Benhabib, the issue that divides them is whether postmodernist proclamations of "the death of man," "the death of history," and "the death of metaphysics" can support a feminist politics. For Butler, the question is whether postmodernism really exists except in the paranoid fantasies of those seeking secure foundations for fem-inist politics in unproblematized metaphysical notions.

Evidently, Benhabib and Butler disagree not only about postmodernism but also about the relative merits of Critical Theory and poststructuralism. At first sight, their views seem irreconcilably opposed. Certainly, each believes her position excludes the other's. Thus, despite their manifold disagreements, there is one issue on which they agree. Both assume that the only way to resolve this dispute is to choose between Critical Theory and poststructuralism; there is no way that feminists can have both. But is that really the only possibility? The apparent necessity of opting for one approach and rejecting the other creates difficulties for theorists, like me, who think each has something important to offer to feminists.

I contend that feminists do not have to choose between Critical Theory and poststructuralism; instead, we might reconstruct each approach so as to reconcile it with the other. Thus, in what follows, I shall argue that the Benhabib-Butler exchange poses false antitheses and unnecessary polarizations. To make my case, I shall identify the respective strengths and weaknesses of each theorist's position, subjecting to special scrutiny those formulations that purport definitively to rule out the other. In particular, I shall indicate points at which each theorist has overreached herself by extrapolating to the point of implausibility an insight that is otherwise sound. In those cases, I shall propose more modest and defensible alternative formulations that avoid generating a false antithesis between Critical Theory and poststructuralism. My overall aim is to preserve the best elements of each paradigm, thereby helping to prepare the ground for their fruitful integration in feminist theorizing.

Let me begin with Seyla Benhabib's position, which evinces her usual clarity, comprehensiveness, and political commitment. Benhabib argues that feminists should not rush too quickly into an alliance with postmodernism despite certain apparent affinities. To be sure, postmodernists and feminists have both criticized traditional philosophical concepts of man, history, and metaphysics, but their criticisms do not necessarily converge. On the contrary, there are postmodernist versions of "the death of man," "the death of history," and "the death of metaphysics" that are not compatible with feminism. Thus, it is necessary to distinguish strong and weak versions of those theses. Feminists may, indeed should, accept the weak versions, but the strong versions must be decisively rejected.

According to Benhabib, a strong, postmodernist version of "the death of man" undermines the principles of autonomy and self-reflective subjectivity on which feminist politics depends. Likewise, a strong, postmodern interpretation of "the death of history" precludes the possibility of an emancipatory interest in the past, including the reconstruction of women's history. Finally, a strong version of "the death of metaphysics" undermines the possibility of a genuinely radical feminist critique that goes beyond merely immanent social criticism. Together these three strong, postmodernist theses are tantamount to a disabling "retreat from utopia." Feminists should therefore reject them in favor of weaker, nondisabling, versions of the death of man, the death of history, and the death of metaphysics.

Here Benhabib has elaborated a clarifying and fruitful argumentative strategy. By identifying three postmodernist theses and distinguishing strong and weak versions of each, she suggests a way to overcome problems that typically plague debates about postmodernism. Too often, such debates swirl confusedly around sweeping statements that conflate analytically distinct claims. Benhabib's approach of sorting out weaker and stronger versions of such claims enables more nuanced and fruitful discussion.

However, Benhabib does not herself use this approach to fullest advantage. In each case, she targets for criticism a postmodernist thesis that is too strong and too easily refutable. Then, having "refuted postmodernism," she claims to have established her critical-theoretical alternative. The latter claim is not persuasive, however, since she has not considered other, more defensible, versions of the theses. She overlooks medium-strength versions that do not pose a false antithesis between Critical Theory and poststructuralism, versions that are theoretically defensible and politically enabling.

Take, for example, her discussion of the death of history. This theme has been salient in poststructuralist criticisms of Marxism, some of which propose to throw out the baby of politically engaged historical reflection with the bathwater of a teleological philosophy of history.[2] In the face of such overreactions, Benhabib quite sensibly wants a view that allows for engaged historiography while ruling out essentialist, monocausal metanarratives that enshrine a single group as the subject of history. The thrust of her argument is to define a middle ground between modernist metanarratives and strong postmodernisms that would liquidate history altogether. But just when the argument demands some characterization of that middle ground, and of the sort of historiography that might occupy it, Benhabib's reasoning wavers. Instead of staking out the middle position that her own argument requires, she concludes by doubting that feminist historiography can be postmodern in *any* sense and still retain an interest in emancipation.

En route to this conclusion, Benhabib responds ambivalently to one approach that *does* stake out the middle position: the version of postmodernist feminism elaborated by Linda Nicholson and me in our essay "Social Criticism without Philosophy: An Encounter between Feminism and Postmodernism."[3] There Nicholson and I opposed interpretations of the death of history that would preclude "big" histories of male dominance. We distinguished metanarratives, which claim to provide foundational grounding in a philosophy of history, from large-scale empirical narratives, which are fallibilistic, revisable, and nonfoundational. This distinction permits feminists to reject metanarrative but still affirm historiography that discerns broad patterns of gender relations over long stretches of time.[4] It thereby helps secure one of the intellectual tools we need to understand a phenomenon as complex and pervasive as male dominance. Moreover, because our view allows both for large historical narrative and for smaller local narrative, it permits each to counteract the distorting tendencies of the other: local genealogizing narratives correct the tendency of large-scale accounts to congeal into "quasi metanarratives," while larger contextualizing accounts help prevent local narratives from devolving into simple demonstrations of "difference." Nicholson and I concluded that the result would be a postmodernist, pragmatic, fallibilistic mode of feminist theorizing that would retain social-critical, emancipatory force even as it eschewed traditional philosophical foundations. It would also be a mode of feminist theorizing that overcomes the false antithesis between Critical Theory and poststructuralism by integrating the best insights of each.

Benhabib's response to our position is curious. She endorses our defense of "big" historiography but rejects our model of postmodernist, pragmatic, fallibilistic feminist theorizing. She contends the latter precludes historiography guided by an emancipatory interest and permits only value-free social science. Unfortunately, she offers no argument in support of this contention. Does she mean to imply that only metanarrative can guarantee an emancipatory interest in history?[5] That view posits a false antithesis between antifoundationalism and emancipation. Not only is it at odds with Benhabib's own professed position, it is also belied by the many forms of engaged historiography now being successfully practiced by feminist scholars without any recourse to metanarrative. These include local histories that recover lost traditions of female agency or resistance; narratives that restore historicity to female-centered practices heretofore misapprehended as natural; histories that revalue previously derogated forms of women's culture; and genealogies that denaturalize gender-coded categories like "production" and "reproduction" or that reconstruct the hidden gender subtexts of concepts like "class" and the "state."[6] *Pace* Benhabib, all these genres of feminist historiography can be characterized as postmodern insofar as they refuse to legitimate themselves by recourse to the philosophy of history. Yet all are clearly guided by an interest in women's liberation, and all have emancipatory effects. Even their refusal to ground themselves by appeal to a foundational metanarrative is motivated by an interest in emancipation, moreover: the interest in avoiding the vanguardism associated with claims about the subject and telos of history.[7]

For these reasons Nicholson's and my view still seems to me a theoretically defensible and politically enabling version of the death of history. It is a version, moreover, that fulfills Benhabib's stated aim of avoiding the untenable extremes. Why then does she shrink from accepting it? Perhaps she fears that unless we can anchor the feminist interest in emancipation in a metanarrative, that interest will be arbitrary and unjustified. If that is Benhabib's real worry, then the question of the death of history collapses into the question of the death of metaphysics.

Benhabib's treatment of the death of metaphysics is marred by analogous difficulties. She begins, quite appropriately, by seeking the defensible middle ground. Thus, she rejects a strong version of the thesis, which would preclude warranted social critique altogether, while also eschewing the project of grounding critique in a foundationalist epistemology. She is poised therefore to articulate a weak version of the death of metaphysics. However, in the course of her argument, she swerves from that goal and posits a series of false antitheses.

The steps in her argument run like this. First, Benhabib endorses the view, shared by Rorty, Lyotard, Nicholson, and me, that there can be no justificatory metadiscourse that articulates the validity criteria for every first-order discourse. Next, she rejects the alternative of a naturalized epistemology that would merely describe existing practices of social criticism and surrender all normative claims. Somewhere between these extremes, she implies, is a third alternative, which would elaborate a view of *situated* social criticism and account for its possibility. Yet, Benhabib does not develop this alternative. Instead of pursuing the logic of her argument, she concludes that situated criticism is not good enough and that therefore there can be no social criticism without philosophy.[8]

Why does Benhabib believe that situated social criticism is not good enough? She offers two arguments to support her view, but neither is ultimately persuasive. The first is that situated criticism presupposes an "unjustified hermeneutical monism of meaning." It supposes, in other words, that cultural practices have a single, consistent, univocal meaning, which the critic can read off straightforwardly and unproblematically. But this is belied by the fact that traditions are contested, interpretations conflict, and social practices do not wear their meanings on their sleeves. It follows, claims Benhabib, that social criticism cannot consist merely in elucidating cultural norms that are given in social practices and traditions. There is no avoiding the *philosophical* task of clarifying and reconstructing the norms to which criticism appeals. Thus, according to Benhabib, social criticism without philosophy is impossible.

But is it really? Everything depends on what is meant by the terms "situated criticism" and "philosophy." The position Benhabib has criticized here is associated with Michael Walzer, whose *Spheres of Justice* does assume an "unjustified hermeneutical monism of meaning."[9] This position is indeed vulnerable to her criticism. What she overlooks is that Walzer's is not the only available view of situated criticism. Other versions appreciate the essential contestedness of culture and the need to clarify and reconstruct cultural norms. But they hold that practices of clarifying and reconstructing norms are themselves culturally and historically situated and cannot escape that condition. Thus, on this view, both criticism and its self-clarification are situated. Neither requires philosophy, moreover, if "philosophy" means discourse aspiring to the God's-eye view of foundationalist thought. As a matter of fact, the self-clarification of social criticism need not take the form of general conceptual reflection pursued in isolation from historical, legal, cultural, and sociological inquiry. It may also take the form of contextualizing historical narrative that genealogizes norms and thereby situates them more precisely.[10] It is worth noting, finally, that situated criticism does not preclude general claims or appeals to general norms; it requires only that these, too, be regarded as situated.[11] Thus, for a variety of reasons, Benhabib's first objection to situated criticism misses the mark.

Her second objection can be handled more briefly. She asserts that situated criticism cannot account for cases in which a culture or society is so bad that the social critic is driven into exile (either literally or metaphorically). In those cases, a more radical, external criticism is called for. This objection is not persuasive, however, since it is not a true counterexample. When the exiled critic leaves her country, she doesn't go without any cultural baggage; she goes, rather, as a culturally formed and culturally situated critic with a culturally formed set of normative standards. This was the situation of exiles from the Third Reich, arguably the worst society in human history. It was also, until recently, the situation of exiled members of the African National Congress, who left South Africa but took with them a complex culture of resistance comprising elements of Marxism, democratic theory, Christianity, and in many cases Xhosa tradition. Even the lone exile is a member of an "imagined community" and thus is also a situated critic.

I remain convinced, therefore, that social criticism without philosophy *is* possible, if we mean by "philosophy" what Linda Nicholson and I meant, namely, ahistorical, transcendental discourse claiming to articulate the criteria of validity for all other discourses. Nothing in this view precludes that the situated feminist critic is a radical critic, nor that she engages in critical self-clarification. Thus, what Benhabib considered mutually antithetical ideas are reconcilable after all.

In general, Benhabib has unnecessarily polarized the debate by positing a set of false antitheses: antifoundationalism versus political engagement, situated criticism versus critical self-reflection and radical opposition to one's society. Consequently, she has constructed a scenario in which she must reject poststructuralist thought altogether if she is to defend Critical Theory. However, since the wholesale rejection of poststructuralist ideas is neither theoretically defensible nor politically sound, the result is to provoke an equally one-sided poststructuralist riposte that jeopardizes the insights of Critical Theory.

This brings me to Judith Butler's position, which presses an unnecessarily polarizing argument from the opposite direction. Butler's is a provocative stance, which displays her characteristic genius for insubordination. Seeking to rebut the frequently bruited charge that postmodernism is politically disabling for feminism, she questions the existence of postmodernism as anything other than a fevered figment of foundationalist paranoia. Thus, she turns the tables on her antagonists by charging that they have constructed a straw person in order to whip up support for an ailing and untenable foundationalist project. She claims that far from undermining feminist commitments, poststructuralist views of subjectivity, identity, and human agency actually enable and promote them.

Like Benhabib, Butler seeks to disaggregate the analytically distinct claims that are often lumped together under the labels 'postmodernism' and 'poststructuralism'. In fact, it is precisely in order to counter the conflation of different views that she rejects the very word 'postmodernism'.[12] Thus, although she doesn't herself use these terms, she, too, can be read as distinguishing weak and strong versions of such claims in order to defend a poststructuralist feminism that escapes the critics' objections. Butler is especially interested in countering the charge, endorsed by Benhabib, that the poststructuralist view of the subject undermines feminism by rendering it inconceivable that anyone could criticize, resist, or act to change her or his society. Moreover, the objection continues, even if poststructuralist theory could account for individual agency, its relentless nominalism and antiessentialism would evacuate and delegitimate the category "women," thereby undermining the basis of female solidarity and of feminist movements.

In seeking to rebut these objections, Butler simultaneously provides a rejoinder to Benhabib's discussion of "the death of man." Benhabib distinguishes two interpretations of this thesis: a weak version, which holds that the subject is situated in relation to a social, cultural, and discursive context; and a strong version, which holds that the subject is merely another position in language. And she argues that only the weak version is compatible with feminism. Referring to Butler's performative account of gender in *Gender Trouble,* Benhabib asks: If we are no more than the sum total of gendered performances, how can we possibly rewrite the script?[13] Much of Butler's subsequent work can be read as an extended answer to this question.[14] She seeks to show how a subject that is "merely" a discursive position can indeed rewrite the script.

To clarify what is at stake in this dispute, I shall distinguish and treat separately two sorts of claims—ontological and normative—that are intermingled in Butler's argument. I begin with the ontological. Butler elaborates a poststructuralist ontology of the subject. She claims, *pace* Benhabib, that it is not sufficient to view the subject as *situated* vis-à-vis a setting or context that is external to it. Instead, we should see the subject as *constituted* in and through power/discourse formations. It follows that there exists no structure of subjectivity that is not always already an effect of a power/discourse matrix; there is no "ontologically intact reflexivity," no reflexivity that is not itself culturally constructed.

To be sure, Butler also believes that people have what I shall call "critical capacities"; we are not preprogrammed pawns but are able to engage in novel actions and to modify social conditions. Thus, I take her point here to be that critical capacities are culturally constructed. If that is right, then one way of focusing her dispute with Benhabib is around the question, Where do critical capacities come from? Butler suggests that critics of poststructuralism like Benhabib treat critical capacities as a priori ontological structures of subjectivity, "ontologically intact," as opposed to culturally constructed. Benhabib does not address this issue, and I am unsure whether she really holds that view.[15] In any case, there is no need for feminist theorists to hold it. On the contrary, it is perfectly possible to give an account of the cultural construction of critical capacities. Thus, nothing in principle precludes that subjects are *both* culturally constructed *and* capable of critique.

Suppose, therefore, we leave aside the question, Where do critical capacities come from in the past? Suppose we ask instead, What do they look like in the present? And how can we best characterize their future-directedness, the ways in which they point beyond their matrices of constitution? Here it is important to note that Butler's idiom privileges linguistic metaphors. She characterizes the subject as a "site of resignification" and a "permanent possibility of a certain resignifying process." This is her way of saying that the culturally constructed subject can rewrite the script. Thus, although the subject is itself the product of prior signifying processes, it is capable of *re*signification. Moreover, according to Butler, the subject as a site of resignification represents "power's own possibility of being reworked."

Let me make two observations about Butler's language. First, it is deeply antihumanist. What I have been referring to as "people's capacities" she describes as "power's own possibility" and as an impersonal "signifying process." This idiom is far enough removed from our everyday ways of talking and thinking about ourselves to require some justification. Why should we use such a self-distancing idiom? What are its theoretical advantages (and disadvantages)? What is its likely political impact? Why, above all, use an antihumanist rhetoric when one's aim is to explain how *agency* is possible given the constitution of subjects by power regimes? For this purpose, might not such a rhetoric be counterproductive?[16]

Second, in Butler's usage the term "resignification" carries a strong, if implicit, positive charge. In this respect, "resignification" functions in her discourse as "critique" has been functioning in mine. But in another respect the two terms differ sharply. "Critique" is logically connected to the concepts of warrant and justification, so its positive connotations are rooted in a claim to validity. This is not the case, however, with "resignification." Since Butler's term carries no implication of validity or warrant, its positive connotations are puzzling. Why is resignification good? Can't there be bad (oppressive, reactionary) resignifications? In opting for the epistemically neutral "resignification," as opposed to the epistemically positive "critique," Butler seems to valorize change for its own sake and thereby to disempower feminist judgment.

Moreover, Butler's ontology of the subject has some significant conceptual limitations. It does not theorize the relation of embodied individuals, with their relatively enduring dispositions (habitus), to the dispersed subject positions they successively occupy. Nor does it theorize intersubjectivity, the relations to one another of such individuals. Part of the difficulty here stems from Butler's tendency, when theorizing subjectivity, to shift too quickly and without adequate differentiation among various conceptual levels—from, for example, the structural-linguistic level (at which she invokes a quasi-Saussurean account of the function of the shifter "I") to the psychoanalytic level (at which she invokes a quasi-Kristevan account of the *intra*psychic process of individual, ontogenetic subject formation by means of abjection) to the institutional level (at which she invokes a quasi-Foucauldian account of the constitution of various different and distinct *subject-positions* at various different and distinct institutional sites) to the level of collective identifications (at which she invokes a quasi-Žižekian account of the phantasmatic and exclusionary character of politicized collective identities such as "women"). Failing to distinguish these levels, Butler never considers the important and difficult problem of how to theorize their relations to one another.[17]

This brings me to the second set of claims implicit in Butler's poststructuralist account of subjectivity—normative, as opposed to ontological, claims. Such claims arise, first, in relation to the social practices through which subjects are constituted. Here Butler follows Foucault in asserting that practices of subjectivation are also practices of subjection. Like him, she insists that subjects are constituted through exclusion; some people are authorized to speak authoritatively because others are silenced. Thus, in Butler's view, the constitution of a class of authorized subjects entails "the creation of a domain of deauthorized subjects, pre-subjects, figures of abjection, populations erased from view."[18]

But is it really the case that no one can become the subject of speech without others being silenced? Are there no counterexamples? Where such exclusions do exist, are they all bad? Are they all equally bad? Can we distinguish legitimate from illegitimate exclusions, better from worse practices of subjectivation? Is subject-authorization *inherently* a zero-sum game? Or does it become one only in oppressive societies? Can we overcome or at least ameliorate the asymmetries in current practices of subjectivation? Can we construct practices, institutions, and forms of life in which the empowerment of some does not entail the disempowerment of others? If not, what is the point of feminist struggle?[19]

Butler offers no help in thinking about these issues. Nor can she, I submit, so long as she fails to integrate critical-theoretical considerations into her poststructuralist Foucauldian framework. The latter's internal normative resources—reification of performativity is bad, dereification is good—are far too meager for feminist purposes. Revealingly, Butler's own applications of her approach presuppose strong normative commitments; a moral objection to "exclusion" runs consistently through *Bodies That Matter,* and antiracism informs her essay on the May 1992 acquittal of the police officers who assaulted Rodney King.[20] Like Foucault, however, Butler has explicitly renounced the moral-theoretical resources necessary to account for her own implicit normative judgments.[21] Recently, however, she has begun to appeal to "radical democracy."[22] Although so far this appeal remains largely rhetorical, I read it as an acknowledgment that feminist politics requires a more comprehensive moral-political vision than mere dereification of performativity.

In addition to her claims about the social practices of subjectivation, Butler also makes normative claims about the relative merits of different *theories* of subjectivity. She claims that some such theories are "politically insidious," whereas others are progressive or emancipatory. On the insidious side is the view of subjectivity as possessing an ontologically intact reflexivity that is not an effect of cultural processes of subjectivation. This view, according to Butler, is a "ruse of power" and an "instrument of cultural imperialism."

Is it really? There is no denying that foundationalist theories of subjectivity have often functioned as instruments of cultural imperialism. But is that due to conceptual necessity or historical contingency? In fact, there are cases where such theories have had emancipatory effects—witness the French Revolution and the appropriation of its foundationalist view of subjectivity by the Haitian "Black Jacobin" Toussaint l'Ouverture.[23] These examples show that it is not possible to deduce a single, univocal political valence from a theory of subjectivity. Such theories, too, are bits of cultural discourse whose meanings are subject to "resignification."[24]

How, then, should we resolve the Benhabib-Butler dispute over "the death of man"? I conclude that Butler is right in maintaining that a culturally constructed subject can also be a critical subject, but that the terms in which she formulates the point give rise to difficulties. Specifically, "resignification" is not an adequate substitute for "critique," since it surrenders the normative moment. Likewise, the view that subjectivation necessarily entails subjection precludes normative distinctions between better and worse subjectivating practices. Finally, the view that foundationalist theories of subjectivity are inherently oppressive is historically disconfirmed, and it is conceptually incompatible with a contextualist theory of meaning. The upshot, then, is that feminists need to develop an alternative conceptualization of the subject, one that integrates Butler's poststructuralist emphasis on construction with Benhabib's critical-theoretical stress on critique.

Let me turn briefly to Butler's discussion of the problem of "women" in feminist theory. She provides an account of the processes by which U.S. feminists' descriptions of women have functioned covertly as prescriptions, thereby provoking protest and factionalization within the movement. Butler maintains that these processes exemplify an inescapable logic. On the one hand, feminist movements cannot avoid making claims in the name of "women"; on the other, the category "women" that is constructed by means of those claims is necessarily subject to continual deconstruction. Butler concludes that feminists should view this dialectic not as a political disaster but as a political resource. We should prize the fact that 'women' "designates an undesignatable field of differences . . . that cannot be totalized or summarized by a descriptive identity category."[25]

What should we make of this discussion? For the most part I find Butler's account illuminating and apt. I am persuaded by her claim that the self-deconstructing tendencies within feminism are endemic to identity movements and cannot be eliminated by fiat. But I am not convinced that these tendencies should be treasured or prized. The idea of 'women' as the sign of an untotalizable field of differences is susceptible to two interpretations, one strong and indefensible, the other weak and defensible but hardly cause for celebration. The strong thesis is the one associated with "New French Feminist" theory, according to which 'woman' cannot be defined but signifies difference and nonidentity. This, of course, is a paradoxical claim, since to make the term 'woman' the sign of the undefinable is thereby precisely to define it. Moreover, this (anti)definition is mystifying. Why should 'woman' or 'women' be the sign of the nonidentical? Isn't everything Butler says about 'women' also true of 'men', 'workers', 'people of color', 'Chicanos', or any collective nomination? There is no privileged relation between the appellation 'women' and what is actually the general political problem of how to construct cultures of solidarity that are not homogenizing and repressive.[26]

A more defensible interpretation of Butler's suggestion would follow the Fraser-Nicholson view discussed earlier. According to this view, generalizing claims about "women" are inescapable but always subject to revision; they should be advanced nonfoundationally and fallibilistically. Further, the assumptions underlying such claims should be genealogized, framed by contextualizing narrative and rendered culturally and historically specific.[27]

This interpretation of Butler's claim is defensible, but it is hardly cause for celebration. Although a fallibilistic orientation is epistemically appropriate and politically useful, it cannot by itself solve the deeper underlying political problem. That problem, which is dissimulated in Butler's discussion, is whether there are not real conflicts of interest among women of different classes, ethnicities, nationalities, and sexual orientations, conflicts so intractable as not to be harmonizable, or even finessable, within feminist movements. Certainly, there *are* conflicts when interests are defined relative to present forms of social organization; an example is the clash in interests between professional white middle-class First World women and the Third World women of color they employ as domestic workers. In the face of this sort of conflict, uncritical, celebratory talk about women's "differences" is a mystification. The hard question feminist movements need to face is one Butler's proposal elides: Can "we" envision new social arrangements that would harmonize present conflicts? And if so, can "we" articulate "our" vision in terms that are sufficiently compelling to persuade other women— and men—to reinterpret their interests?

Butler's essay misses those questions, I think, because of the inadequacy of her conception of liberation. At the deepest level, she understands women's liberation as liberation *from* identity, since she views identity as inherently oppressive. It follows that deconstructive critique—critique that dereifies or unfreezes identity—is the privileged mode of feminist theorizing, whereas normative, reconstructive critique is normalizing and oppressive. But this view is far too one-sided to meet the full needs of a liberatory politics. Feminists *do* need to make normative judgments and to offer emancipatory alternatives. We are not for "anything goes." Moreover, it is arguable that the current proliferation of identity-dereifying, fungible, commodified images and significations constitutes as great a threat to women's liberation as do fixed, fundamentalist identities. In fact, dereifying processes and reifying processes are two sides of the same postfordist coin.[28] They demand a two-sided response. Feminists need both deconstruction *and* reconstruction, destabilization of meaning *and* projection of utopian hope.

I conclude that Butler, too, has generated a series of false antitheses: identity versus difference, subjectivation versus reciprocity, dereification versus normative critique, deconstruction versus reconstruction. She, too, has unnecessarily polarized the debate by insinuating that feminists face an either/or choice between Critical Theory and poststructuralism.

It is unfortunate that Benhabib and Butler should finally find common ground in subscribing to a false antithesis between Critical Theory and poststructuralism. By framing their debate in such dichotomous terms, they miss the chance to try another, more promising tack. I have suggested that instead of assuming we must choose between these two approaches, we might reformulate the claims of each so as to render them mutually compatible. Thus, instead of clinging to a series of mutually reinforcing false antitheses, we might conceive subjectivity as endowed with critical capacities *and* as culturally constructed. Similarly, we might view critique as simultaneously situated *and* amenable to self-reflection, as potentially radical *and* subject to warrants. Likewise, we might posit a relation to history that is at once antifoundationalist *and* politically engaged, while promoting a field of multiple historiographies that is both contextualized *and* provisionally totalizing. Finally, we might develop a view of collective identities as at once discursively constructed *and* complex, enabling of collective action *and* amenable to mystification, in need of deconstruction *and* reconstruction. In sum, we might try to develop new paradigms of feminist theorizing that integrate the insights of Critical Theory with the insights of poststructuralism. Such paradigms would yield important intellectual and political gains, while finally laying to rest the false antitheses of our current debates.

Notes

1. Seyla Benhabib, "Feminism and the Question of Postmodernism," and Judith Butler, "Contingent Foundations: Feminism and the Question of 'Postmodernism,'" both in Seyla Benhabib, Judith Butler, Drucilla Cornell, and Nancy Fraser, *Feminist Contentions: A Philosophical Exchange* (New York: Routledge, 1994).

2. The paradigm case of teleological Marxian metanarrative is Georg Lukacs's view of the proletariat as the subject-object of history in *History and Class Consciousness*, trans. Rodney Livingstone (Cambridge: MIT Press, 1985). For a critique of Marxian metanarrative in the name of postmodernism, see Jean-François Lyotard, *The Postmodern Condition: A Report on Knowledge*, trans. G. Bennington and B. Massumi (Minneapolis: University of Minnesota Press, 1984). For a more extreme view, which threatens to evacuate history altogether, see Jean Baudrillard, *Simulations* (New York: Semiotext(e), 1983). For a recent neoconservative appropriation of the death-of-history theme, see Francis Fukuyama, "The End of History?" *National Interest*, summer 1989, pp. 3–18. All of these critics fail to consider alternative versions and aspects of Marxism that do not rely on teleological metanarrative.

3. Nancy Fraser and Linda J. Nicholson, "Social Criticism without Philosophy: An Encounter between Feminism and Postmodernism," in *Feminism/Postmodernism*, ed. Nicholson (New York: Routledge, 1989), pp. 19–38.

4. Examples of such large narratives are Linda J. Nicholson, *Gender and History: The Limits of Social Theory in the Age of the Family* (New York: Columbia University Press, 1986); and Eli Zaretsky, *Capitalism, the Family, and Personal Life* (New York: Harper & Row, 1986).

5. Thomas McCarthy has suggested an alternative interpretation. Perhaps Benhabib's claim is that large-scale histories cannot be sharply distinguished from metanarratives because they utilize general categories. That view assumes that general categories cannot also be categories whose status is nonfoundational. Thus, it too posits a false antithesis. I discuss this issue below in the context of Benhabib's treatment of "the death of metaphysics."

6. Among the many examples I could cite are Linda Gordon, *Heroes of Their Own Lives: The Politics and History of Family Violence, Boston 1880–1960* (New York: Penguin Books, 1988); Carroll Smith-Rosenberg, "The Female World of Love and Ritual: Relations Between Women in 19th Century America," *Signs* 1, no. 1 (1975): 1–29; Joan Wallach Scott, *Gender and the Politics of History* (New York: Columbia University Press, 1988).

7. In her response to these criticisms, Benhabib poses what I take to be another false antithesis. She suggests that one must choose sides in the exchange between the historians Joan Scott and Linda Gordon, that one cannot split the difference between them. I disagree. Both these historians seem to me to have a piece of the right in this exchange, although neither adequately integrates the other's points. Here, too, I would prefer to depolarize. See Benhabib, "Subjectivity, Historiography, and Politics," in Benhabib, Judith Butler, Drucilla Cornell, and Nancy Fraser, *Feminist Contentions* (New York: Routledge, 1994). See also Joan Scott, "Review of Gordon's *Heroes of Their Own Lives*," and Linda Gordon, "Review of Scott's *Gender and the Politics of History*," both in *Signs* 15, no. 4 (summer 1990): 848–60. For my views on Scott, see Fraser, "Review of Linda Nicholson, *Gender and History* and Joan W. Scott, *Gender and the Politics of History*," *NWSA Journal* 2, no. 3 (summer 1990): 505–8. For my own attempts at a genealogy that avoids disabling metaphysical entanglements, in a chapter coauthored with Gordon, see "A Genealogy of 'Dependency'," chapter 5 of this volume.

8. Benhabib's rejection of situated social criticism is especially puzzling in the light of her endorsement of a theory of the situated subject. One might think that the two went together, since it is not clear how a situated subject could produce unsituated criticism. I discuss the question of the situated subject below.

9. Michael Walzer, *Spheres of Justice: A Defense of Pluralism and Equality* (New York: Basic Books, 1983).

10. My own view is that the latter is often more useful than the former. Insofar as "pure" conceptual reflection, untainted by empirical content, undertakes to justify principles of, say, democracy and equality, it trades in relatively uncontroversial abstractions and side-steps the hard questions about how to apply such principles in social life. *Those* questions are more fruitfully addressed by means of "impure" interdisciplinary efforts integrating normative and empirical considerations. But this kind of empirical-cum-normative reflection is not sharply separated from first-order social criticism; it is the latter's immanent self-clarification.

11. For an approach that retains a high level of conceptual abstraction and generality even while acknowledging its own situatedness, see John Rawls, "Kantian Constructivism in Moral Theory," *Journal of Philosophy* 77, no. 9 (1980): 515–571. Here Rawls interprets his general theorizing about justice as an attempt to seek "reflective equilibrium" among tradition-laden intuitions and principles.

12. I do not agree that the problems Butler discusses warrant rejecting the term 'postmodernism'. I prefer, rather, to use this term in a broad but precise sense to designate an epochal shift in philosophy and social theory from an epistemological problematic, in which mind is conceived as reflecting or mirroring reality, to a discursive problematic, in which culturally constructed social meanings are accorded density and weight. Such a shift carries with it the condition diagnosed by Lyotard in *The Postmodern Condition*. Belief in philosophical metanarratives tends to decline with the linguistic turn, since to accord density and weight to signifying processes is also to cast doubt on the possibility of a permanent neutral matrix for inquiry. Postmodernism in this sense is larger than post-structuralism. It encompasses not only Foucault, Derrida, and Lacan but also such theorists as Habermas, Gramsci, Bakhtin, and Bourdieu, who provide alternative frameworks for conceptualizing signification. If we understand postmodernism as the imperative of theorizing from within the horizon of the linguistic turn, then we can view a large group of thinkers as offering different ways of doing just that, and we can assess their relative merits from a feminist perspective. If, however, we follow Butler in rejecting the term 'postmodernism', we do more than simply protest reductive polemics that con-flate different views; we also risk balkanizing the theoretical field—segregating various camps from one another, refusing to entertain questions posed from other perspectives, and foreclosing debate concerning the full range of options. But of course such debate can be foreclosed just as well by tendentious, sectarian definitions of postmodernism. If we follow Benhabib in associating the term 'postmodernism' with the aestheticization of historical inquiry and the rejection of universalist norms, we risk dismissing out of hand some ways of taking language seriously that are potentially useful for feminist theorizing. (See Benhabib, "Subjectivity, Historiography and Politics.") The trick, once again, is to avoid false antitheses.

13. Judith Butler, *Gender Trouble: Feminism and the Subversion of Identity* (New York: Routledge, 1990).

14. In addition to her contributions to Seyla Benhabib, Butler, Drucilla Cornell, and Nancy Fraser, *Feminist Contentions* (New York: Routledge, 1994), see Judith Butler, *Bodies That Matter* (New York: Routledge, 1993).

15. Benhabib certainly rejects the self-authorizing subject of instrumental reason, which Butler evokes in her discussion of American militarism and the Gulf War. On this point, there is no disagreement between them. Neither Butler nor Benhabib defends a theory of the self-authorizing subject that could entirely master its milieu. Both agree that that is a masculinist "fantasy of autogenesis" predicated on a disavowal or repression of "feminine" dependence.

16. In an earlier version of this essay I suggested that in the absence of attention to such issues, Butler's language projects an aura of estericism unredeemed by any evident gains. Responding to this point, she has noted that I, too, use esoteric theoretical language. (See Judith Butler, "For a Careful Reading," in Seyla Benhabib, Butler, Drucilla Cornell, and Nancy Fraser, *Feminist Contentions* [New York: Routledge, 1994].) My point, however, is not that the use of difficult theoretical language is never justified. I am questioning, rather, whether *her* use of antihumanist language is, i.e., whether it provides theoretical clarity and/or political gains.

17. This conflation of levels is apparent in Butler's response to some of my criticisms. See note 19 below.

18. Butler, "Contingent Foundations."

19. Butler's response to this criticism oscillates confusedly among the subjective and intersubjective levels. She claims, on the one hand, that I am mistaken in attributing to her a concern with the question "who is authorized to speak, and who is de-authorized into silence" despite her appeal to "deauthorized subjects, pre-subjects, figures of abjection, populations erased from view." She claims that her primary interest, rather, is the "exclusionary formation of the subject" understood as a constitutive intrapsychic operation, not an intersubjective process or relation. Yet she also claims this "psychoanalytic premise . . . might [be] usefully employ[ed] in the service of a political critique." To explain how the premise might be so employed, however, she reverts to the example of masculinist figures of mastery, which "have required the de-subjectivation of the feminine," and she then goes on to endorse my questions about *intersubjective* equity: "can we overcome or at least ameliorate the asymmetries in current practices of subjectivation?" (See Butler, "For a Careful Reading.") In general, then, Butler oscillates between intrasubjective and intersubjective claims, and between claims that she is and is not interested in intersubjectivity. As I see it, her framework is still primarily that of a philosophy of subjectivity, albeit in the mode of a reversal or abstract negation. As such, it has difficulty dealing with issues involving intersubjectivity, including the justice of relations among subjects. Yet Butler does (sometimes) want to deal with such issues. And she seems to appreciate that her claim to political relevance ultimately depends on the ability of her framework to connect up with and to illuminate such matters. Hence her oscillation between the standpoints of subjectivity and intersubjectivity.

20. Judith Butler, "Endangered/Endangering: Schematic Racism and White Paranoia," in *Reading Rodney King, Reading Urban Uprising,* ed. Robert Gooding-Williams (New York: Routledge, 1993).

21. For an argument that Foucault's framework is structurally incapable of providing satisfactory answers to the normative questions it unfailingly solicits, see Nancy Fraser, "Foucault on Modern Power: Empirical Insights and Normative Confusions," in Fraser, *Unruly Practices: Power, Discourse and Gender in Contemporary Social Theory* (Minneapolis: University of Minnesota Press, 1989).

22. Butler, *Bodies That Matter.*

23. See C. L. R. James, *The Black Jacobins: Toussaint l'Ouverture and the San Domingo Revolution* (New York: Vintage, 1963).

24. I develop a more extensive version of this argument in "Foucault's Body-Language: A Post-Humanist Political Rhetoric?" in Fraser, *Unruly Practices.* In "For a Careful Reading," Butler appears to misunderstand my point about the political implications of foundationalist theories of subjectivity. I am not claiming that Toussaint subversively cited an otherwise politically insidious Jacobin view and thereby redeemed it for progressive politics. I am saying, rather, that, like Toussaint, the Jacobins themselves put a foundationalist view to emancipatory uses—an assessment I share with Toussaint. My point in any event bears restating: one cannot deduce a single univocal political valence from a theory of subjectivity in the abstract, as Butler does in "Contingent Foundations." In any case, there have surely been "politically insidious" as well as politically progressive citations. So the problem of normative judgment remains.

25. Here Butler seems close to Theodor Adorno's attempt to articulate a nonidentitarian mode of thinking, although she does not share his focus on reconciliation. See Adorno, *Negative Dialectics,* trans. E. B. Ashton (New York: Continuum Press, 1973).

26. For critical discussion of "New French Feminist" theories of 'woman' as sign of nonidentity, see my "Structuralism or Pragmatics?" in this volume. See also my introduction to *Revaluing French Feminism: Critical Essays on Difference, Agency, and Culture,* ed. Nancy Fraser and Sandra Bartky (Bloomington: Indiana University Press, 1991).

27. This point is elaborated in Fraser and Nicholson, "Social Criticism without Philosophy."

28. It is widely appreciated that in *Gender Trouble,* Butler vastly overestimated the emancipatory potential of gender-bending performance in everyday life. She missed its susceptibility to commodification, recuperation, and depoliticization—especially in the absence of strong social movements struggling for political-economic justice. (For a more balanced and sober assessment of gender-bending, see the film *Paris Is Burning,* which captures both the aspirations for transcendence in, and the limitations of, transvestite ball culture among poor gay men of color in New York.) Butler's misestimation of such phenomena seems to me to be symptomatic not only of her one-sided emphasis on deconstruction but also of her tendency to privilege the local. That tendency presents obstacles to the provisional totalization that is necessary to contextualize—and thereby to assess realistically—the seemingly expansive, gender-bending performative possibilities of everyday life in relation to structural dynamics involving large-scale institutions, such as states and economies.

10

Beyond the Master/Subject Model
On Carole Pateman's The Sexual Contract

I take enormous pleasure in the boldness and originality of Carole Pateman's 1988 book, *The Sexual Contract.*[1] Yet I am ultimately not persuaded by several of its central claims. In trying to understand why not, I have found myself returning again and again to the book's core conceptions of dominance and subordination.

As I read her, Pateman follows a long line of feminist thinkers, stretching from Mary Wollstonecraft and John Stuart Mill to Catharine MacKinnon, who construe dominance and subordination on the model of mastery and subjection. In this tradition, women's subordination is understood first and foremost as the condition of being subject to the direct command of an individual man. Male dominance, accordingly, is a dyadic power relation in which a male superordinate commands a female subordinate. It is a master/subject relation.

This, at any rate, is the conception I find implicit in Pateman's account of what she calls "the sexual contract." That idea appears in her book in three different guises, which are not always adequately distinguished from one another. But in each the master/subject model is presupposed.

In one guise, the sexual contract is an unspoken presupposition of classical social contract theory. It is the shadow myth that Pateman claims to discover behind that theory's official account of the foundation of political power—or, as I would prefer to say, it is the suppressed gender subtext of the theory. Thus, when apparently anti-patriarchal-contract theorists like Locke rejected

225

"paternal right" as the model for "political right," they nevertheless assumed husbands' conjugal rights over wives, while redefining such rights as "nonpolitical." This shows, according to Pateman, that even before the theorists conceived the social contract, they had tacitly presupposed a prior "sexual contract." This latter "contract" was an agreement among the "brothers" to democratize the "male sex-right" that had previously been monopolized by the "father." The sexual contract authorized the right of every individual man to command an individual woman—in labor and especially in sex. It established a private sphere of male/female master/subject dyads.

The sexual contract also appears in a second guise in Pateman's book, in real-life contracts in contemporary society. The contracts in question involve "property in the person" and thus include the wage-labor contract, the marriage contract, the "surrogate-motherhood" contract, and what Pateman calls "the prostitution contract." All such contracts necessarily establish relations of subordination, she claims, since they involve odd commodities such as "labor power," "gestational services," and "sexual services," which are not detachable from the persons of their "owners." The use of these commodities thus requires the presence, and indeed the subordination, of their owners, the latters' subjection to a user's command. Contracts involving labor power, gestational and sexual services, and so on thus establish master/subject dyads; the boss acquires the right of command over the worker, the husband over the wife, the john over the prostitute, and so on. When the commodity is attached to a woman's body, moreover, the specifically sexual contract is in play. Then the contract establishes a real-life relation of "male sex-right." An individual man commands the labor and/or sex of an individual woman. He is master, she is subject.

The sexual contract also appears in a third guise in Pateman's book, as the central interpretive schema of patriarchal culture. On this level, which is far less developed than the other two, the sexual contract establishes the patriarchal meaning of sexual difference. It defines masculinity as mastery and femininity as subjection, paradigmatically with respect to sexuality. What it means to be a man, then, is to command a woman sexually, to have right of access to some individual female body. What it means to be a woman, correlatively, is to be sexually subject to some man. Thus, in Pateman's view, the dyadic master/subject model constructs our understandings of masculinity, femininity, sexuality, and sexual difference. It is the symbolic template of patriarchal culture.

As I read her, then, Pateman conceives male dominance—in political theory, in modern society, and in culture—on the master/subject model. Not only is this view presupposed in her discussions of contract theory and of real-life contracts, it is central to her historical thesis as well. Pateman contends that contract is not really antipatriarchal and that modern societies are "fraternal, contractual patriarchies." She also holds that "subordination," not exploitation, is the crux of unfreedom in capitalist wage labor and in other contracts involving property in the person. By "subordination" she means subjection to a master's command. One way to read *The Sexual Contract*, then, is as an argument that late-capitalist contractual relations are really disguised master/subject relations. What appears to be a major historical transformation in the mode of domination is actually the same old wine of "male sex-right" in new, contractual, bottles.

Several important questions follow from this reading of *The Sexual Contract*. Is the master/subject model adequate for analyzing gender inequality in contemporary late-capitalist societies? Are contemporary relations of marriage, wage labor, prostitution, and "surrogacy" most fruitfully understood in these terms? Does this model obscure larger structural or systemic processes that underlie and support hierarchical dyads? Does it obscure gendered constraints on women's lives that take the form not of the authoritative will of a superior but of processes in which the actions of many people are abstractly or impersonally mediated? In any case, how useful is the master/subject model for analyzing contemporary cultural meanings of sexual difference? Do notions of mastery and subjection exhaust the full meanings of masculinity, femininity, and sexuality? Are late-capitalist cultural struggles best theorized, and best intervened in, in these terms?

In what follows, I shall attempt to address these questions by reexamining three of the real-life contracts discussed in Pateman's book: the marriage contract, the employment contract, and the prostitution contract. I shall argue that none is adequately understood on a master/subject model. In these discussions, I shall also consider the sexual contract as a model for analyzing the cultural meanings of sex and gender in contemporary society, contending that here, too, it is not wholly satisfactory. Throughout, I shall argue against the assimilation of contract to subjection, of commodification to command. My aim is not to defend contract as inherently emancipatory but, rather, to open a space for more nuanced thinking about desirable alternatives to contemporary modes of domination.

The Marriage Contract

Let me begin with marriage. Pateman is right and illuminating about the anomalies of "the marriage contract," which is unlike most commercial contracts in that it establishes a long-term, hierarchical status relation whose terms are predetermined and unalterable, and whose roles are assigned according to sex. (The recent rush of the U.S. Congress and state legislatures to explicitly rule out same-sex marriages before a Hawaiian court authorizes them amply confirms Pateman's account on this point.) She is also right and illuminating on the persistence in the late twentieth century of the legal disabilities of wives, including the nonrecognition in many jurisdictions of rape within marriage. Yet for all that, it still seems misleading to understand husbands' power over wives today solely or primarily in the master/subject terms of the sexual contract. Equally important are the sorts of structural and processual constraints that Susan Okin has characterized as "a cycle of socially caused and distinctly asymmetric vulnerability by marriage."[2]

In Okin's cycle, women's traditional responsibility for child rearing helps shape labor markets that disadvantage women; the result is unequal power in the economic marketplace, which in turn reinforces, and exacerbates, unequal power in the family. Initially, women are disadvantaged by anticipation of marriage, since the expectation of primary domestic and child-care responsibilities burdens their decisions about education, training, and degree of commitment to employment. Women's vulnerability is then compounded within marriage, since they enter it with inferior labor-market opportunities and, hence, with less leverage than their husbands. Vulnerability in marriage increases over time, moreover, as the gap in spouses' earning power, and thus in exit options, widens. Finally, women become vulnerable by separation or divorce, which usually brings a precipitous drop in their standard of living, if not outright destitution.[3]

I find this account more useful in accounting for power dynamics within marriage today than Pateman's appeal to "the sexual contract" and "male sex-right." The reason is that Okin looks beyond the marital dyad itself, as legally constituted, to the larger institutional context in which it is situated. If marriage still too often resembles a master/subject relation, this is due in large measure to its social embeddedness in relation to sex-segmented labor markets, gender-structured social-welfare policy regimes, and the gender division of unpaid labor. Such structural constraints certainly help to explain why women sometimes endure such direct forms of subjection as battery and rape within marriage, if not why men engage in such behaviors. (Meanwhile, Pateman's own explanation for the men is unsatisfactory because question-begging; her appeals to "male sex-right" or "the sexual contract" are tantamount to positing a given, unexplained male proclivity to rape and battery.) In general, then, although the legal reform of marriage remains significantly incomplete, the institution in the United States today is probably better understood as an unequal partnership in which "voice" correlates inversely with opportunities for "exit" than as a master/subject relation.

Suppose, however, we ask whether "the sexual contract" figures in marriage at another level, namely, as a schema of cultural interpretation. Then the question would be whether the structural asymmetries theorized by Okin are currently lived through an interpretive grid that equates masculinity with mastery and femininity with subjection; and if so, whether that grid influences behavior. Here I believe we should proceed with caution. Doubtless the master/subject interpretation of sexual difference mediates the marital experience of some people in late-capitalist society, but it is doubtful that this is the case for everyone, nor for everyone in the same degree. Today the master/subject schema seems, rather, to coexist with other mediating interpretive schemata, such as the companionate egalitarian heterosexuality that is represented as an ideal in much late-capitalist middle-brow mass culture. In general, today's meanings of gender, sex, and sexuality are highly fragmented and contested. The meanings inscribed in Pateman's sexual contract are but one component of the mix. They do not dictate a univocal, shared, authoritative interpretation of marriage as a master/subject relation.

The Employment Contract

If the master/subject model does not fit the marriage contract, still less does it fit the other everyday-life contracts Pateman discusses. The latter are all unlike marriage in the crucial respect of involving direct commodification. Whereas the marriage contract involves the withdrawal of major aspects of social reproduction from the cash nexus, wage labor, prostitution, and "surrogacy" are precisely market transactions. They therefore involve a different, more abstract form of social mediation or coordination, which is further removed from the master/subject model.[4]

Consider first "the employment contract." It seems closest to Pateman's view of marriage, since it too establishes a relatively long-term relationship in which a subordinate agrees (under structural constraints) to take orders from a superordinate in exchange for the means of subsistence. But the latter, significantly, is rendered in cash, as opposed to in kind, and thus in a form that confers some leverage in spheres of life outside the place of employment. Pateman, however, focuses chiefly on the employment relation itself, viewed in abstraction from the surrounding context. Thus, she stresses the boss's power to command the worker, which belies the conventional ideological view of the wage contract as a free exchange among equals. She is right about that, I think, and also about the deeper point that "labor power" is not detachable from the worker's person, and hence is an odd sort of commodity whose use requires the worker's presence and subordination. But her decontextualized master/subject focus is too limited to permit an adequate critique. It leads her to judgments that are in some respects too severe and in others too lenient.

Pateman is too severe in holding that capitalist employment is akin to "wage slavery." To be sure, it was painfully experienced in just that way by some early-nineteenth-century proletarianized (male) artisans and yeoman farmers who were losing not only tangible property in tools and in land but also prior control over their work. But their response was contextually specific and gendered. Consider, by way of contrast, the very different experience of the young single women who left farms—with open-ended work hours, pervasive parental supervision, and little autonomous personal life—for mill towns, where intense supervision in the mill was combined with relative freedom from supervision outside it, as well as the increased autonomy in personal life conferred by cash earnings. From their perspective, the employment contract was a liberation.[5]

The mill girls' perspective alerts us to important features of the institution of wage labor that are obscured in Pateman's analysis. Even as the wage contract establishes the worker as subject to the boss's command in the employment sphere, it simultaneously constitutes that sphere as a limited sphere. The boss has no right of direct command outside it.[6] "The outside" here includes both a market in consumer commodities into which the wage buys entry and a noncommodified domestic sphere in which much of the work of social reproduction is performed without pay by women. In those arenas, which are themselves permeated by power and inequality, the wage functions as a resource and source of leverage. For some women, it buys a reduction in vulnerability through marriage.[7]

The moral is that assessing the wage contract requires looking beyond the boss/worker dyad. At the very least, one must balance subordination in paid work against the potential for relative freedom from subordination outside it. The latter will vary with people's social location, as determined in part by their place in the gender division of unpaid labor. Pateman, certainly, wants to include such considerations. That is why, I think, she asserts that women are not and cannot be workers in the same sense as men, that the sexual contract underlies the employment contract. But I do not find these formulations satisfactory. For one thing, they imply too seamless a fit between marital power and capitalist power, thereby missing the possibility of trade-offs. For another, they suggest that the terms "woman" and "worker" are given once and for all as monolithically patriarchal, whereas in fact their meanings are contested and subject to change.[8] Finally, by claiming that the sexual contract underlies the employment contract, Pateman merely redoubles, but does not transcend, the master/subject model of domination.

To appreciate this last point, consider that although Pateman's assessment of the employment contract is too severe in one respect, it is simultaneously too lenient in another. If the institution of wage labor were at base a series of dyadic master/subject relations, the remedy for capitalist domination would be workplace democracy at the level of the firm. Desirable though that is, it would leave unaddressed a number of problems. Pateman is aware of one of these: the disproportionate benefit to full-time workers with few unpaid domestic responsibilities, usually men, as opposed to homemakers, part-time workers, and full-time workers with a "double-shift," for whom meeting attendance is especially onerous, nearly all of whom are women. But other major problems, too, are unresolved by workplace democracy and obscured by Pateman's master/subject focus.

First, workplace democracy is androcentric in its neglect of sites for democratic participation that are associated with "reproduction" as opposed to "production," for example, neighborhoods, child care, health care, and education; with respect to such public goods, public services, and public spaces, it is not just workers but also parents, consumers, and citizens who deserve rights of representation and participation. Second, workplace democracy at the level of the firm fails to remedy the wholesale irrationality of an economic system in which profitability, rather than human need and environmental sustainability, dictates the use of social resources. Finally, it does not overcome the undemocratic character of a social order in which many of the most important social questions are removed from collective deliberation and decided behind citizens' backs through market mechanisms. If none of these problems would be remedied by workplace democracy at the level of the firm, the reason is that none is rooted in a dyadic relation of mastery and subjection. All, rather, are problems that escape that conceptual grid, since they involve more abstract forms of social mediation and impersonal mechanisms of action coordination.

The Prostitution Contract

So far I have been considering Pateman's sexual contract primarily as a model for analyzing institutionalized power relations. And I have argued that it is insufficiently structural to account for gender inequality in late-capitalist society. Yet I have also suggested that there is another way of understanding her model, namely, as a template for the cultural meanings of sex and gender. It is worth considering whether the sexual contract understood as an interpretive grid illuminates contemporary *cultural* dimensions of male dominance and female subordination.

Recall that for Pateman the sexual contract establishes the cultural meaning of sexual difference—hence, of masculinity and femininity, which it defines in terms of sexual mastery and subjection. These meanings, she claims, are institutionalized in contemporary practices such as prostitution and "surrogate motherhood." Her analyses of these practices, then, can be read on two levels: the social level of power relations and the symbolic level of cultural meanings. An analysis that fails to persuade as an account of power relations may be more successful as an account of cultural meaning.

To explore these possibilities, consider "the prostitution contract." Along with "surrogate motherhood," prostitution is analyzed by Pateman as a real-life commercial manifestation of the sexual contract, a case of "male sex-right" gone public. To speak of the sale of sexual (or gestational) services is a distortion, she claims, since the prostitute's sexual parts, like the "surrogate mother's" womb, cannot be used without her presence, nor without her subordination. (It is unfortunate that Pateman did not compare prostitution with pornography, where the use, as opposed to the production, of the commodity requires only a representation of the woman's body. One wonders whether that difference would count in favor of pornography in her view.) The prostitution contract thus establishes a master/subject relation in which a man commands a woman's body. It thereby enacts the patriarchal meanings of masculinity as sexual mastery and femininity as sexual subjection. Far from being a simple free market exchange, then, prostitution institutionalizes male sex-right.

Pateman's use of the master/subject model here is both social and symbolic. On the social level, she appears to hold that in prostitution the john acquires the right of command over the prostitute. But there are some reasons to doubt whether this is so. For one thing, as Pateman notes, prostitution involves a "contract of specific performance," nearly a simultaneous exchange; unlike marriage, it does not establish a long-term relation of dependence. (The master/subject model seems better suited to the pimp/prostitute relation than to the john/prostitute relation, but Pateman does not try that tack.) For another, the transaction is often governed by advance negotiations over specific services, which limit the power of the john. (To say this is not to deny the vulnerability of prostitutes to rape, coercion, and violence, especially where prostitution is illegal and the "contract" is unenforceable.) Some (feminist) ethnographers report, moreover, that prostitutes at the upper end of the occupational scale enjoy considerable control in the sexual transaction itself and considerable autonomy outside it.[9] Finally, in some (though not all) masculine cultures today, resort to prostitution is a token not of power or mastery but of shame, suffused with the embarrassment of having to pay for "it." For all these reasons, the john does not usually have that much power over the prostitute, nor does he have what he has for very long.

To acknowledge this is not to claim that prostitution is liberating for women. It is, on the contrary, to suggest that male dominance can persist even in the absence of master/subject relations. Put differently, if the commodification of women's bodies does not bring gender equality, the reason is not that females who assume the stance of possessive individuals must take orders from male superiors. It is, rather, that prostitution encodes meanings that are harmful to women as a class.

This brings me to the sexual contract as a template for cultural meanings. If the master/subject model is not very helpful in analyzing prostitution on the social level, it does strike a symbolic chord. Certainly Pateman is right to stress that contemporary prostitution is gendered; in its heterosexual form, it is overwhelmingly men purchasing sex from women. (She neglects, however, to consider gay male prostitution, as well as the ways in which both gay and straight varieties are structured not only by gender but also by age and racial-ethnic stratification.) In heterosexual prostitution, the buyer belongs to a higher-status gender than the seller, and the transaction is often permeated by symbolic associations that link masculinity with sexual mastery and femininity with sexual subjection.

Far from implying the solidity of those associations, however, contemporary prostitution rather implies their fragility. I suggest that what is often sold in late-capitalist societies today is a male fantasy of "male sex-right," one that implies its precariousness in actuality. Far from acquiring the right of command over the prostitute, what the john gets is the staged representation of such command. A staged representation of command, however, involves a performative contradiction. The fantasy of mastery that is sold through prostitution is undermined even as it is enacted.

What, then, should we conclude about the value of Pateman's conception of the sexual contract as a symbolic template of patriarchal culture? The moral I draw is that contemporary meanings of masculinity and femininity do have some associations with mastery and subjection, but that those associations are neither exclusive nor fully authoritative. They coexist with a range of other associations—including some that paint women as insatiable dominatrices, others that cast us as nurturant mothers, and still others that envision us as sexually autonomous pleasure-seeking equals. Within this field of rival interpretations of sexual difference, the master/subject model is intensely contested. It does not provide the template for the whole.

If that is right, then Pateman's approach is too absolutist to do justice to the inherent complexity of contemporary cultural politics. An adequate approach ought not to assume that mastery and subjection exhaust the full meanings of masculinity and femininity. Nor that the meanings of those terms are impervious to contestation and change. Doubtless much about our current situation is murky, but at least this much is clear: we live in a time of intense contestation concerning gender, sexuality, and sexual difference. Far from being monolithically patriarchal, the interpretation of these terms is at every point subject to dispute. (The same holds for the concept of "the individual," which Pateman unhelpfully claims is inherently patriarchal.) We need an approach that can analyze the current cultural politics of gender in all its complexity and heterogeneity.

Conclusion

Let me conclude by summarizing my overall argument. In reconsidering the marriage, employment, and prostitution contracts, I have offered assessments of Pateman's notion of the sexual contract in two of its three distinct guises. (I have not discussed its merits as a device for interpreting classical social contract theory.) First, I have evaluated the sexual contract as a model for theorizing contemporary relations of power, and I have argued that it is insufficiently structural to account for the social mechanics of male dominance in late-capitalist society. Second, I have examined the sexual contract as a template for analyzing contemporary cultural meanings of sex and gender; here I have claimed that the master/subject model is but one interpretive grid among others, that it ought not to be unitarized and absolutized, nor treated as impervious to resistance and change.

My larger point is that male dominance today is not best viewed as old master/subject wine in new contractual bottles. Nor are contract and commodification properly understood as command and subjection in disguise. Rather, gender inequality is today being transformed by a shift from dyadic relations of mastery and subjection to more impersonal structural mechanisms that are lived through more fluid cultural forms. One consequence is the (re)production of subordination even as women act increasingly as indi

viduals who are not under the direct command of individual men. Another
is the creation of new forms of political resistance and cultural contestation.

Notes

1. Carole Pateman, *The Sexual Contract* (Stanford: Stanford University Press, 1988).
   Research for this essay was supported by the Center for Urban Affairs and Policy
   Research, Northwestern University. I am grateful to Moira Gatens and Marion Tapper
   for the invitation that provided the occasion for writing it. For helpful comments and
   stimulating discussion, I thank John Deigh, Jane Mansbridge, Eli Zaretsky, and the participants in the Sexual Contract Workshop, Australian National University, December
   1992.

2. Susan Moller Okin, *Justice, Gender, and the Family* (New York: Basic Books), p. 138.

3. Okin's account draws on Robert Goodin's conception of socially created asymmetric vulnerability and on Albert O. Hirschman's account of the effects of people's differential
   potentials for exit on their power within relationships. See Robert E. Goodin, *Protecting
   the Vulnerable: A Reanalysis of Our Social Responsibilities* (Chicago: University of
   Chicago Press, 1985); and Albert O. Hirschman, *Exit, Voice, and Loyalty: Responses to
   Decline in Firms, Organizations, and States* (Cambridge: Harvard University Press,
   1970).

4. This may tempt one to conclude that commodification-of-the-person contracts belong to
   a different, more modern, historical episteme than the marriage contract. But, as we shall
   see, it is precisely their contemporaneity with modern marriage, their coimplication with
   it in a single structured social setting, that helps explain why they, too, manifest gender
   hierarchy—of a non-master/subject sort.

5. For one version of this argument, see Christine Stansell, *City of Women: Sex and Class in
   New York, 1789–1860* (New York: Knopf, 1986).

6. John Deigh has reminded me of some recent cases in which employers have sought to
   dictate workers' off-the-job behavior with respect to things like smoking in order to
   lower health-insurance costs. And of course, gays and lesbians have never enjoyed the liberty of declaring their off-the-job sexuality to be outside the purview of their employers'
   legitimate concern. Nevertheless, heterosexuals today enjoy considerable freedom from
   employer command outside the workplace.

7. See Amartya Sen, "Gender and Cooperative Conflicts," in *Persistent Inequalities: Women
   and World Development,* ed. Irene Tinker (Oxford: Oxford University Press, 1990).

8. For interesting accounts of the contested and changing character of these terms, see Alice
   Kessler-Harris, *A Woman's Wage: Historical Meanings and Social Consequences*
   (Lexington: University Press of Kentucky, 1990); and Joan W. Scott, "'L'ouvrière! Mot
   impie, sordide . . .': Women Workers in the Discourse of French Political Economy,
   1840–1860," in *Gender and the Politics of History* (New York: Columbia University Press,
   1988).

9. See, for example, Lizzie Borden's film *Working Girls.*

Index